NEW MEDIA AND INTERNATIONAL DEVELOPMENT

New Media and International Development is the first in-depth examination of microfinance's enduring popularity with Northern publics. Through a case study of Kiva.org, the world's first person-to-person microlending website, and other microfinance organizations, the book argues that international development efforts have an affective dimension. This is fostered through narrative and visual representations, through the performance of development rituals and through bonds of fellowship between Northern donors and Southern recipients. These practices constitute people in the global North as everyday humanitarians and mobilize their affective investments, which are financial, social and emotional commitments to distant others to alleviate their poverty. This book draws on ethnographic material from the US, India and Indonesia and the anthropological and development studies literature on humanitarianism, affect and the public faces of development. It opens up novel avenues of research into the formation of new development subjects in the global North.

This book will appeal to researchers and students of international development, anthropology, media studies and related fields, as well as practitioners and professionals in the field of international development.

Anke Schwittay is a Senior Lecturer of Anthropology and International Development at the University of Sussex, UK.

RETHINKING DEVELOPMENT

Rethinking Development offers accessible and thought-provoking overviews of contemporary topics in international development and aid. Providing original empirical and analytical insights, the books in this series push thinking in new directions by challenging current conceptualizations and developing new ones.

This is a dynamic and inspiring series for all those engaged with today's debates surrounding development issues, whether they be students, scholars, policy makers and practitioners internationally. These interdisciplinary books provide an invaluable resource for discussion in advanced undergraduate and postgraduate courses in development studies as well as in anthropology, economics, politics, geography, media studies and sociology.

Popular Representations of Development
Insights from novels, films, television and social media
Edited by David Lewis, Dennis Rodgers and Michael Woolcock

Celebrity Advocacy and International Development
Daniel Brockington

International Aid and the Making of a Better World
Reflexive practice
Rosalind Eyben

New Media and International Development
Representation and affect in microfinance
Anke Schwittay

Art, Culture and International Development
Humanizing social transformation
John Clammer

NEW MEDIA AND INTERNATIONAL DEVELOPMENT

Representation and Affect in Microfinance

Anke Schwittay

Routledge
Taylor & Francis Group

LONDON AND NEW YORK

First published 2015
by Routledge
2 Park Square, Milton Park, Abingdon, Oxon OX14 4RN

and by Routledge
711 Third Avenue, New York, NY 10017

Routledge is an imprint of the Taylor & Francis Group, an informa business

British Library Cataloguing-in-Publication Data
A catalogue record for this book is available from the British Library.

Library of Congress Cataloging-in-Publication Data
Schwittay, Anke Fleur, 1971-
New media and international development : representation and affect in microfinance / Anke Schwittay.
    pages cm. – (Rethinking development)
    Includes bibliographical references and index.
    1. Microfinance–Social aspects. 2. Poverty. 3. Economic assistance–International cooperation. 4. Economic development–International cooperation. 5. Digital media–Social aspects. 6. Charities.
    7. Humanitarianism. I. Title.
    HG178.3.S39 2015
    338.9–dc23   2014013053

ISBN: 978-0-415-85607-2 (hbk)
ISBN: 978-0-415-85608-9 (pbk)
ISBN: 978-0-203-71418-8 (ebk)

Typeset in Bembo
by Wearset Ltd, Boldon, Tyne and Wear

For my two families
Paul, Finley and Rory
and
Helga, Gerold and Henning

"*New Media and International Development* takes us on a journey across the emotional, social, technical and financial landscapes of 'everyday humanitarianism'. From photography competitions to person-to-person loans on Kiva.org and the growth of microfinance tourism, Schwittay offers a fresh and compelling analysis that moves anthropology and development studies in exciting new directions."

Heather A. Horst, *RMIT University, Australia*

"Increasing global interconnectivity facilitated by new media has spurred the fantasy that we can each individually alleviate global poverty and redress economic inequality one person at a time. Anke Schwittay explodes this myth by incisively revealing the neoliberal principles and practices that undergird this illusion. In so doing, *New Media and International Development* shows us that problems of global injustice are far more complex than can be resolved through the click of a mouse."

Daromir Rudnyckyj, *University of Victoria, Canada*

"*New Media and International Development* provides a grounded and critical examination of the management of affect in North–South relations. Schwittay demonstrates how the branding of caring is most effective when the Western self is actually the product on offer."

Lisa Ann Richey, *Roskilde University, Denmark*

"This book brings together two sets of development questions usually considered separately: the affective investments in humanitarian and development aid and the latter's use of visual representation and digital media. The author interweaves analysis of both to directly address young people's investments in charitable giving, mediated through websites and tours."

Meena Khandelwal, *University of Iowa, USA*

"Anke Schwittay's original and engaging study of digital micro-financing as a panacea to global poverty not only offers new insights into the relationship between technology, development and affect but also provides a succinct problematization of the neoliberal assumptions that drive development today. A valuable resource for all those concerned with the critical study of global governance."

Lilie Chouliaraki, *London School of Economics, UK*

"*New Media and International Development* offers a novel account of the ways that people in the global North are moved to give their money and time to microfinance initiatives in the global South. The book brings readers up to date with attempts to extend financial services to the world's poor and focuses attention on the power of social media to produce feelings of humanitarian support for 'distant others'. This book takes anthropology of development into new arenas and is set to become an important reference point in debates about poverty alleviation and entrepreneurship."

Jamie Cross, *University of Edinburgh, UK*

"Speculation and sentiment, reality tours and self-reinvention: *New Media and International Development* captures the technologically mediated labor of mustering and managing affective investments – emotional connections to the world's poor – in the business of aid in the 21st century. Focusing on the financial and information apparatuses animating international development today, Schwittay shows that perhaps the most important contribution of new techniques of aid is to the emotional economy of the global North, which, despite the obvious critiques, presents openings for political change."

Bill Maurer, *University of California, Irvine, USA*

CONTENTS

FIGURES

ACKNOWLEDGMENTS

New Media and International Development owes its existence to many people and institutions, and any book, especially one on affect, would be incomplete without acknowledging their financial, logistical, academic and emotional support.

A grant from the Institute for Money, Technology and Financial Inclusion (IMTFI), which was shared with Paul Braund, enabled this research to get under way, funding field research in Mexico and Indonesia. IMTFI's co-founder and director, Professor Bill Maurer, has remained an engaged supporter of this work over the years. Thank you, Bill. Further research was funded by the Faculty of Arts at the University of Auckland, through its Faculty Research Development Fund and Emerging Research Excellence Fellowship.

At CGAP, I thank Jeanette Thomas for her time and interest in my work. Michael Rizzo and Jake-Anthony Pauig helped with finding images and photographers' email addresses. I especially thank Kushal Gangopadhyay, Dave Larson, Sourav Karmakar, Mohammad Rakibul Hasan, Sandipan Majumdar and Jashim Salam for allowing me to reproduce their photographs.

In Indonesia, I thank the staff at INM for receiving me and my family so warmly. Richard Barter provided a valuable introduction. Pak Alit, Debbie, Pasty, Zeruya, Made and Anna were patient interlocutors and spent many hours explaining the benefits and drawbacks of being a Kiva partner. Last but not least, a great thanks to our driver Ketut for keeping me and my family safe and keeping his cool amid much backseat madness.

At Opportunity International, I thank John and Adele, who were instrumental in making my participation in the Insight Tour possible. I also thank Wendell, Angela, Fred, Chris, Richard and Grant for allowing me to be a part of their journey and answering my numerous questions before, during and after the trip. In Chennai, Sam was a great inspiration who did not shy away from the tough questions. To the dedicated staff of his organization and the many borrowers, thank you for your kind hospitality.

At Kiva, I thank Jessica Jackley for early interactions. To the many Kiva lenders and Fellows who answered my questions over the years, thank you. The Kiva website itself (www.kiva.org) was a treasure trove of information and I am grateful for the opportunity to use especially the Fellows blog (www.kiva.org/updates/kiva) for my analysis.

This book was also nurtured by many academic interactions, which helped its ideas become more focused. First and foremost, I am greatly indebted to Daromir Rudnyckyj and Lisa-Ann Richey for their close reading of the final manuscript. Your many suggestions have allowed me to sharpen my arguments and made this book a much better one. Where Dar's interest in the ideas of this book provided early confidence that helped make it a reality, Lisa's encouragement provided energy for the final push. Thank you! Shameem Black, Meike Fechtner, Jamie Cross and Meena Kandelwal gave helpful comments at different stages of the writing process. At the University of Auckland, Susanna Trnka, Anita Lacey, Cris Shore, Julie Parks, Christine Dureau, Jane Horan, Jean-Jacques Courtin and Sun Hee Koo gave valuable comments on various parts of the manuscript. I also thank my colleagues at the Centre for Development Studies, and especially Yvonne Underhill-Sem, my HoD and mentor, for their support over the years.

I presented parts of this book at the University of Auckland, RMIT, the University of Edinburgh, Sussex University and Roskilde University. I thank everybody who attended these talks for their interest in my work and for their comments and feedback.

Over the years, I have had a number of capable research students and summer scholars working on various parts of the book: Shayne Misselbrook, Sopheary Ou, Sofia Pereira, Labiba Rahman, Kirsty Towers, Bryce Turner, Tom Wilson, Lisa Young and Ya-Wen Ho. I thank all of you for your thorough work. All of my students continue to be an inspiration.

At Routledge, Khanam Virjee's early enthusiasm for the book project and her support during its growth were instrumental for materializing my ideas. Helen Bell was a most capable editorial assistant. In addition, Susan Timberlake patiently accommodated my many ideas for the book cover and turned them into a beautiful visual representation of the book's main ideas. Thank you for the elevator pitch.

In the end, however, this book would not have been possible without the love, patience and support of my family. I am deeply grateful to Paul Braund and to Finley and Rory for giving me the time and space to write. Paul, thank you for being a constant companion and intellectual interlocutor during this research. Not only did we share the IMTFI grant and conduct some of our fieldwork together, but we also had countless conversations and joint writing sessions afterwards, during which many of the ideas in this book were developed and fleshed out. Some of the sections, especially in Chapter 3, were first written by you and then made it into joint draft papers submitted to IMTFI and ICTD2010 throughout 2010. I am deeply indebted to your own scholarship and to the ways in which you push those around you to think in new and creative ways. Thank you for being such good sports during those research trips you shared with me and also during those you did not. Especially when things got deadline-crazy at the end, thanks for hanging in there. I love you! I hope that one day you will read this book and think that it was all worth it.

ABBREVIATIONS

CGAP	Consultative Group for the Advancement of the Poor
GCAAP	Global Campaign for Action Against Poverty
IC	Invisible Children
ICT	Information and communication technology
INM	Indonesian microfinance organization
LRA	Lord's Resistance Army
MDG	Millennium Development Goals
MFI	Microfinance institutions
MPH	Make Poverty History
NGO	Non-governmental organization
ROs	Religious organizations
UN	United Nations

PROLOGUE

In July 2010, I conducted research at INM,[1] an Indonesian microfinance institution (MFI) and partner organization of Kiva.org, the world's first person-to-person microlending website. Kiva lets people make loans of as little as US$25 to hundreds of "Kiva entrepreneurs" listed on the website, bypassing traditional charities in the process. On the final day of interviews at INM's local headquarters on the outskirts of Denpasar, Bali's largest city, the director insisted on taking me and my family to visit what he called a success story of the organization's work. In fact, we were told that everybody who came to INM to learn about its programs was taken to meet this particular client, a woman called Annisa who worked as an "agent waste collector." Previous visitors had included a women's group from New Zealand, which came with a professional photographer and followed her and other collectors around for a morning. A group of German tourists visited Annisa and her lending group as part of an Opportunity International Insight Tour. One of them later commented on the women's shyness, but also on their curiosity about the visitors. For this German woman, the pride that the garbage collectors showed in their work jarred greatly with their tiny one-room homes made of straw, wood and corrugated iron roofs.[2] Another tour participant described the women's lives as "pitiful and miserable." Uprooted from their homes in Java to seek a better life in Bali, to this German man it seemed that they had found only more poverty.[3]

On our way to Annisa, Ketut, her male loan officer and our self-proclaimed "tour guide," handed us a sheet of paper, with a description of how Annisa had started collecting garbage for a wholesaler. After she learned about INM, she joined one of its lending groups and began taking out microloans. Five loan cycles later, she had doubled her loan amount, graduated to individual loans, built a three-room house and become a wholesaler herself, employing two people to pick garbage for her. She and her husband had specialized in assorting and preparing recyclables and had also started a side business selling fragrant coconut charcoal to local restaurants.

Annisa's achievements are an example of what I call "microfinance's obligatory success story," a story of loans invested in a growing business, whose profits contribute to the improvement of borrowers' and their families' lives. In the process, Annisa became empowered to manage a successful microenterprise that now provided jobs for people in the community.

After a 30-minute drive through Denpasar's busy streets, we arrived at the site of a new, high-end housing complex under construction. Right next to it was a narrow dirt lane, flanked by mountains of trash and coconut shells. Navigating their overwhelming smell and passing a skinny cow on the way to a small house made of gray cinder blocks, we met Annisa's husband. She herself was away in Java, where their young daughter was being treated for cancer. Her husband paused his work to sit down with us, politely but hesitantly, in the shade provided by the tin roof sheets jutting out over the porch. Ketut translated our greetings and obligatory questions about how the business was going. Feeling awkward and intrusive, we did not ask enough questions for Ketut's taste, who therefore asked them for us in a seemingly well-rehearsed conversation: "What is your dream?" "To build a nice house in Java and move back there." "When will you be able to do that?" "The house is almost finished, thanks to the business." While my partner said under his breath how he felt the husband hated the whole situation, I had the sense that I was being treated to a performance put on for us.

This was only reinforced when Ketut pulled out some paperwork to undertake one of microfinance's key rituals, repeated countless times in borrowers' homes or microfinance offices the world over – the weekly payment collection. While the husband went to get his wallet, from which he pulled a number of crisp bills and his yellow repayment card, Ketut spread out an assortment of pens, stamps and papers on the small wooden table between them. He then wrote the date, payment amount, interest payment and balance remaining on the husband's card, which he signed and stamped, explaining to us that "without a stamp nothing is official." He also filled out a numbered receipt in triplicate, one copy of which he gave to the husband who added it to all his other repayment receipts, while the two remaining copies would go to the INM office. Lastly, Ketut entered the transaction into his own report book, complete with stamp and signature. It was then that INM's director, who had been observing the exchange with us, asked us whether we could see why this whole process was so time-consuming and in need of technological innovation.

It is this time- and labor-intensive nature of microfinance transactions, often taking place after long motorcycle rides by loan officers to reach remote clients, that has been cited to justify microfinance's high interest rates. When Compartamos, a Mexican MFI that was the first of its kind to go public in 2009, was shown to charge close to 100 percent annualized interest from its poor clients, while netting millions of dollars for its founders and investors, this only added fuel to the fire of microfinance's public castigation (Cull, Demirgüç-Kunt & Morduch, 2010). The popular press has long reported stories of over-indebtedness (Brück, 2006), which reached a high point in 2010 with accounts of a wave of borrower suicides in Southern India (Biswas, 2010; Polgreen & Bajaj, 2010). Academic critiques have centered on the contested impact of microfinance on poverty alleviation (Bateman, 2010; Dichter & Harper, 2007), on its complex and sometimes questionable gender dynamics (Karim, 2011; Rankin, 2001) and on microfinance's connections to neoliberalism (Elyachar, 2002; Weber, 2004), which has been confirmed through its incorporation into mainstream financial systems (Roy, 2010). This book takes many of these criticisms into account, but focuses on a different set of questions that have not yet been asked and that arose from my virtual encounter with Annisa and actual meeting with her husband.

This encounter heightened my own skepticism of microfinance. Granted, Annisa had probably improved her life in material terms, but she was still living on a garbage dump, which may have contributed to her daughter's cancer. And why was a garbage collector paraded around as a success story in the first place, when many other professions would have done a more convincing job? Were my feelings of guilt and embarrassment, but also curiosity and sympathy, at all representative of development or, more accurately, poverty tourists? It is these sentiments that gave rise to my interest in the role of affect in the constitution of microfinance as a popular global poverty alleviation practice. By popular, I mean not only microfinance's continued deployment by development organizations, but also its increasing support from lay people in the global North.[4] How do the representations and recipients of microfinance move such people who encounter them, not as professional managers, but as potential supporters? Indeed, how do such encounters constitute the latter as microfinance supporters in the first place? And how do microfinance encounters, representations and rituals contribute to its continued embrace, in spite of growing criticisms in the popular and academic press?

It was my research on Kiva that had brought me to INM, a Christian MFI operating in the world's largest Muslim country, in the first place. While I was there, I met Heike, a young Austrian woman who had just graduated from medical school and was volunteering as a Kiva Fellow to help INM become a better Kiva partner. My conversations with her and her temporary colleagues at INM made me reflect on the religious roots of much of the charity work that still surrounds microfinance, in spite of its increasing commercialization, and on the practices of caring and commitment implicit in the notion of fellowship. Because of the phenomenal success of Kiva, which connects over 1 million lenders mainly from the global North with an equal number of borrowers predominantly from the global South through stories and images, I knew that my questions were relevant. *New Media and International Development*, whose journey began on that day in July 2010, is my attempt at an answer. Even though I never met Annisa, I thank her for helping me take the first step.

Notes

1 INM and names associated with the organization are pseudonyms.
2 Retrieved August 4, 2010, from http://oid.org/dokumente/service/reisebericht-nafziger-bali.html.
3 Retrieved August 4, 2010, from http://oid.org/dokumente/service/reisebericht-bley-bali-09.html.

4 Having resided in New Zealand during the research and writing of the book, I am very aware of the faulty development geography invoked in the terminology of global North and South. Nevertheless, for me it is less problematic than developed/developing or First/Third World because of the latter's normative implications.

Bibliography

Bateman, M. (2010). *Why doesn't microfinance work? The destructive rise of global neoliberalism.* London: Zed Books.

Biswas, S. (2010, December 16). India's micro-finance suicide pandemic. *BBC News.*

Brück, C. (2006, October 30). Millions for millions. *New Yorker.*

Cull, R., Demirgüç-Kunt, A. & Morduch, J. (2010). Microfinance meets the market. *Contemporary Studies in Economic and Financial Analysis, 92,* 1–30.

Dichter, T. & Harper, M. (Eds.). (2007). *What's wrong with microfinance?* Rugby, UK: Practical Action Publishing.

Elyachar, J. (2002). Empowerment money: The World Bank, non-governmental organizations and the value of culture in Egypt. *Public Culture, 14*(3), 493–513.

Karim, L. (2011). *Microfinance and its discontents: Women in debt in Bangladesh.* Minneapolis: University of Minnesota Press.

Polgreen, L. & Bajaj, V. (2010, November 17). India microcredit faces collapse from defaults. *New York Times.*

Rankin, K. (2001). Governing development: Neoliberalism, microcredit and rational economic woman. *Economy and Society, 30*(1), 18–37.

Roy, A. (2010). *Poverty capital: Microfinance and the making of development.* New York and London: Routledge.

Weber, H. (2004). The "new economy" and social risks: Banking on the poor? *Review of International Political Economy, 11*(2), 356–386.

PART I

Foundations

1

INTRODUCING *NEW MEDIA AND INTERNATIONAL DEVELOPMENT*＊

New Media and International Development examines the role of affect, representation, performance and fellowship in international development. It argues, first, that global poverty-alleviation efforts have an affective dimension, which is fostered through narrative and visual representations, through the performance of development rituals and through establishing personal connections. These relations are imagined to link (affluent) people in the global North with (poor) people in the global South. Increasingly, they are forged with the help of new media technologies, although more often than not these technologies establish connections among Northern publics and continue to exclude Southern ones. Second, the book shows how affect works on everyday citizens in the global North who are supportive of poverty-alleviation efforts. It asks how Northern publics come to learn and care about geographically, culturally and materially distant others and how they share some of their money and time to improve far-away lives. I call these Northern publics *everyday humanitarians* and argue that they need to be studied as development subjects in their own right, much like poor aid recipients and development managers have been until now. Their subject formation is (almost) always mediated by organizations, so that the practices of development supporters cannot be separated from the institutional context in which they occur and that often enables them in the first place. In presenting these two central arguments, *New Media and International Development* contributes to current anthropological and development studies debates over the nature of popular interventions in global poverty alleviation.

It does so by focusing on one particularly popular development technology – microfinance, which I have situated in a larger financial inclusion assemblage (Schwittay, 2011). Over the last 40 years, various subjects, technics and rationalities have come together into an "identifiable terrain of action and debate" (Li, 2007, p. 266) to develop formal small-scale financial products and services that are seen as an essential part of helping poor people enterprise themselves out of poverty. The assemblage also includes practices that make them knowable as financial and entrepreneurial subjects, so that their financial inclusion becomes a cause worthy of popular support. This support is not distributed evenly, but, not unlike microfinance, is structured by logics of inclusion and exclusion. While the empowering, beneficial and harmonious sheen of inclusion appeals to microfinance supporters, it is also a dangerous term – similar to community (Williams, 1976) and participation (Kothari, 2001) – that can mask practices of control and coercion. Similarly, digital technologies such as those used by Kiva can connect but also distance people. By analyzing these dynamics, *New Media and International Development* deepens our understanding of affective engagements with poverty alleviation, their limits but also their possibilities, and thereby sheds light on a fundamental problem of our times: the persistence of global poverty.

The formation of microfinance supporters, through technological mediations, organizational strategies and representational practices, is framed by an increasing interest in poverty that has led to the proclamation of "the new millennium … as the *age of poverty*, one in which a concern for poverty not only shapes social life but also serves as a key part of the remaking of the global economy" (Roy, 2012a, p. 105). Microfinance is central to this constellation, constituting "the panacea of choice" situated at the emerging frontier of finance capitalism (Roy, 2010, p. 22). Its continuing popularity is grounded in the discursive and material constitution of poverty in financial terms, because only as a financial problem can poverty be alleviated by financial means (Schwittay, 2014).

The Financialization of Poverty

Poverty's financialization is visible in a number of ways. Most importantly, the World Bank's global poverty line and its translation into the first Millennium Development Goal (MDG) adhere to an "essentially mono-dimensional conception of 'extreme poverty' (as lack of income or consumption)" (Edward, 2006, p. 381). The global poverty line defines the extremely poor as those who live on less than $1/day and thereby firmly yokes poverty to a financial indicator. This insufficient amount of money is explained by a lack of income, whether from microentrepreneurship as advocated by microfinance supporters (Yunus, 1999) or from formal waged jobs as advocated by its opponents (Karnani, 2007). Consequently, efforts by the microfinance industry aim to create "social value [through the] maximization of the disposable income of the poor" (Chu, 2005, p. 14). This is not to deny that being poor means not having enough money to live. However, as Amartya Sen has shown, "real incomes can be rather poor indicators of important components of well-being and quality of life that people have reason to value" (1999, p. 80). Even though Sen's own work has led to the emergence of broader definitions of poverty that pay attention to what poor people themselves value, easy-to-measure, income-tied dimensions of poverty continue to be seen as fundamental to enabling poor people to make other choices, from housing to education to healthcare. This means that the multidimensional character of poverty is acknowledged, but remains represented as a financial problem (Edward, 2006).

One effect of the financialization of poverty is poverty's universalizing definition as a common condition shared by poor people the world over. This not only neglects the heterogeneity and diversity of poor people's lives, but also enables the global poverty-alleviation interventions of which microfinance is exemplary (Ilcan & Lacey, 2011).[1] These are, by necessity, of a financio-technical nature, calling for the better design of poor-appropriate financial services, often through the use of mobile technologies (Maurer, 2012) or the creation of new asset classes to tap into commercial capital (Matthäus-Maier & von Pischke, 2009). All of these strategies focus on the expansion of formal financial services to the poor, in an attempt to ameliorate what is perceived to be the major cause of their impoverishment, namely their lack of capital. In the process, the poor are reconceptualized as financial subjects, who can escape the "tyranny of emergency" (Appadurai, 2001, p. 31) that rules their lives through gaining access to microfinance. These lives are made knowable as financial lives through financial diaries (Collins, Morduch, Rutherford & Ruthven, 2009), producing the knowledge on which financial inclusion interventions are built. Such interventions aim to instill fiscal prudence and foresight through financial literacy education, often delivered through microfinance lending groups, and the increasing emphasis on savings, insurance and pension as forms of asset-building. This in turn inculcates practices of planning for the future, rather than succumbing to day-to-day struggle. The director of the Consultative Group for the Advancement of the Poor (CGAP), a microfinance think tank housed at the World Bank, concurs: "Microfinance allows poor households to move from everyday survival to planning for the future, investing in better nutrition, improved living conditions and children's health and education" (Littlefield, Morduch & Hashemi, 2003, p. 1). Even though research has shown that poor people do not usually live from hand to mouth, such arguments against mere survival strategies and for forward-looking planning are central to the constitution of poor people as financial subjects. They also say more about how Northern publics imagine people below the poverty line live than how they actually do.

Affective Investments

To focus only on the politics of numbers, however, is to miss a crucial aspect of financial inclusion, because it is microfinance's affective dimension, constituted through myriad acts of representations, performance and fellowship, that contributes to its current popularity. The question I ask in this book is how the participation of microfinance supporters in global poverty-alleviation efforts is shaped by affective sentiments, relationships and collectivities. These materialize in feelings of caring for strangers who are geographically and materially distant, and in practices of sharing through financial and labor contributions. Departing from the observation that "people care if they are invested" (Harding & Pribram, 2004, p. 879), I argue that the mobilization of *affective investments* is at the heart of the constitution of microfinance supporters. Such investments are emotional, social and financial commitments to distant others to alleviate their poverty. While financial contributions are the most visible of the three, they are embedded in a moral grammar of affective sentiments and relationships, which sometimes spurs financial donations in the first place. In fact, it is precisely the articulation of the different dimensions of affective investments that makes them so powerful.

Kiva is one of the most visible, and by now most studied, examples of the mobilization of affective investments in the financial inclusion assemblage (Black, 2009, 2013; Gajjala, 2012; Moodie, 2013). Established in 2005 in California's Silicon Valley by a husband-and-wife team, it is the world's first person-to-person micro-lending website and one of the fastest-growing non-profits in US history (Coates & Saloner, 2009). As of February 2014, more than 1 million lenders from dozens of countries, but predominantly from the United States and Northern Europe, have lent over US$500 million to over 1 million borrowers in 73 countries, including the United States itself. Lenders come from all walks of life, ages and political persuasions, and assort themselves into lending teams based on self-selected affiliations such as geography, religion, professions and interests. Kiva's success shows that, on the one hand, the small scale of affective investments, manifesting in millions of US$25 transactions and one-paragraph stories, makes them easily manageable and consumable (Black, 2009). Taken together, they constitute a noteworthy public engagement with global poverty alleviation.

On the other hand, affective investments are imagined to empower not only their poor beneficiaries in the global South, but also donors in the global North. As Kiva's President states, on Kiva, "the average person can be like a Bill Gates or a Rockefeller" (cited in Heim, 2006). Such feelings drive Kiva's growth, together with the personal relationships between lenders and borrowers that are imagined to be established through the website. However, its call to emulate mega-capitalists-cum-philanthropists forces us to question the very nature of Kiva's project: is it really a tool that allows everyday people in the global North to reinvent themselves, making poor borrowers instruments in others' search for meaningful identities? This shift is in line with an ever-growing emphasis in international development on Northern publics and the corresponding disappearance of the global South from popular development representations (Cameron & Haanstra, 2008). While my book contributes to this move, the latter is too important to go without critical analysis. What is called for is an awareness of the consequences of each scholarly project, on those who are its subjects and on those who are by necessity excluded.

Kiva is also a good example of how the financialization of poverty mobilizes affective investments by framing poverty in a way that is accessible to Northern publics. As levels of income and access to financial resources open up or foreclose choices in their lives as well, Northern supporters can comprehend, or at least try to, what it would be like to live on $1 a day. Initiatives like Live Below the Line, which challenges people in the United States, United Kingdom, Australia and New Zealand to survive on between US$1.25 and NZD2.25 for 5 days each year, aim to raise awareness and donations. They make the struggles of distant others less different and more real, at the same time as they are reinforcing the financialization of poverty. This in turn gives development supporters the sense that they can take actions that will make an impact. For example, donating money through sites like Kiva promises visible improvements in the lives of its borrowers, as communicated in regular email updates. Whereas focusing on the structural complexities of global poverty could easily become overwhelming and inhibit action, presenting its problem in a simplified, financial way makes it wieldy and actionable. Microfinance institutions (MFIs) play an important role in these reimaginings. Not only does Muhammad Yunus, who received the Nobel Peace Prize in 2006 for his work with the Grameen Bank, argue that "the poor know that credit is their only opportunity to break out of poverty" (1999, p. 59), but in the process of legitimizing their own work by presenting it as the most appropriate solution to poverty, MFIs also claim that previous development interventions have failed. Microfinance, then, becomes a sound and efficient business practice that brings benefits to poor individuals, their families and communities. It becomes a cause that everyday humanitarians can and should support.

Development Made Popular

The entrance of lay Northerners into the global development arena in general, and into microfinance in particular, is a manifestation of the popularization of development, a phenomenon that goes by many names. Proponents of Global Development 2.0, termed this way to index its affinity with the emergence of social media and thus mark its fashionable newness, observe that "the fight against poverty, which was once almost exclusively restricted to aid officials and learned experts, has become one of the twenty-first century's most popular causes" (Brainard & LaFleur, 2008, p. 9). Corporations are joining new government donors, celebrities, the global public and a new generation of philanthropists in generating financial support surpassing that of official development assistance from traditional donors. The predominance of new mega-foundations has given rise to philanthrocapitalism (Bishop & Green, 2008), which marries the agency of the super-wealthy with the sentiments of compassionate capitalism and the structures of venture philanthropy to create new centers of development power and authority. However, philanthrocapitalists are only one of development's new constituencies, albeit a highly visible and influential one. The "widespread ownership of the ideas and practices of development that defies centralized edifices such as the World Bank or even the Grameen Bank" has also resulted in a "democratization of development" (Roy, 2010, pp. 3, 4). Microfinance, which as a practice has its main origin in Grameen in the global South and has been embraced by Northern development institutions,[2] is paradigmatic of that process, even though the center of authority has now shifted to the latter in the form of CGAP (Roy, 2010).

Popularized development also includes lay people. The hundreds of thousands of online lenders, together with their fellow volunteers, child sponsors or campaign donors, feel empowered to make poverty history and are finding, or creating, the tools to do so. Situating this emergence at the beginning of the 21st century, Ananya Roy calls this "millennial development,"[3] which "relies greatly on the modern, Western self who is not only aware of poverty's devastation but is also empowered to act upon it in responsible ways" (2010, p. 12). In addition, the term signals the involvement of the millennial generation, young people who were born after 1980, have come of age in the new millennium and have enthusiastically embraced the cause of poverty alleviation (Tatarchevskiy, 2011). Their empowerment manifests the emotional dimension of affective investments and is in part driven by the convenient power of micro, the persuasive force of images and the increasing involvement of celebrities in international development. Coupling such celebrity appeal with an invitation to consume, Brand Aid is another way in which Northern publics can gain emotional satisfaction from helping distant others (Richey & Ponte, 2011).

Practices of caring and sharing create relationships, however imaginary they may be, which foster the social dimension of affective investments. Often, these relationships are mediated by new digital technologies; their increasing importance in philanthropy is sometimes referred to as Giving 2.0 (Arrillaga-Andreessen, 2012).[4] By forging new connections, first and foremost among development supporters in the global North, and, to a smaller extent, between these supporters and their beneficiaries in the global South, these technologies contribute to the popularization of development. There are web-based campaigns, crowd-sourcing platforms and online marketplaces that combine the reach of the Internet with the stickiness of social media and the aggregation of scalable models. Not incidentally, the millennial generation has been dubbed the Facebook generation and posting one's Kiva loan on Facebook and Twitter profiles adds cultural capital to their owners. However, technological innovation cannot mask that these are "unidirectional cross-cultural encounters that encourage and reinforce a Western gaze at the 'Third World'" (Gajjala & Birzescu, 2011, p. 100). Through their mediations, digital technologies make small Southern organizations and their clients visible to Northern publics, who can then pool their microtransactions into a form of "connected capital," as Kiva's CEO calls the money flowing through the organization's site (Flannery, 2009). It is an apt description of the ways in which the financialization of poverty and the popularization of development merge to mobilize affective investments. Their articulation creates a space that enables everyday practices of humanitarianism.

Everyday Humanitarianism

Didier Fassin begins his recent book on *Humanitarian Government* with reference to Adam Smith's notion of moral sentiments as "the emotions that direct our attention to the suffering of others and make us want to remedy them" (Fassin, 2012, p. 1). The Scottish moral philosophers who shared Smith's thoughts argued that morality derived not from reason but from emotions.[5] Rather than a rational sense of obligation, moral feelings of love, friendship, trust and solidarity incite action to help

distant others (Rorty, 1993). Consequently, Fassin argues for the crucial importance of a " 'humanitarian emotion': the affect by virtue of which human beings feel
personally concerned by the situation of others" (2010, p. 269). In a similar way,
Lisa Malkki has shown that the "historical shaping of 'international opinion' has
much to do with the shaping and circulation of affect. There is research to be done
on the effects of representations in educating the distribution of sentiments" (2010,
p. 83). I take these arguments as the conceptual point of departure for an analysis of
everyday humanitarianism. While some scholars foreground humanitarianism's
interventionist and emergency nature (Calhoun, 2010), for Fassin it is precisely the
articulation of values and affects that has come to define contemporary humanitarianism. Because I am similarly focusing on the work of affect, I do not draw analytical distinctions between humanitarianism, development and poverty alleviation.[6]
They come together in a broad definition of "a structure of feeling, a cluster of
moral principles, a basis for ethical claims and political strategies, and a call for
action" (Redfield & Bornstein, 2010, p. 17).

Within this ensemble, Raymond Williams' notion of structure of feeling
allows us to situate humanitarianism temporally and culturally. As a "periodizing
concept," structure of feeling refers to "the felt sense of the quality of life at a
particular place and time" (Williams, 1975, p. 47). By framing how individuals'
feelings are variously anchored, structures of feeling also "indicate a productive
process that constructs subject identities" (Harding & Pribram, 2004, p. 870).
Thus, when Thomas Laqueur claims that "we are, in fact, more likely today to
have sympathy for, and even to do something to alleviate, the suffering of people
and animals distant from ourselves – geographically, culturally, in their species
being – than were men and women three centuries ago" (2009, p. 32), he speaks
to the existence of contemporary moral and affective collectives that are enabled
by globalization and inhabited by certain kinds of political subjects. Such distinctions show that humanitarian sentiments are not inborn human faculties, but have
been cultivated over time.

Thomas Haskell has identified four preconditions for the historical emergence of
humanitarianism, from the existence of ethical maxims to help suffering strangers,
which were grounded in religious tenets, to the perception of involvement in the
causes of this suffering, to the ability, by way of techniques, to see a way to end it.
Most importantly, "the recipes for intervention available to us must be ones of sufficient ordinariness, familiarity, certainty of effect and ease of operation" (1985,
p. 358). In other words, the practices enabled by these technologies must, by their
fit with what people know and are used to, create the confidence that taking action
would make a difference, and create the conscience that not taking action would
make people complicit in the perpetuation of suffering. Such awareness, techniques,
confidence and conscience were, and continue to be, unevenly distributed. At the
same time, humanitarian organizations work to "compel care" among ever more
people (Feldman, 2010, p. 201).

For the Scottish moral philosophers, Christian compassion, "a quintessential
humanitarian sentiment" (Suski, 2009, p. 200), became sympathy. The German

translation of this word as *Mitgefühl* captures its meaning as "feeling with some-body," alluding to a certain distance between the spectator and the sufferer. The former "does not identify with [the latter] and does not imagine himself to be in the same situation" (Boltanski, 1999, p. 38). More recently, it is empathy that has gained purchase (Wilson & Brown, 2009). As *Einfühlungsvermögen*, or "the ability to feel into," in the sense of stepping into someone else's shoes, empathy is a more involved identification with suffering. It is "nonjudgmental and can be positive or negative … it does not guarantee benevolence" (Bornstein, 2012, pp. 145–146). This shift from sympathy to empathy represents an intensification of humanitarian sentiments that is in part fostered by the increasing emphasis on affect in con-temporary public discourse and politics (Mazzarella, 2009; Woodward, 2004). It also corresponds to the individualization of suffering, where "empathy differs from sympathy in that it entails seeking the individual perspective of another rather than generalizing or stereotyping" (Halpern & Weinstein, 2004, p. 568). Another shift has taken place from guilt about Northern publics' wealth in the face of abject poverty to a celebration of their ability to contribute to its alleviation. These diverse emotions are part of a politics of pity that works through "tender-heartedness" and beneficent actions (Boltanski, 1999, p. 48). While all have the potential to lead to action aimed at alleviating distant suffering, the ethical implications of pity, guilt or sympathy are distinct.

Similar differentiations are necessary for the recipients of humanitarian senti-ments, since "the emotional pull of humanitarian appeals is always dependent upon the worthiness of those suffering" (Suski, 2009, p. 201). Their constitution is dynamic and includes aspects of performance by those under the humanitarian gaze and by the apparatus itself (Sandvik, 2009). While historically a category of "needy victim" has been constituted through evaluations of entitlement and moral worth (Redfield & Bornstein, 2010, p. 13), in the financial inclusion assemblage, it is the female, self-actualizing, responsible microentrepreneur who is regarded as most deserving. Her prominence points not only to the gendered nature of humanitari-anism, but also to the particularities by which microfinance inflects everyday humanitarian sentiments.

First, microfinance is subject to the more general tension between the intimate connections fostered by everyday humanitarianism and the generic nature of the monetary donations by which they are most often made manifest (Bornstein, 2003). As Marx argued, "the exchange of money indiscriminately for all qualities and objects seems to make all of our particular human essential powers indifferent, thus distorting our relationships to each other and the world and undermining our powers to create social bonds" (paraphrased by Hardt, 2011, p. 679). In the humanitarian realm, that means that money's "general equivalent obliterates the singularity of both the donor and the recipient" (Boltanski, 1999, p. 18). Both become undifferentiated abstractions and as such stand in the way of humanitarian sentiments. This does not mean that money is a non-affective entity, as it evokes strong positive and negative sentiments that can be considered a kind of "financial affect" (Konings, 2014, p. 37). Neverthe-less, as an impersonal medium, money obscures the donor and his commitment, opening the door for accusations of superficial engagement. It also hides the recipient, and as a result "the bond created between the donor and the unfortunate is minimal and abstract" (Boltanski, 1999, p. 18). The exchange of letters and photos between care-giver and cared-for aims to counter this flattening.

Second, in its predominant form of micro-credit, which makes small loans to poor women to start or grow their own businesses, microfinance is not only a financial transaction, but also an exchange. The unidirectional charitable impulse becomes a two-way interchange (Bornstein, 2012). This opens up the possibility of a connection, which Kiva, by coupling financial repayments with stories about borrowers' progress, has turned so successfully into imaginary relationships between its lenders and borrowers. According to the organization's leaders, these relationships distinguish Kiva from mere philanthropy and produce business partnerships. Trading in debt creates risks, however, and while Kiva warns its lenders of the risks they are taking in making loans to strangers on the other side of the world, it does not acknowledge the risks for borrowers, which are amplified by commercial microfinance's increasing focus on profitability (Maclean, 2013; Moodie, 2013; Roy, 2012b). A focus on finance thus also draws attention to humanitarianism's connections to capitalism.

Lastly, microfinance does not dwell on "sad and sentimental stories" (Rorty, 1993, p. 114) but capitalizes on narratives of empowerment, entrepreneurial success and material improvement. Women are represented not as quintessential passive victims but as distinctly (neo)liberal subjects: strong, dignified, independent and powerful economic actors who are in charge of improving the lives of their families. The reality of this representation has been problematized by several grounded academic studies of microfinance (Karim, 2011; Rahman, 1999), but as a central aspect of microfinance's legitimization, the empowered microentrepreneurial woman continues to dominate its visual and narrative terrain. In spite of these unique features, microfinance presents an exemplary case from which to examine affective investments of Northern publics in distant others. It also allows me to interrogate the possibilities of critical engagement, in this case with microfinance's obligatory success story, through affective encounters.

Over the years, a number of arguments have been brought against the emotionalism of humanitarian action (Arendt, 2006 [1963]; Fassin, 2012). According to Luc Boltanski,

> emotions can be discredited as foundations and symptoms of a moral disposition due to their circumstantial character – bound up as they are with a particular situation in which they are tethered to the real or imaginary presence of a particular unfortunate – which does not enable one to construct a moral duty with general validity.
>
> *(1999, p. 100)*

His observations regarding the tension inherent in a politics of pity – between the necessary detachment from local circumstances but their simultaneous requirement to inspire pity in the first place – leads to a humanitarian double bind. Drawing on

Gregory Bateson's foundational work (1972), Peter Redfield argues that a double bind "motivates by a desire to satisfy competing injunctions" (2012, p. 361). For everyday humanitarians, this is the tension between the satisfaction of helping to make a difference, sometimes repeatedly, in the life of one person, and the recognition that this does not alter the structural conditions that perpetuate poverty for that person's neighbors, town or country. For the latter to happen, sponsoring a child or making a Kiva loan does not suffice, however good it may feel. An entirely different set of actions is necessary, which leads to the "choice between two states which are *equally valued* and so *equally insufficient* that a self-perpetuating oscillation is engendered by any active choice between them" (Wilden & Wilson, 1976, p. 276). While everyday humanitarians can both protest against trade injustice and sponsor a Kiva entrepreneur, either action feels somewhat inadequate. This is accompanied by a tension between fundamentally neoliberal individualized action and a more collective vision of social and political change.

Humanitarian sentiments also provide unstable ground for action: "compassion needs to be translated into action, or it withers" (Sontag, 2003, p. 90; Cohen, 2001). However, their transformation to charitable or political practices is far from guaranteed. Last but not least, humanitarian sentiments can lead to hatred, racism and chauvinism (Ahmed, 2004; Rozario, 2003). In light of this "crisis of pity," Lilie Chouliaraki has argued for the emergence of a post-humanitarian sensibility that disengages from the grand emotion of Pity and its ensemble of guilt/indignation and empathy/gratitude. Although these traditional affective registers persist, they "do not appear as immediate emotions that may inspire action but rather as objects of contemplation to be reflected upon" (2010, p. 118). Such reflexivity by Northern spectators leads to self-inspection that can cause them to question their judgments and motivations, but still does not sustain political action.

Ultimately, affective humanitarianism is characterized by a "remarkable paradox" – namely the tension between compassion giving rise to a politics of inequality (by focusing on the poor) and a politics of solidarity (by seeing the other as an equal) (Fassin, 2012, p. 3). If the dimension of assistance wins the day, this is because "the very condition of the social relation between the two parties ... makes compassion a moral sentiment with no possible reciprocity" (Fassin, 2012, p. 3). Even though microfinance's particularities complicate these relations, an examination of the attachment of humanitarianism to older, hierarchical ideas of charity, where those with wealth and resources help those who are (considered to be) less fortunate, is necessary. Similarly, in spite of the frequent and ongoing construction of a common humanity, "humane behavior, the exercise of humanity, certainly did not entail a commitment to human equality, social or juridical" (Laqueur, 2009, p. 43). Affective engagements with international development are not exempt from this paradox.

Affect and International Development

In complement to the recent scholarship on the affective dimension of humanitarianism is an emerging body of work in anthropology and international development studies that takes affect as its central object. This opus sits within a broader multi-disciplinary interest in affect, which makes the subject a contested scholarly terrain following a number of intellectual trajectories (for a good summary, see Anderson, 2006). All agree on William Mazzarella's observation that "affect management [has become] a necessary moment of any institutional practice with aspirations to public efficacy" (2009, p. 298).

My own work draws on scholarship that highlights the role of affect in enabling global connections through subject formation. Here, "affect structures cultural logics of global connection, as affective management techniques shape the situated subjects who enact global networks" (Richard & Rudnyckyj, 2009, p. 63). Inter-subjective ties that express both being affected and affecting are crucial to these connections, and affect's "transitive and reflexive capacity" opens up the possibility of examining how it affects oneself and others, giving rise to forms of conduct whose outcome is indeterminate and unstable (Richard & Rudnyckyj, 2009, p. 59). In addition, while some authors argue for the importance of an analytical and lin-guistic distinction between emotions and affect, most scholars writing in the affec-tive space use the two terms almost interchangeably, sometimes emphasizing emotions' expressibility and affect's inexpressibility. Concretely, the corporeal expression of affect manifests in bodily feelings, so that affect becomes experienced through personal emotions (Anderson, 2006). In this book I mainly use the terms affect and sentiments, but also draw on works that talk about emotions. In doing so I agree with Sarah Wright that "I see no reason to insert cleavage between other-wise friendly terms" (Wright, 2012, p. 1126).

Critical to the constitution of development supporters through the mobiliza-tion of affective investments is circulation, first and foremost of financial resources but also of people, stories and images. All of these draw attention to the material-ity of affect, which is not simply an expression of interior subjectivity, but mani-fests in affective spaces and objects that discharge emotive energy upon their owners (Navaro-Yashin, 2009; Solomon, 2011). As such, affect is part of the ordinary, everyday experiences of individuals (Stewart, 2007). While working in and on individuals, affect can also constitute "affective collectivities" (Richard & Rudnyckyj, 2009, p. 66). In the resulting relationships, affects are critical in establishing and maintaining boundaries, as they "align individuals with com-munities – or bodily spaces with social space – through the very intensity of their attachments" (Ahmed, 2004, p. 119). Often, embodied rituals are integral to the formation of such groups and their members, who are being "govern[ed] through affect" (Rudnyckyj, 2011, p. 65). Part of this process, which highlights the intimate connection between bodies and affect, is a striving for ethical self-improvement that can also motivate microfinance supporters. My conceptualiza-tion of affective investments also draws inspiration from the work of Larry Grossberg, who defines affect as "the coloration or passion within which one's investments in, or commitments to, the world are made possible" (1988, p. 285). Affect shapes what matters to people, within a field of power that circumscribes its effects.

This attention to power is a critical component in thinking about particular modes of engagement of Northern publics with global poverty-alleviation efforts and the ways in which these can become sites for ideological and political contestation. Drawing on Orientalism and post-development scholarship, the literature on the "public faces of development," which refers to the ways in which non-governmental organizations, the media and global civil society organizations mediate how Northern publics perceive issues of poverty and development, engages with such questions of power through representation (Smith & Yanacopulos, 2004). Its scholars reveal the central role of particular constructions of the Other in development interventions, showing how these public perceptions impact the relationship between the global North and South and the practices that stem from the public's understanding of this relationship. Lilie Chouliaraki's work on humanitarian communication, especially in mass media, has been particularly productive in showing the connections between development representations and practice (Chouliaraki, 2006, 2010, 2012).

There lies a danger in examining poverty and its alleviation through an affective lens, which must not neglect poverty's material conditions, political and structural causes and efforts for social change. However, "to understand what it means to be deprived, to experience the world differently and to be motivated to change it means attending to the way in which we are affected by it and how we affect others" (Wright, 2012, p. 1114). Attention to affect does not mean turning away from questions of power and politics, but can enrich our understanding of how these work in the world. This is especially relevant for international development, which works in the emotionally charged terrain of changing human lives under highly unequal relations. Nevertheless, for all inhabitants of this terrain, affect can provide a space of hope made possible by a "politics of affirmation" (Roelvink, 2010, p. 112).

Book Summary

Research for this book began in 2006, when Matt Flannery, the co-founder of a very young Kiva, was a participant at the Silicon Valley Challenge Summit co-organized by the RiOS Institute, for which I was working as the Director of Research. I have followed Kiva's developments since then, mainly through participant-observations as a Kiva lender, the study of its website and through attending public appearances by Kiva leaders. Since 2009, I have studied Kiva systematically, conducting interviews with staff, lenders and Fellows, as well as fieldwork with a former Mexican Kiva partner organization in 2009 and a current Indonesian Kiva partner in 2010. Primary research was also conducted on microfinance tours, which take financial inclusion supporters on site visits to observe the work of microfinance organizations; I undertook participant-observation at one Opportunity International Insight Tour to Chennai, India in 2012. This field research was complemented with visual and narrative analysis of relevant organizational websites. Each of the research projects for this book posed unique methodological challenges, which I address in the individual chapters.

Methodology is only part of the story, however. My various positionalities chart an uneven ground of engagement throughout the book. As an anthropologist of development who is critical of microfinance, I want to advance academic research in new directions by drawing attention to the importance of affect and everyday humanitarians. However, analytical distance proved more challenging in some situations than others. In other words, *New Media and International Development* was an intellectual, geographical and emotional journey, as I was drawn into relations, images and texts much more than I had expected to be, sometimes becoming an everyday humanitarian myself. Writing about affect, I realized that there is no location outside it. Last but not least, I also believe that publics matter, not only to microfinance and Kiva, but also to the kind of engaged scholarship I envision. At times, this demanded a balancing act between public accessibility and scholarly accountability; I leave it to the readers of my book to judge whether I have been successful.

New Media and International Development is divided into three parts: a conceptual (Chapter 1) and historical (Chapter 2) introduction; mediated connections with distant others through the Kiva website (Chapter 3) and photographs (Chapter 4); and personal encounters by way of microfinance tourism (Chapter 5) and volunteering for Kiva (Chapter 6). Taken together, these six chapters present a continuum of engagement from virtual and passive to active and involved.

While this first chapter has introduced my main arguments and grounded them in the academic literature, Chapter 2 provides a general historical foundation. Here I examine several modes of affective engagement of development supporters, namely campaign, emergency, spectacle, sponsorship and consumption. The chapter's focus is on key events and practices that have produced particular kinds of caring subject and made their affective investments manifest: the sugar boycott during the abolition movement, the Make Poverty History campaign, the LiveAid and Live 8 concerts and child sponsorship, among others. I pay particular attention to the role of various media in forging affective connections, from the pamphlets of the abolitionists to letters exchanged between child sponsors and their children to the televised spectacle of Band Aid and the virtual relationships established via social media. The chapter shows the ongoing tensions between ideas of a common humanity and hierarchical relationships of assistance, as well as the shift toward Northern actors and positive sentiments of engagement.

This leads to the second part of the book, titled "Mediations," in which I explore how affective investments in the financial inclusion assemblage are forged through narrative and visual representations on the Internet. Its power lies in its ability to broadcast dynamic information to widely dispersed and diverse audiences, to establish virtual connections and to aggregate micro-transactions for greater impact. Practices of representation, both narrative and visual, are central to these mediations.

In Chapter 3, I examine the work of Kiva's virtual stories in the mobilization of affective investments. I analyze the organizational discourses and practices by which Kiva cultivates affective investments in itself, in its cause of online person-to-person microfinance and in its over 1 million Kiva "entrepreneurs" who have received Kiva lenders' money via MFI partners. Central to the constitution of dedicated "Kivans" is the creation of humanitarian micronarratives, which are scripted representations of borrowers as worthy of lenders' support. These stories, together with pictures of borrowers and regular updates about their progress, promise virtual connections between lenders and borrowers. These are secondary to connections among lenders, however, who come together in lending teams organized around social, religious and geographic affiliations. These teams are particular manifestations of affective collectivities that give rise to practices of caring and sharing "Kiva love." Still, Kiva claims that a person-to-person relationship between lenders and borrowers is at the heart of its operations, an illusion that is successfully maintained by various forms of mediation. The success of the Kiva website, especially in the United States, calls for an examination of the political potential of love.

In Chapter 4, I analyze the importance of microfinance photographs through the lens of the CGAP Microfinance Photo Contest. I situate a number of its winning images within a well-established history in development representations, through which Northern publics learn about poverty and the possibilities of its alleviation. The chapter traces a shift from negative to positive imagery and examines how gendered representations legitimize particular practices of microfinance. Microfinance representations show especially poor women as agents of their own destiny, and are therefore particularly well suited to constitute financial inclusion supporters, by enabling personal identifications and showing the visible effect their financial contributions will have on the lives of poor borrowers.

The third part of the book, titled "Encounters," explores the experiences of financial inclusion supporters who come into direct contact with distant others, either through participating in organized microfinance tours or volunteering as Kiva Fellows at Kiva partner MFIs. In Chapter 5 I focus on microfinance tourism as an embodied engagement of financial inclusion supporters with their cause. Undertaking an affective journey to visit microfinance organizations to observe their work and its effects produces personal encounters, usually meant to reinforce the obligatory microfinance success story and cement support for it. Based on participant-observation at a microfinance tour to Chennai, India, I examine the performative and photographic aspects of microfinance tourism and the ways in which these create, confirm and, to a much smaller extent, contest subject positions of financial inclusion supporters. This chapter also takes a more explicit look at the role of religion in microfinance and international development.

More intense and involved than a microfinance tour is volunteering at a microfinance organization, which I analyze as a form of affective labor in Chapter 6. The chapter focuses on the experiences of Kiva Fellows, who are young professionals mostly from technological, financial and business backgrounds who volunteer for at least 4 months at a Kiva partner organization. Based on a content analysis of the extensive Kiva Fellows blog on the Kiva website, as well as interviews with Kiva Fellows and observation of their work, I examine volunteering as the most personal and emotionally invested form of financial inclusion support. Focusing on Kiva

Fellows' ambiguous status as Kiva's eyes and ears at the partner MFIs, on their changing representations of microfinance and development and on their journeys of self-discovery and transformation, this chapter directly engages the notion of fellowship. Through encounters with MFI staff and borrowers, Kiva Fellows' affective labor shapes their identities and relationships between self and other and ultimately cements their support for microfinance. Finally, the book's Conclusion interrogates the possibility of a politics based on affect.

Notes

* Parts of this chapter were previously published in the *Journal of International Development*, 26(4) (May 2014).
1 The quantitative dimension of the financialization of poverty also accords with the increasing emphasis on metrics to enable global rankings, impact assessments and monitoring and evaluation activities. Even social impact assessments and social performance indexes rely on quantitative data about changes to lives and livelihoods (Merry, 2011).
2 Although it is commonly assumed that microfinance originated with the Grameen Bank, in the 1970s there were similar experiments with microfinance by Accion in Latin America and what later became Opportunity International in Indonesia.
3 For anthropologists, millennial development invites reflections of "millennial capitalism," which, if rightly harnessed, also promises to transform the lives of the poor (Comaroff & Comaroff, 2000).
4 The moniker 2.0 reveals the origins of many of these ideas in the wealthy hi-tech culture of the US West Coast.
5 The trajectory of humanitarian reason is pursued by scholars of human rights.
6 While financial inclusion professionals debate whether microfinance is a tool for development or poverty alleviation, in practice it is used in both contexts.

Bibliography

Ahmed, S. (2004). Affective economies. *Social Text, 22*(2), 117–139.
Anderson, B. (2006). Becoming and being hopeful: Towards a theory of affect. *Environment and Planning D: Society and Space, 24*(5), 733–752.
Appadurai, A. (2001). Deep democracy: Urban governmentality and the horizon of politics. *Environment and Urbanization, 13*(2), 23–44.
Arendt, H. (2006 [1963]). *On revolution.* London: Penguin Classics.
Arrillaga-Andreessen, L. (2012). *Giving 2.0: Transform your giving and our world.* New York: Jossey-Bass.
Bateson, G. (1972). *Steps to an ecology of mind.* Chicago: Chicago University Press.
Bishop, M. & Green, M. (2008). *Philanthrocapitalism: How the rich can save the world.* New York: Bloomsbury Press.
Black, S. (2009). Microloans and micronarratives: Sentiments for a small world. *Public Culture, 21*(2), 269–291.
Black, S. (2013). Fictions of humanitarian responsibility: Narrating microfinance. *Journal of Human Rights, 12*(1), 103–120.
Boltanski, L. (1999). *Distant suffering: Morality, media and politics.* Cambridge: Cambridge University Press.
Bornstein, E. (2003). *The spirit of development: Protestant NGOs, morality and economics in Zimbabwe.* London: Routledge.

Bornstein, E. (2012). *Disquieting gifts: Humanitarianism in New Delhi*. Palo Alto, CA: Stanford University Press.

Brainard, L. & LaFleur, V. (2008). Making poverty history? How activists, philanthropists, and the public are changing global development. In L. Brainard & D. Chollet (Eds.), *Global development 2.0: Can philanthropists, the public, and the poor make poverty history?* (pp. 9–41). Washington, DC: Brookings Institution Press.

Calhoun, C. (2010). *The idea of emergency: Humanitarian action and global (dis)order*. New York: Zone Books.

Cameron, J. & Haanstra, A. (2008). Development made sexy: How it happened and what it means. *Third World Quarterly, 29*(8), 1475–1489.

Chouliaraki, L. (2006). *The spectatorship of suffering*. London: Sage.

Chouliaraki, L. (2010). Post-humanitarianism: Humanitarian communication beyond a politics of pity. *International Journal of Cultural Studies, 13*(2), 107–126.

Chouliaraki, L. (2012). The theatricality of humanitarianism: A critique of celebrity advocacy. *Communication and Critical/Cultural Studies, 9*(1), 1–21.

Chu, M. (2005). Microfinance: The next ten years. In A. Pakpahan, E. M. Lokollo & K. Wijaya (Eds.), *Microbanking: Creation opportunities for the poor through innovation* (pp. 111–115). Jakarta: Bak Rakyat Indonesia.

Coates, B. & Saloner, G. (2009). The profit in nonprofit. *Stanford Social Innovation Review*, Summer, 68–71.

Cohen, S. (2001). *States of denial: Knowing about atrocities and suffering*. Cambridge: Polity.

Collins, D., Morduch, J., Rutherford, S. & Ruthven, O. (2009). *Portfolios of the poor: How the world's poor live on $2 a day*. Princeton, NJ: Princeton University Press.

Comaroff, J. & Comaroff, J. L. (2000). Millennial capitalism: First thoughts on a second coming. *Public Culture, 12*(2), 291–343.

Edward, P. (2006). The ethical poverty line: A moral quantification of absolute poverty. *Third World Quarterly, 27*(2), 377–393.

Fassin, D. (2010). Heart of humaneness: The moral economy of humanitarian intervention. In D. Fassin & M. Pandolfi (Eds.), *Contemporary states of emergency: The politics of military and humanitarian interventions* (pp. 269–294). New York: Zone Books.

Fassin, D. (2012). *Humanitarian reason: A moral history of the present*. Berkeley: University of California Press.

Feldman, I. (2010). The humanitarian circuit: Relief work, development assistance, and CARE in Gaza, 1955–67. In E. Bornstein & P. Redfield (Eds.), *Forces of compassion: Humanitarianism between ethics and politics* (pp. 203–226). Santa Fe, NM: SAR Press.

Flannery, M. (2009). Kiva at four. *Innovations: Technology, Governance, Globalization, 4*(2), 31–49.

Gajjala, R. (2012). *Cyberculture and the subaltern: Weavings of the virtual and real*. Lexington, KY: Lexington Press.

Gajjala, R. & Birzescu, A. (2011). Digital imperialism through online social/financial networks. *Economic and Political Weekly, 66*(13), 95–102.

Grossberg, L. (1988). Postmodernity and affect: All dressed up with no place to go. *Communication, 10*(3–4), 271–293.

Halpern, J. & Weinstein, H. (2004). Rehumanizing the other: Empathy and reconciliation. *Human Rights Quarterly, 26*(3), 561–583.

Harding, J. & Pribram, E. (2004). Losing our cool? Following Williams and Grossberg on emotions. *Cultural Studies, 18*(6), 863–883.

Hardt, M. (2011). For love or money. *Cultural Anthropology, 26*(4), 676–682.

Haskell, T. (1985). Capitalism and the origins of humanitarian sensibilities. *American Historical Review, 90*(2), 339–361.

Heim, K. (2006, December 18). Web of giving. *Seattle Times*.

Ilcan, S. & Lacey, A. (2011). *Governing the poor: Exercises in poverty reduction, practices of global aid*. Montreal and Kingston: McGill-Queen's University Press.

Karim, L. (2011). *Microfinance and its discontents: Women in debt in Bangladesh*. Minneapolis: University of Minnesota Press.

Karnani, A. (2007). Employment, not microcredit, is the solution. *Journal of Corporate Citizenship, 32*, 45–62.

Konings, M. (2014). Financial affect. *Distinktion: Scandinavian Journal of Social Theory, 15*(1), 37–53.

Kothari, U. (2001). Power, knowledge and social control in participatory development. In B. Cooke & U. Kothari (Eds.), *Participation: The new tyranny?* (pp. 139–152). London: Zed Books.

Laqueur, T. (2009). Mourning, pity, and the work of narrative in the making of "humanity." In R. A. Wilson & R. D. Brown (Eds.), *Humanitarianism and suffering: The mobilization of empathy* (pp. 31–57). Cambridge: Cambridge University Press.

Li, T. M. (2007). Practices of assemblage and community forest management. *Economy and Society, 36*(2), 263–293.

Littlefield, E., Morduch, J. & Hashemi, S. (2003). *Is microfinance an effective strategy to reach the Millennium Development Goals?* Washington, DC: CGAP.

Maclean, K. (2013). Gender, risk and micro-financial subjectivities. *Antipode, 45*(2), 455–473.

Malkki, L. (2010). Children, humanity and the infantilization of peace. In I. Feldman & M. Ticktin (Eds.), *In the name of humanity: The government of threat and care* (pp. 58–90). Durham, NC: Duke University Press.

Matthäus-Maier, I. & von Pischke, J. D. (2009). *New partnerships for innovation in microfinance*. Berlin: Springer Verlag.

Maurer, B. (2012). Mobile money: Communication, consumption and change in the payments space. *Journal of Development Studies, 48*(5), 589–604.

Mazzarella, W. (2009). Affect: What is it good for? In S. Dube (Ed.), *Enchantments of modernity: Empire, nation, globalization* (pp. 291–309). London: Routledge.

Merry, S. (2011). Measuring the world: Indicators, human rights and global governance. *Current Anthropology, 52*(S3), 83–95.

Moodie, M. (2013). Microfinance and the gender of risk: The case of Kiva.org. *Signs, 38*(2), 279–302.

Navaro-Yashin, Y. (2009). Affective spaces, melancholic objects: Ruination and the production of anthropological knowledge. *Journal of the Royal Anthropological Institute* (N.S.), 15, 1–18.

Rahman, A. (1999). *Women and microcredit in rural Bangladesh: Anthropological study of the rhetoric and realities of Grameen Bank lending*. Boulder, CO: Westview Press.

Redfield, P. (2012). The unbearable lightness of ex-pats: Double binds of humanitarian mobility. *Cultural Anthropology, 27*(2), 358–382.

Redfield, P. & Bornstein, E. (2010). An introduction to the anthropology of humanitarianism. In E. Bornstein & P. Redfield (Eds.), *Forces of compassion: Humanitarianism between ethics and politics* (pp. 3–30). Santa Fe, NM: SAR Press.

Richard, A. & Rudnyckyj, D. (2009). Economies of affect. *Journal of the Royal Anthropological Institute* (N.S.), 15, 57–77.

Richey, L. A. & Ponte, S. (2011). *Brand aid: Shopping well to save the world*. Minneapolis: University of Minnesota Press.

Roelvink, G. (2010). Collective action and the politics of affect. *Emotions, Space and Society, 3*, 111–118.

Rorty, R. (1993). Human rights, rationality, and sentimentality. In S. Shute & S. Hurley

(Eds.), *On human rights: The Oxford Amnesty lectures* (pp. 111–134). New York: Basic Books.

Roy, A. (2010). *Poverty capital: Microfinance and the making of development.* New York and London: Routledge.

Roy, A. (2012a). Ethical subjects: Market rule in an age of poverty. *Public Culture, 24*(1), 105–108.

Roy, A. (2012b). Subjects of risk: Technologies of gender in the making of millennial modernity. *Public Culture, 24*(1), 131–155.

Rozario, K. (2003). "Delicious horrors": Mass culture, the Red Cross, and the appeal of modern American humanitarianism. *American Quarterly, 55*(3), 417–455.

Rudnyckyj, D. (2011). Circulating tears and managing hearts: Governing through affect in an Indonesian steel factory. *Anthropological Theory, 11*(1), 63–87.

Sandvik, K. B. (2009). The physicality of legal consciousness: Suffering and the production of credibility in refugee settlement. In R. A. Wilson & R. D. Brown (Eds.), *Humanitarianism and suffering: The mobilization of empathy* (pp. 223–244). Cambridge: Cambridge University Press.

Schwittay, A. (2011). The financial inclusion assemblage: Subjects, techniques, rationalities. *Critique of Anthropology, 31*(4), 381–401.

Schwittay, A. (2014). Making poverty into a financial problem: From global poverty lines to Kiva.org. *Journal of International Development, 26*(4), 508–519.

Sen, A. (1999). *Development as freedom.* New York: Doubleday.

Smith, M. & Yanacopulos, H. (2004). The public faces of development: An introduction. *Journal of International Development, 16*(5), 657–664.

Solomon, H. (2011). Affective journeys: The emotional structuring of medical tourism in India. *Anthropology and Medicine, 18*(1), 105–118.

Sontag, S. (2003). *Regarding the pain of others.* New York: Picador.

Stewart, K. (2007). *Ordinary affects.* Durham, NC: Duke University Press.

Suski, L. (2009). Children, suffering, and the humanitarian appeal. In R. A. Wilson & R. D. Brown (Eds.), *Humanitarianism and suffering: The mobilization of empathy* (pp. 202–222). Cambridge: Cambridge University Press.

Tatarchevskiy, T. (2011). The "popular" culture of internet activism. *New Media and Society, 13*(2), 297–313.

Wilden, A. & Wilson, T. (1976). The double bind: Logic, magic and economics. In C. Sluzki & D. Ranson (Eds.), *Double bind: The foundation of the communicational approach to the family* (pp. 263–286). New York: Grune & Stratton.

Williams, R. (1975). *The country and the city.* Oxford: Oxford University Press.

Williams, R. (1976). *Keywords: A vocabulary of culture and society.* Oxford: Oxford University Press.

Wilson, R. A. & Brown, R. D. (2009). Introduction. In R. A. Wilson & R. D. Brown (Eds.), *Humanitarianism and suffering: The mobilization of empathy* (pp. 1–28). Cambridge: Cambridge University Press.

Woodward, K. (2004). Calculating compassion. In L. Berlant (Ed.), *Compassion: The culture and politics of an emotion.* New York: Routledge.

Wright, S. (2012). Emotional geographies of development. *Third World Quarterly, 33*(6), 1113–1127.

Yunus, M. (1999). *Banker to the poor: Micro-lending and the battle against world poverty.* New York: Public Affairs.

2

A BRIEF HISTORY OF AFFECTIVE INVESTMENTS

In the early 1970s, Bangladesh became a hotspot for humanitarian activities. The confluence of Cyclone Bhola in 1970, the war of independence from Pakistan in 1971 and a devastating famine in 1974, and the suffering that these crises created, brought numerous humanitarian organizations into the country. They led George Harrison to stage the first prominent humanitarian concert, mobilizing celebrity performers to raise money for the afflicted nation. And they motivated a young Bangladeshi named Muhammad Yunus to return from the United States to help establish his new country. By 1976 Yunus had created a microlending program that was to become the Grameen Bank.

While Grameen contributed to the birth of modern microfinance, the origins of modern humanitarianism lie more than 200 years earlier, in the second half of the 18th century. It was at that time that events such as the Lisbon earthquake and the anti-slavery campaign came together with changing ideas about causal action at a distance to create the conditions under which sentiments of caring for far-off suffering others could emerge. These sentiments drew on older religious ideas of brotherly love and the equal worth of all human beings (Redfield & Bornstein, 2010), as well as contemporary texts such as Adam Smith's *The Theory of Moral Sentiments*, which had been published in 1759. The 1776 US Declaration of Independence and the French Declaration of the Rights of Man and of the Citizen 12 years later also inspired followers of the nascent humanitarian movement (Wilson & Brown, 2009). It was a time when "moral sentiments became the driving force for politics" more broadly (Fassin, 2010, p. 272) and when capitalism's expansion provided new insights into what caused human affairs and how they could be made predictable across space and time. Capitalism also produced the discipline and technologies to act on these insights (Haskell, 1985a, 1985b).

A century later it was the expansion of international trade that made Northern consumers aware of how their own actions linked them causally to distant others. This awareness became tied up with ideas of progress and improvement that were driven by the rise of modern industry, the early achievements of modern science and technology and modern state notions of equivalent subjects. All of these led to the emergence of a "new sense of interconnectedness" and a new understanding of responsibility, obligations and rights (Calhoun, 2010, p. 42). At around the same time, poverty came to be seen as a solvable problem through the application of secular solutions. Finally, "mass humanitarianism" emerged in the United States in the 1920s, together with the sensationalistic mass culture forged in the crucible of World War I propaganda films, advertising and marketing campaigns and pulp fiction (Rozario, 2003, p. 425).

Taking the historical location of the 18th century as a starting point, in this chapter I rewrite the emergence of everyday humanitarian as a history of affective engagements. In particular, I trace the unfolding of various modes of affective engagements through which Anglo-American everyday humanitarians contribute to alleviating the poverty and suffering of distant others, who are usually located in the global South. My analysis of the modes of campaign, emergency, spectacle, sponsorship and consumption proceeds roughly along chronological lines within each section, which results in some temporal back-and-forth between sections. What unites these modes is the ways in which they provide appropriate recipes that constitute everyday people as humanitarians and mobilize their affective investments. All of them are also characterized by the ongoing tension between notions of a common humanity and hierarchical differences among those who expend care and those who receive it. In addition, I pay attention to the various media by which states of suffering and poverty as well as the possibility of action against them are communicated. This shows that popular attention has been moving from passive distant sufferers toward active Northern helpers, with corresponding shifts in humanitarian sentiments from guilt and pity to empathy to self-gratification and pride.

Campaign

Humanitarian campaigns bring together large numbers of people who show their support for the alleviation of distant suffering through attending public events such as demonstrations, speaker tours or concerts, and through lobbying elected representatives to bring about political change. The movement to abolish slavery is often identified as one of the earliest humanitarian campaigns and fostered many of the sentiments animating its successors (Calhoun, 2010; Redfield & Bornstein, 2010). In the 21st century, the Make Poverty History campaign is exemplary in its dramatized call for global engagement, while KONY2012 showed the power and reach of social media to engender debates about everyday humanitarianism.

Abolitionist Movement

In the late 18th century, the abolitionist movement that had begun among progressive Quakers in America gained popular momentum (Haskell, 1985b). It was a time when the "ethical subject was democratized" (Laqueur, 2009, p. 38), so that more people felt obligated to care about a widely expanded range of distant others, which included African slaves. In Britain, the Society for the Abolition of the Slave Trade was established in 1787 by a group of men who had gathered in a London printing shop, a location that signals the importance of the public distribution of information about the slave trade by means of pamphlets, books and posters. Through such means, the "reformers succeeded in arousing sympathy and in awakening moral qualms so powerfully as to mobilize political action" (Wilson & Brown, 2009, p. 10). At the heart of the campaign were textual and visual "humanitarian narratives [that] created 'sympathetic passions' that bridged the gulf between fact, compassion and action" (Laqueur, 1989, p. 179).

Thomas Clarkson's *Essay on the Slavery and Commerce of the Human Species, Particularly the African* was written in 1785; his book tour 2 years later drew much public attention to the Society and its abolitionist cause. His broadsheet *The Slave Ship* depicted in great detail how 482 bodies were crammed into the *Brookes* for the horror of the Middle Passage; it was one of the first publications that made the evils of slavery visible. The autobiography of freed slave Olaudah Equiano not only showed the cruelty of slavery, but also that Africans were able to produce great literature. Together, these works constituted African slaves as fellow human beings, sharing a common humanity with British people that was based on their ability to *feel* that they have been wronged. Other criteria for this inclusion were variously located in physical appearance, reason, sensibility and capacity to care for others (Festa, 2010).

These narratives mobilized popular antislavery sentiment by appealing to British minds and hearts alike. Representations played a central role in this process; while abolitionists presented slaves as deserving of compassion, the British public was shown as political subjects who held the necessary power to effect change for them. A good example of this is Josiah Wedgwood's medallion depicting a kneeling African man in shackles, looking upwards, with the words "Am I not a man and a brother?" printed underneath. The slave is shown "supplicating" to outside forces on which he is dependent to be granted his freedom (Coleman, 1994, p. 342). On the one hand, the image presented the slave and the viewer as members of a common family joined together by ties of Christian brotherhood. On the other, it encouraged viewers to consider slaves primarily as individuals, albeit stereotyped and anonymous, who required care and to adopt the role of the carer, thereby reinforcing a set of hierarchies consistent with the gap between humane behavior and human equality (Laqueur, 2009). After its original publication by the Society in 1787, the image began to appear on kitchenware, coins, medals, flags, bracelets, hair pins, snuff boxes and other domestic accessories (Sheller, 2011). In this way, support for the antislavery movement became something that could easily be packaged, communicated and displayed in British households, also winning British women for the abolitionist cause. What was important in this early mobilization of humanitarian sentiment was the generic individualization of suffering slaves, where not the abstract wrong of slavery, but awareness of individual pain turned people into abolitionists by arousing their sympathy. This individualization continues in current humanitarian appeals, although the feelings it engenders have changed.

Make Poverty History

Nearly 200 years later, in February 2005, Nelson Mandela invoked the specter of slavery in front of 20,000 people assembled in London's Trafalgar Square to argue against the "social evil" of persisting poverty and inequality in the current age of scientific, technological and industry advances. According to him, the Global Campaign for Action Against Poverty (GCAAP) that had organized the demonstration "can take its place as a public movement alongside the movement to abolish slavery and the international solidarity against apartheid."[1] Mandela thereby established a direct link between today's humanitarian campaigns and its predecessors. The Make Poverty History (MPH) campaign was the British branch of the international GCAAP[2] and brought together over 500 non-governmental organizations (NGOs), ranging from large international ones such as Oxfam to smaller, often more radical groups. All denounced the inaction of global leaders and pressed for concrete measures by G8 governments toward the achievement of the United Nations' Millennium Development Goals (MDGs). Demands focused on increasing foreign aid, granting debt relief[3] and pursuing trade justice. MPH focused on 2005 because the Blair government hosted the G8 Summit in Gleneagles, Scotland, the United Nations reported on MDG progress during its Millennium Summit and a World Trade Organization forum in December promised to bring the Doha Round to a successful conclusion.

On January 1, 2005, during a popular prime-time BBC sitcom, *The Vicar of Dibley* implored her parishioners to support MPH. Its organization as a yearlong media campaign ensured that the public's awareness of MPH remained high (Nash, 2008). Throughout the year, TV documentaries and drama shows reminded people of its importance, and all major British newspapers ran stories, commentaries and op-ed pieces on the campaign. High-profile events such as Mandela's speech and the Live 8 concert coinciding with the G8 Summit brought thousands of MPH supporters together. These mass gatherings generate their own emotional states of being that sustain collective actors (Goodwin, Jasper & Polletta, 2001). Rather than pity, MPH fostered indignation; its slogan was "Justice not Charity" and its demand was reform of international institutions and trade relations. Instead of donating money, the British public was asked to sign petitions, write letters to their MPs, demonstrate and vote for trade justice via the Internet.

Nevertheless, MPH was heavily dramatized and suffused with emotions. According to Bono, "this is show business, we are creating drama" (cited in Nash, 2008, p. 173). Central to this drama was the constitution of its main character – MPH supporters – as a unique, heroic and great generation: the first one with the opportunity, and the responsibility, to make poverty history. The emphasis was on individuals, who recognized each other by their white wristbands and came together to "change the world for good" (*Guardian*, May 15, 2005, cited in Nash, 2008, p. 173). As such, MPH mobilized feelings of empowerment and pride, rather than shame or guilt. While compassion for distant suffering was "an important subtheme, the heroic rescue narrative was much more prominent" (Nash, 2008, pp. 173–174).

The British public, indignant about persistent poverty, denounced the global system that perpetuated it and demanded actions from politicians.

The latter did deliver promises of more foreign aid, spurred on in part by the large numbers of people mobilized by MPH. Ultimately, however, the campaign failed to achieve its goals especially around trade justice, as even its organizers admitted (DATA, 2007). Critics have attributed this to the campaign's operation from within existing global capitalist structures and governance institutions, to the absence of critical African and Western voices and to the limited mandate given to politicians (Biccum, 2007). More importantly for my argument, MPH's emotional character meant that the sentiments for distant suffering it aroused "degenerate[d] from a collective understanding of 'our' moral obligation to do something to alleviate that suffering into narcissistic sentimentalism" (Nash, 2008, p. 177). Action was ultimately contained to consuming music, wristbands and mobile technology, while the power to enact change was given to an elite group of "eight men who can change the world," as Bob Geldof, one of MPH's organizers, put it. Indignation is not sufficient when it is not based on theories of power that show the necessity of changing international political-economic structures of domination (Boltanski, 1999).

Still, MPH cast a spotlight on the power of the Internet to mobilize large constituents for a cause. Information and communication technologies (ICTs) and social media have become central to humanitarian efforts since then, based on a number of promises they are seen to hold. First, they enable people directly affected by crises to become citizen journalists and report first-hand from the front lines, resulting in presumably more authentic and legitimate "sites of witnessing" (Madianou, 2013, p. 250). Second, ICTs allow for disintermediation, because its users do not have to rely on traditional gatekeepers such as mainstream media conglomerates to quickly disseminate news to widely dispersed audiences. Third, ICTs facilitate action, which is only a click away and includes forwarding links, donating money or adding one's name to a petition. On the one hand, such "clicktivism" (White, 2010) condenses the time between knowing and acting and thereby lessens the chances for "implicatory denial" in the form of "arguments, reasons or rationalizations for not responding sympathetically to distressing information" (Cohen, 2001, p. 211). On the other, Internet action can slide into "slacktivism" that is too easy, singular and decoupled from understanding the causes and contexts of suffering (Madianou, 2013; Waldorf, 2012). Moreover, its effortless instantaneity, while acknowledging that humanitarian emotions cannot be sustained for long periods, shows its close connections to contemporary consumer culture (Chouliaraki, 2010). Action becomes routinized when people are told exactly what they should write to whom. This is not to say that the global justice movement has not used ICTs to great effect (Juris, 2008), but when the Internet becomes the primary medium of action, it "contributes to the circulation of affect and opinion and involves a profound passivity, one that is interconnected, linked, but passive nonetheless" (Tatarchevskiy, 2011, p. 306). All of this played out in an exemplary manner in the KONY2012 campaign.

KONY2012

Tapping into the millennial Facebook generation, this campaign broke all records for the use of social media for humanitarian causes. It began on March 5, 2012, when Invisible Children (IC), an organization established in 2004 in San Diego, California, posted a 30-minute video on YouTube. The video showed the atrocities committed by Joseph Kony and his Ugandan Lord's Resistance Army (LRA), especially their abduction of children who become child soldiers or prostitutes. The video went viral and within a week had been watched more than 100 million times.[4] Its accompanying website posted the Twitter accounts of 20 celebrities and 12 politicians whom viewers were to contact for support of the campaign's ultimate goal – military intervention to arrest Kony and stop the LRA's abductions. The campaign organizers claimed that in the end over 3.7 million people had pledged their support, forming a self-proclaimed "'army of peace,' that, if successful, 'will change the course of history'" (cited in Gomberg-Muñoz, 2013, p. 293). Through such language, especially young people in the global North were constituted as a dramatic force for good.

In later videos, IC linked its work to the dispatch of an international military advisory force to the region, the capture of two top LRA commanders, the African Union's 5,000-men-brigade to hunt down Kony, the US Senate passing a resolution to arrest Kony and ultimately to President Obama passing legislation to extend the Reward for Justice program that allows the State Department to offer monetary rewards leading to the capture of human rights abusers, Kony being at the top of the list.[5] It is important to note that this attention and action was not just the result of a 30-minute social media campaign. For 10 years, IC had created a physical support network through its presence in the everyday lives of young people in schools, concerts, music videos and other television shows. The success of this strategy – to meet young people "on their own terms," according to IC's Communication Director – is shown in the fact that the video's biggest promoters were 13–17-year-old girls and 18–24-year-old men (Karlin & Matthew, 2012).[6]

The video itself was heavily criticized for its slickness, lack of historical context and accuracy, and its general "missionary zeal and traffic in ... tired tropes about Africa" (Waldorf, 2012, p. 469). Anthropologists and African scholars were among the leading critical voices, drawing attention to the danger of calling for international military intervention that would destabilize the region and prop up the Ugandan army, which itself was known to perpetrate crimes against civilians. As is often the case with international development efforts, such calls ignore, or can work against, local efforts at reconciliation. According to KONY2012's creator, IC views itself as "the Pixar of human rights stories," in reference to the successful animation company founded by the late Apple CEO Steve Jobs and now owned by Walt Disney. This reveals the ways in which humanitarian campaigns have become "post-modern mash-ups [and] spectacular happenings" (Waldorf, 2012, p. 469). Indeed, at the center of KONY2012, which aimed to make Kony as famous as George Clooney, was a Pop Art "Wanted" poster showing Kony in front of

Bin Laden and Hitler. The campaign's supporters were asked to blanket the night with these posters in April 2012 to make Kony visible to the unconnected masses. That the turnout for this event was much smaller than the video audience shows the difficulty of sustaining online action and taking it into the physical world.

Although KONY2012 has been analyzed as an instance of de-emotionalized post-humanitarian communication (Madianou, 2013), it draws heavily on standard humanitarian affective registers. From the cuteness of the narrator's 4-year-old blond son, who functions as a reminder of the childhood Kony's victims should be having, to Jacob, an escaped child soldier, sobbing when he recounts how he witnessed the slaughter of his brother by the LRA, to the narrator himself seemingly overwhelmed when Jacob tells him that he would rather be dead than alive, to the brief images of mutilated children, the video deploys conventional representations to evoke both empathy and indignation. Juxtaposed to these representations of LRA victims are "the positive emotions associated with the celebration of (Western) publics' ability to change the world through social media" (Madianou, 2013, p. 259). Viewers were told over and over again that now we know what to do about people like Kony, utilizing the tools of technology to make the invisible visible on a number of levels. Kony himself must be tracked down in his hiding place in the jungle and the plight of child soldiers must be shown to the world. Furthermore, campaign supporters, sporting red T-shirts and wristbands, waving posters and flashing V-signs, "perform[ed] visual labor" that drew attention to Kony's atrocities, made support for KONY2012 visible to the world and in the process legitimized IC (Tatarchevskiy, 2011, p. 298). Ultimately, the video became about the power of the millennial generation to make history. For its members, who made up the great majority of the campaign's supporters, participating in KONY2012 became part of the narrative they told about themselves in their Facebook profiles and Twitter updates, where self-presentation is built into the medium and provides temporary celebrity status (Mostafanezhad, 2013b). Like MPH, KONY2012 turned attention away from Africans and toward their self-proclaimed Western protectors and saviors, replicating a colonial narrative and reinforcing a denunciatory and narcissistic engagement with humanitarianism that has come to characterize its current stage.

Emergency

The emergency mode of affective engagements encompasses responses to exceptional states from what are considered normal conditions. These include, among others, natural disasters, famines and wars. In addition to many of these events being human-made, the very category of emergency is culturally constructed, giving rise to a moral "emergency imaginary" that centers on the perceived unpredictability, suddenness and immediacy of emergency events (Calhoun, 2010, p. 31). These not only demand urgent responses but also enable the mobilization of resources from governments, humanitarian organizations and Northern publics. Emergencies thus incite humanitarian actions and sentiments in their purest form, operating according to a calculus of bare life counted in numbers of dead bodies and saved survivors (Agamben, 1998).

Emergencies are also always highly mediated, dramatized and often sensationalized to bring forth affective investments. From the 1755 Lisbon earthquake to the 1984/1985 Ethiopian famine and the 2004 Indian Ocean tsunami, "major natural disasters produce the greatest waves of charitable donations, as well as graphic visuals of suffering that obviate the need for advocacy or advertising" (Redfield, 2008, p. 211). The representation of innocent victims, most often women and children, to report the suffering on the ground does not allow for the complex causes of emergencies to be conveyed. It also presents the strongest resonance with colonial images of helpless, powerless Southerners depending on external help from the North, and thereby neglects existing local responses to emergencies (Brauman, 2009). Such representations drive fundraising appeals to bring in assistance, channeled through agencies that present themselves as ready and efficient dispensers of relief. By supporting these agencies, based on an emotional response to the mediatized witnessing of far-away suffering, Northern publics can do their part to aid distant others who are also fellow human beings. Emergencies are thus a central mode of affective engagement, and it is no coincidence that an emergency is often considered to be one of the founding moments of modern humanitarianism.

The Lisbon Earthquake

November 1, 1755 was by all accounts a beautiful day in Lisbon, then the splendid capital of an enormous and powerful colonial empire and home to 275,000 people. It was the Catholic feast of All Saints Day, and in Lisbon, a stronghold of the Inquisition at the time, "the air was ripe with incense, church bells and the collective drone of prayers" (Sliwinski, 2009, p. 25). The churches were filled for morning mass, when at 9:40 a.m. the priests' chanting was interrupted by the violent clanging of bells, shattering glass and the swaying of church walls. People who rushed outside saw that the once clear sky had turned dark and that gigantic fissures had opened up in the ground, from which white sand rose like steam. Several aftershocks, a devastating tsunami and a fire that raged for 6 days killed between 30,000 and 40,000 people.

In its magnitude, the Lisbon earthquake is an important early moment in the formation of humanitarian sentiment. Long-standing religious ideas about the causes of natural disasters were shaken to their core, which reinforced the general confidence of the time in the human ability to bring about progress (Haskell, 1985b). Enlightenment thinkers such as Voltaire questioned whether a just and compassionate God would have allowed this earthquake to happen. More perceptively, Rousseau, in his response to Voltaire's "Poem on the Lisbon Disaster," noted "the artificiality of natural disasters, created as much by urban crowding and hazardous construction as by geological instability" (Redfield & Bornstein, 2010, p. 15). He thereby foreshadowed the insights of contemporary scholars like Sen and de Waal about the political nature of so-called natural disasters. Four years after the earthquake, Smith published his *Theory of Moral Sentiments*, in which he argued that a moral sense arises from the experience of seeing another person's misfortune. Lastly, Burke and Kant's ideas about the sublime as an overwhelming experience of suffering that causes pleasure motivated by "a sympathetic pity based on love" took shape in response to the quake (Sliwinski, 2009, p. 31).

News about the earthquake spread quickly throughout Europe; newspapers in Berlin reported on it only 10 days after it happened, with their Paris and London counterparts not far behind. "For the first time in the Western world, the press helped to create the illusion of proximity and unity among the peoples of different European nations" (Araujo, 2006, p. 2). The focus of the media reports was on the survivors' panic, which was described so vividly that people as far away as Germany imagined that they had felt the earth shaking on November 1.[7] In addition to this official print news, hundreds of tracts of supposed eyewitness accounts were written in many European languages, often by people who had not been in Lisbon. They fed and reinforced the public's curiosity with sensational, fantastic and terrifying accounts of the quake and its aftermath. The most popular media of dissemination were pamphlets and chapbooks, which were produced in the many printing shops that existed at the time in all major European cities. Available for pennies at every pub and fairground, these publications often contained prints and engravings of imagined scenes that represented the catastrophe as felt by the inhabitants of Lisbon, showing people with their hands over their heads and despairing faces.

Both the official eyewitness accounts and their imaginative recounting focused on the suffering of ordinary people and thereby "brought into consciousness a global, imagined empathy with the sufferings of distant strangers" (Sliwinski, 2009, p. 24). The affective intensity of the calamity and of its representation heightened existing feelings of sympathy into empathetic identification that supported emerging notions of a singular, shared humanity. There was one important difference to later emergencies, however. While spectators in other countries empathized with the innocent victims of Lisbon, they did not have the "recipe knowledge" to rush to their aid (Haskell, 1985b, p. 561). Rather, assistance came from the main European powers at the time, also because the quake appeared at a complex political time for the continent (Araujo, 2006). There was also charity channeled through the churches, which took months to arrive. This shows not only the limited capacity to respond to a major disaster in 1755, but also the inability of ordinary people to imagine that they could help its victims. Some 250 years later, sophisticated communication, finance and transportation infrastructures, as well as the professionalization of the humanitarian sector, have given Northern publics the means to assist in relief efforts, mainly through financial contributions (Calhoun, 2010). Action seems possible, and, according to relief organizations, is of moral urgency. This is especially visible in famine relief.

Famines

The first major famine to reach the consciousness and hearts of especially British publics took place in 1968 in Biafra. The famine was in part caused by the country's failed struggle for independence from Nigeria, but it was not news about the war but the graphic images of emaciated children with flies in their eyes and bloated bellies that touched the British public and aroused its compassion. The intensity of these images was heightened by the innovation of color television broadcasts that had begun in the United Kingdom only the year before.[8] The Biafra famine was also one of the first humanitarian efforts dominated by NGOs rather than multilateral institutions such as the United Nations, and resulted in a number of important humanitarian organizations such as Médecins Sans Frontières (Doctors without Borders; MSF) being founded or growing significantly (de Waal, 1997). Together with the media, these organizations relocated their activities from Biafra to Bangladesh in the early 1970s.

A little over 10 years later, the Ethiopian famine in 1984/1985 became a watershed moment for affective humanitarian engagements, resulting in new ways of visual media use, the high-profile engagement of celebrity humanitarians and the foregrounding of pity. The famine "foster[ed] a moral economy based on affect and sentimentality" that neglected the complex situation at its root, which arose from a combination of drought, poor soil conditions, a state-led program of agricultural collectivization, the forced resettlement of thousands of people and armed conflict (Müller, 2013, p. 472). The British public began to take note after a BBC News broadcast on October 23, 1984. The anchorwoman who introduced the report briefly mentioned that two secessionist wars in Northern Ethiopia had complicated the famine, which had been caused by drought and lack of food, but the sight of rocket launchers and the sounds of fighter jets had been edited out of the images beamed into the homes of millions of TV viewers that night. Rather, the report by BBC reporter Michael Buerk portrayed a scene of epic devastation:

> Dawn, and as the sun breaks through the piercing chill of night on the plain outside Korem, it lights up a biblical famine, now, in the twentieth century. This place, say workers here, is the closest thing to hell on earth. Thousands of wasted people. They come for help and find only death. They flood in every day from villages hundreds of miles away, dulled by hunger, driven beyond the point of desperation.[9]

These words were uttered against a backdrop of overwhelming images of a sea of humanity (Malkki, 1996), consisting of countless dark faces covered in dust and flies, emaciated limbs and protruding ribs, wrapped corpses on stretchers, and rows and rows of people staring with hollow eyes into the dirt in which they were squatting. The continuous wailing, crying and shouting of grieving camp residents permeated the air, while Buerk and a female French MSF volunteer were the only people who actually spoke, giving a white voice to African despair.[10] The report was subsequently repeated by 425 broadcasting stations around the world.

Those who viewed the broadcast were presented with an essentialized, seemingly timeless, image of a famine perpetuated by natural forces outside human control, producing unspeakable suffering that could only be alleviated by donations to Western relief organizations (Müller, 2013). As Buerk stated repeatedly, "the relief agencies are doing all they can," marking the sickest and poorest like cattle so that they could receive a piece of second-hand clothing and be loaded onto government trucks for transport to already overcrowded sheds, where food, shelter and medicine was provided. The report produced tears and unprompted donations from usually unsentimental BBC News staffers and jammed Oxfam's switchboard for 3 days (Lidchi, 1999). It was Bob Geldof who realized "how this direct gaze at destitute victims would elicit widespread compassion" (Müller, 2013, p. 475). Only a month after the Korem report, he had assembled a group of fellow musicians and released the Band Aid charity record "Do They Know It's Christmas?" I will show below how this song and the subsequent Live Aid concert became part of the spectacle mode of engagement. Their emotional appeal was based on representations of innocent victims that reinforced the image of Africa as "the archetypical continent of suffering that requires charitable interventions" (Müller, 2013, p. 475).

In more recent famine appeals, such as for the 2011 famine in the Horn of Africa, similar representations were distributed via YouTube and exhorted viewers to keep sharing the clips via Facebook and Twitter. Technological change has been accompanied by affective shifts, from charitable pity for innocent victims to anger at the failure to prevent such emergencies. While in 1985, the Korem report closed with a brief mention that the relief organizations were angry that governments were not doing more, in 2011 it was viewers who were invited, by angry celebrities, to become indignant themselves. They were to click, not to make a donation but to lobby their politicians to stop the famine (Müller, 2013). A campaign video by ONE, an organization co-founded by Bono, showed a cacophony of irritated celebrities arguing that "drought is an act of nature. Famine is man-made. And we know how to stop this." Here, images of starving Africans had been replaced by celebrity faces, facts and expletives.[11] Even though some of famine's broader issues were acknowledged in the video, the political conflict in which the Somali famine must be situated continued to be ignored.

2004 Tsunami

An examination of the emergency mode of affective engagement would be incomplete without mention of the 2004 Indian Ocean tsunami, which killed hundreds of thousands of people, mostly in Indonesia, Thailand, India and Sri Lanka. The subsequent outpouring of compassion was unprecedented, resulting in US$5.7 billion donated to NGOs.[12] Contributions were so overwhelming that after 1 week, MSF refused to accept any more money for relief efforts. This decision was controversial, also because "any attempt to tone down the discourse or view the situation in perspective was perceived as heartlessness, while sensationalism and excess were seen as manifestations of compassion" (Brauman, 2009, p. 114). A number of factors came together to produce this new magnitude of affective investments: Christmas is already a period of high charitable engagement; the victims included not just distant others but also recognizable Western tourists and amateur videos of the destruction spread instantly over the Internet. Their continuous repetition on television contributed to the sense that they showed raw, immediate suffering of innocent victims.[13] In the resulting "emotional frenzy" (Brauman, 2009, p. 114), created by eyewitness accounts of material destruction, dead and hurt tourists and locals and heart-rending searches for kin by children and parents alike, viewers felt that it could have been them in the waves. This "experiential proximity" (Forstorp, 2005, p. 17) produced a strong sense of worldwide empathetic identification with the victims, re-energizing feelings of a common humanity. On the other hand, the sensationalist character of the reports ultimately offered this emergency up for consumption and commodification, complete with the requisite Hollywood blockbuster.

The emergency mode of affective engagement reveals the tension between the urgent need to keep people alive that is at the heart of the humanitarian sentiment and the complex conditions of humanitarian situations. There is no space for the latter in the affective appeals to Northern publics, which necessarily present dramatic, heart-rending stories in order to reinforce the need for making a donation, now. These representations focus on suffering individuals, often women and children, who are shown as innocent victims of forces beyond their, and often beyond human, control. It is their combination of immediacy and disaster, where saving bare lives takes precedence over anything else, that gives emergency appeals their power. But it is that same power that reveals at its most problematic the binary of helpless Southern victim and active Northern rescuer that continues to permeate representations of emergencies with the aim of mobilizing affective investments. As an employee of a large New Zealand NGO, in a discussion of his organization's use of images of starving children to raise funds for the Horn of Africa famine victims, asked an audience of development studies students in 2011: "how else would we convey the urgency of the situation and the magnitude of need?" This binary becomes even more problematic when such representations are turned into spectacles for Northern publics' entertainment.

Spectacle

In 1954 American actor Danny Kaye became the first UNICEF ambassador; 9 years later the Beatles held a benefit concert to support Oxfam's *No Child Should Die of Hunger* fundraising campaign and in 1971, the Concert for Bangladesh took place. These early examples of humanitarianism's "dependence on spectacle" (Chouliaraki, 2012, p. 2) gave rise to the spectacle mode of affective engagement that grew into full force in the 1980s and carries on today, albeit with important differences. The spectacle mode encompasses concerts and celebrities, which are closely intertwined. Even though they work on different emotional registers, both use entertainment to incite Northern publics to care and share in order to alleviate the suffering of distant others. From Live Aid in 1985 to its successor 20 years later, spectacles create "a space of performance that produces exemplary dispositions of emotions and action on distant others for publics to identify with" (Chouliaraki, 2012, p. 3).

Live Aid

In his autobiography, Geldof remembered that in 1984, the fortunes of his own band were not looking very good. All of that became seemingly irrelevant when he switched on his television on October 25 and watched Buerk's report from Korem:

> It was something that placed my worries in a ghastly new perspective ... from the first second it was clear that this was a horror on a monumental scale ... I felt disgusted, enraged and outraged, but more than all those, I felt deep shame ... to expiate yourself truly from any complicity in this evil meant that you had to give something of yourself.
>
> *(1986, pp. 269–271)*

In his account, Geldof positioned himself as an individual with appropriate sensibilities and techniques to become a celebrity humanitarian. To alleviate his guilt and shame, he used his time and connections in the music industry to record the Christmas single and organize the Live Aid concerts in 1985.[14]

Geldof's testimonial also draws attention to the fact that celebrities' own performance of care and compassion is a crucial part of the way in which they mobilize affective actions in their fans. This performance is both narrated and embodied, encompassing "the joyful look on [a celebrity's] face in being entertained by ... the locals, the sweat on their brow in digging a new well..., their look of concern while holding a sick orphan" (Goodman & Barnes, 2011, pp. 76–77). It finds expression in travel diaries, tweets and tearful pauses during television interviews. Be it Audrey Hepburn's "cautious verbalization of emotion" and "dispassionate witnessing" in her role as Kaye's successor at UNICEF or Angelina Jolie's, UNHRC's Goodwill Ambassador since 2001, "visible signs of emotionality," celebrities' affective work helps Northern publics to experience similar feelings vicariously (Chouliaraki, 2012, pp. 9, 15). As a result, everyday people feel that they can make a contribution in their own small ways.

Geldof assembled an A-list line-up of British and Irish musicians, all of whom waived their usual recording fees, to record "Do They Know It's Christmas?" The song was released only a month later in time for the Christmas sales season and sold 4 million copies, making it the second most successful single in UK history (Elavsky, 2009). Geldof subsequently went to Africa, where his visits to refugee camps and feeding centers were stage-managed by Ethiopian authorities, who trucked in people from resettlement areas for the media occasion. He returned determined to do more and planned the Live Aid spectacle to combine the "joint raw emotion" of celebrity, musical performance and images of starving children (Müller, 2013, p. 473).

On July 13, 1985, two concerts took place simultaneously in London and Philadelphia, attended by over 170,000 people and broadcast to another estimated 1.9 billion viewers in 150 countries around the world. It was an extraordinary technological feat – one of the largest satellite link-ups and television broadcasts of all time – in the name of global poverty alleviation. One of the most dramatic moments of the concert was a video clip that combined images from Geldof's trip to Africa with highly emotive music. Geldof remembers the moment when the video was first shown to him:

> The video was a short sequence of a child, weakened by hunger, trying and trying and trying again to stand up on his little matchstick legs. They had edited it over [the band] The Cars' *Drive* . . . My eyes filled with tears and my voice caught in my throat.
>
> *(1986, p. 369)*

The reaction was similar when he showed it to the concert's production team, with David Bowie starting to cry and offering one of his spots so that the video could be broadcast during the concert. When that happened, the Band Aid Trust's phone system was overwhelmed by the incoming number of donation calls. For Geldof, through the combination of a song about love and dependence and the footage of the starving Ethiopian boy, "the artificial and at times indulgent world of pop was harnessed in an improbable marriage with the most basic feelings of compassion" (Geldof, 1986, p. 369). It created a story that went straight to the heart.

Live Aid showed that "one must be affective in order to be effective" (Mazzarella, 2009, p. 299). On the day of the concert, between US$60 and 75 million were raised for the Band Aid Charitable Trust, which changed the face of international fund-raising forever (Richey & Ponte, 2011, p. 33). While the concert thus successfully reached its fundraising goal, its emotionalism was criticized by NGO groups who felt not only that their authoritative position had been undermined, but that it de-politicized the famine, glossed over its deeper structural issues and played into local dynamics of corruption (Hague et al., 2008). What audiences were instead left with were images that urged them to assume a neo-colonial role of becoming the savior of emaciated Africans, who would starve to death without their donations.

Live 8

Geldof reactivated his populist "constituency of compassion" (Geldof, 1986, p. 250) on the 20th anniversary of Live Aid, spurred on by the ongoing crisis in Sudan and the MPH campaign. This time, however, the emphasis was not on fundraising but on addressing the systemic global inequalities that perpetuated poverty (Elavsky, 2009). On July 2, 2005, 10 Live 8 concerts took place simultaneously in London, Paris, Berlin, Rome, Philadelphia, Johannesburg, Moscow, Barrie (Canada), Chiba (Japan) and Cornwall (UK), followed by a final show in Edinburgh on July 6 to coincide with the G8 Summit. This show took place at the same time as rallies against the summit, which led to accusations that it undermined more radical protests (Biccum, 2007). The concerts were broadcast on television, radio and the Internet to about 3 billion viewers. Critiques of the Live 8 spectacle were even more numerous than those in 1985. They focused on the concerts' unabashed commercial nature, substantial profits for its corporate partners and "motivational hypocrisy" of some of the performers, who were suspected of wanting to revive their careers and grab lavish gift bags (Elavsky, 2009). Most problematic was the absence of African musicians, except for Nigerian singer Youssou N'Dour, which Geldof justified by saying that "for all their great musicianship, African acts do not sell many records" (quoted in Hague et al., 2008, p. 16). In keeping with his emphasis on the monetary value of music, he wanted to recruit the best-known artists that would allow him to market the concerts and draw record crowds. In response, Peter Gabriel, who himself has been involved in a series of Amnesty International concerts, organized the 10th Live 8 concert in Cornwall in the United Kingdom that featured only African musicians.

After the event, Geldof stated that "all the promises of rock 'n' roll [were] made concrete in one day" (cited in Biccum, 2007, p. 1121). He thereby drew on a musical lineage of individualistic anti-establishment music that allows its followers to make themselves heard, uninhibited by bureaucracy or convention. Geldof called this "punk diplomacy" and declared itself its populist leader (Geldof, 1986, p. 250). Although punk here does not actually refer to punk music, and certainly not to its disdain for corporate power, the name draws attention to music and concerts as particular media of engagement. "The emotional power of a song lyric or melody has long served to motivate individuals, mobilize communities, and stimulate and sustain a diverse array of political activities and social movements" (Elavsky, 2009, p. 384). Music works on an affective level, evoking particular sentiments, associations and bodily sensations. This is heightened in the context of music-media concerts, where the pleasures of music shape the feelings of participants, which are amplified by the presence of thousands of other spectators. Sound, sight, touch and smell come together to produce "affective agitation at the level of individual consciousness ... [and] visceral prospects for envisioning and embracing – at the level of the unconsciousness – alternative ways of hearing, seeing and being in the world" (Elavsky, 2009, pp. 400–401). While the shift from such symbolic internalization to political movement is far from guaranteed, the emotional power of music does offer potential opportunities for political transformation.

Indeed, Live 8 aimed for a politics of commitment rather than compassion. During the concerts, images of starving African children were replaced with the Click Campaign, which showed a series of celebrities clicking their fingers at 3-second intervals to signify how frequently a child dies from extreme poverty. The ad was powerful:[15]

> the regular clicks suggested time passing without action to prevent another death ... and another death ... and another death ... They also created a sense of simultaneity in time: that death happened right now, while I am here watching, another child has died ... and another ... and another...
>
> *(Nash, 2008, p. 173)*

However, highly commercialized and dramatized "poverty-tainment" (Goodman & Barnes, 2011, p. 82) made the near-impossible task of conveying the complexities around global trade politics and poverty even more elusive. What Live 8 audiences got were time-worn charity-concert tropes, hit songs by familiar artists and celebrity testimonials. Audience action was reduced to sending a text message to add one's name to a petition, asking G8 leaders to make good on their promises of more aid money, debt relief and better trade terms for Africa (Biccum, 2007). In spite of 26.4 million people doing so, Live 8's "expectations (or lack thereof) largely eclipsed the immediate affective potential of the performances" (Elavsky, 2009, p. 393). Audiences ended up going through the motions of apathy, fatigue or cynicism and what was celebrated was not their political, but their consumer identities.

Celebrities

Celebrities were central to Live 8 and similar spectacles. They can move thousands of fans to action because they "are able to provide an expression of and an anchoring for affect in contemporary society" (Richey & Ponte, 2011, p. 51). This affect management, which materializes in celebrities' embodiment of manufactured consensus and their substitution of simple moral truths for rational debate, is able to bring together and give voice to diverse constituencies. According to Geldof, in 1985 "they [politicians] had to listen because I had not only the money but the constituency of support which that money represents" (Geldof, 1986, p. 11). Since then, celebrity mediation between fans and politicians has only increased. As celebrities have assumed quasi-professionalized advocacy roles (Brockington, 2014), they have become distanced from their compassionate constituencies. The basis of that mediating relationship, however, remains an affective bond between celebrities and their fans (Müller, 2013). As Angelina Jolie argued, "if I can use this celebrity thing in a positive way, that might mean young people get involved, it has to be worth it" (cited in Mostafanezhad, 2013b, p. 487). This involvement is highly gendered, so that Bono, Geldof, Clooney and Affleck pursue humanitarian politics, while Hepburn, Farrow and Jolie care for women and children in crisis (Mostafanezhad, 2013b).

Celebrity humanitarianism thus stands in a dynamic relationship with everyday humanitarianism. It is one aspect of the mobilization of everyday people for international development, but this is not an automatic response to seeing celebrities sweating and smiling in Africa. Many everyday humanitarians are highly suspicious of the motivations of celebrities and remain unconvinced that their involvement in humanitarian work has the right effects. What both have in common, however, is that mediated affect is one of the central mechanisms of their engagement. While celebrities are primary producers of a highly controlled – some would say contrived – and glamorized affect, everyday humanitarians are its consumers and in turn produce affective investments in distant others.

Similar to the changing relationship between celebrities and their poverty-fighting followers, the objects of affect have changed over time. Celebrity involvement "displaces the affective relationship between spectator and sufferer onto a relationship between spectator and celebrity" (Chouliaraki, 2012, p. 15), where the poor and those working for them become literally invisible. On the one hand, celebrities give voice to the poor; as Bono so infamously remarked: "I represent a lot of people [in Africa] who have no voice at all.... They haven't asked me to represent them. It's cheeky but I hope they are glad I do" (quoted in Richey & Ponte, 2011, p. 62). On the other, development organizations' recruitment of celebrities can end up stealing the spotlight from them. One exasperated UN staffer exclaimed that "when most people think of the UN now they think of Angelina Jolie on a crusade not the work that goes on in the field" (cited in Chouliaraki, 2012, p. 16). This displacement feeds into a broader critique of the development apparatus, manifest in such popular and polemical books as *Dead Aid* (Moyo, 2009) and *The White Man's Burden* (Easterly, 2006), which themselves are skillful at manipulating the affect of their non-expert readers. To the rescue of an increasingly confused public come aid celebrities, "whose identity has been made inseparable from their aid work" (Richey & Ponte, 2011, p. 179). Bono, Jeffrey Sachs and Paul Farmer are exemplary of individuals who have merged development expertise and celebrity status, to become advocates for Brand Aid, development enterprise and finance. In spite of these shifts in the spectacle mode, its reliance on and production of affect has remained constant. The same holds true for affective engagements through sponsorship.

Sponsorship

Sponsorship of an individual, be it a child or an entrepreneur, is a prime example of the mobilization of affective investments. Regular small financial contributions first give rise to and then continue through mediated relationships between sponsor and sponsored. These relationships are fostered through affective objects and result in emotional satisfactions of various kinds. Sponsoring a child has been the oldest and most ubiquitous of this mode of caring and sharing. Through the use of "highly emotive tactics," it is also one of the most successful fundraising strategies of Northern NGOs (Suski, 2009, p. 213) and therefore a prominent way in which everyday people in the global North learn about the global South and its problems.[16]

Child sponsorship is grounded in a particular conception of childhood as a "problematic social [and historical] construction" of a state of vulnerability, dependency and innocence (Aitken, 2001, p. 120). Especially the 19th century ideal of childhood as a time for education and play, free from the burdens of work, has assumed a universal status that is underwritten by a shift from children's economic value to their emotional value (Manzo, 2008; Zelizer, 1985). From this position, children can evoke nostalgia for one's own childhood that draws sponsors in on a personal level and contributes to their desire to ensure a "normal" childhood, meaning one full of play and education and free from hunger and work, for their sponsored children (Pupuvac, 2001).

Child sponsorship works through images of children that produce sympathy and compassion (Cameron & Haanstra, 2008; Mostafanezhad, 2013a). In the guise of the "starving baby" of the 1970s and 1980s famines, children became the "universal icon of human suffering," which led to accusations of development porn (Cohen, 2001, p. 178). As a result, today's child sponsorship appeals show mainly images of smiling children that signal not need but its fulfillment through successful sponsorship programs. Children are still, however, often shown on their own, sometimes with friends or siblings and always without their parents or other non-white adult figures. The focus of these photos is on the child's face as the primary non-verbal channel for the communication of emotions that can be easily read by the viewer (Mittelman & Leighann, 2011). This lone child face is at the crux of affective investments.

On a personal level, this framing mobilizes parental instincts of nurture, protection and care, constituting potential sponsors as surrogate parents who step in where actual parents are not able or willing to provide. It reproduces ideas of a superior global North and an inferior South in need of paternalistic care. On a more general level, without their social surroundings, children become decontextualized abstractions that reinforce their lack of protection, which implicitly can only be provided by outside help (Manzo, 2008). These representations are potently ambiguous, as they can be a testament to international suffering or an embodiment of goodness and thereby hope for the future of humankind (Malkki, 1996). In both cases, they invoke a generic human family, a common humanity that has been expressed in slogans such as "a hungry child has no politics," which was used by USAID during the 1984 famine (cited in Manzo, 2008, p. 641).

Contemporary politics of famine, conflict and market rule belie this rhetoric. They also draw attention to child sponsorship's colonial and missionary lineages, stemming back to the purchase of children from slave markets that allowed the buyer to give the child a baptismal name and receive an image in return (Pieterse, 1995). More recently, the origin story of World Vision tells of the organization's founder, Bob Pierce, preaching at a mission school in China in 1947. When one of the female students was punished by her parents for her new faith, Pierce gave the missionary teacher the $5 he had in his pocket and promised to send the same amount for every month thereafter so that the girl could live at the missionary school (Bornstein, 2003). In both cases, children were saved from fates of suffering and cruel treatment by the intervention of Western Christians. Even today, the largest child sponsorship organizations, such as World Vision, are of a religious nature, but they have been joined by secular ones like ActionAid and Plan International.

The iconic representation of lone children does not require their own voices to be heard. Instead, their facial expressions and bodily states lend themselves to easy translation by adult interpreters (Suski, 2009). Distended bellies and protruding ribs mean starvation, tears or vacant stares from white eyes in dark faces signify suffering and the failure of international development projects, while smiles convey successful development that brings happiness and can restore the childhood these children deserve. The abstraction of the mute child is reinforced through sponsorship's impersonal, monetary exchange and children's corresponding commodification, often in the name of community development. They lend their faces and stories so that money can be raised for their communities. This stands in contrast with the personal, even intimate relations promised by child sponsorship, which manifest in letters and tearful encounters.

Relationships between sponsors and sponsored children are maintained through affective objects. Wallet-sized photographs, sometimes mounted on magnets, allow for children's placement alongside other family members and thus for their symbolic inclusion into sponsors' families. They become part of the daily routine and its "ordinary affects" (Stewart, 2007), be it opening the fridge to take out the milk for morning cereal or opening one's wallet to pull out a bank card. Less personal are standardized annual progress reports that tell sponsors about the achievements of their child and its larger community, focusing on familiar and valued practices such as education, health and sanitation and improved living conditions, all delivered thanks to the sponsors and the organization they support. At the heart of the relationship, however, is an "epistolary engagement" between sponsor and sponsored (O'Neill, 2013, p. 212).

Handwritten letters from sponsored children are priceless treasures that for sponsors increasingly stand out as special and unique among the bills and other official or junk mail flooding today's mail boxes. They prompt return letters in which sponsors share details of their lives and exercise their roles of distant-yet-responsible guardians. Each letter Bornstein read at the World Vision office in Harare, destined for Zimbabwe's sponsored charges, "was simultaneously mundane, with bland and superficial descriptions of everyday life and weather, and intensely intimate and personal, with descriptions of children and grandchildren, husbands and wives, vacation travel, sick pets" (Bornstein, 2003, p. 77). These letters are assembled with care and creativity and as such are central to forging the social relations on which affective investments are built. They also reveal, however, the "absurd" gaps between the lives of sponsors and sponsored (Bornstein, 2012, p. 168).

Moreover, the presumed one-to-one relationship of intimate correspondence is heavily mediated on several levels. NGO staff not only catalog letters and manage their proper flow, aided by the children's all-essential ID numbers, but also translate and censor mail and often help children write return letters. In this process, the content and form of letters becomes tightly controlled. Sponsors receive guidelines for what to write about, and if they transgress, for example by writing about wealth, politics or sex, their letters get snipped. Children's return letters, which in the Guatemalan Protestant organization studied by O'Neill were written right away, under the watchful guidance of staff, become exercises in penmanship, grammar and choice of words to bridge un-relatable worlds through narratives of self and questions to others. In sum, "from correct grammar to suitable stationery, from appropriate topics of conversation to just the right question, letters exchanged between sponsored and the sponsored discipline the at-risk child" (O'Neill, 2013, p. 212). Letters, then, simultaneously produce relationships and their subjects.

Some sponsors choose to visit their children, undertaking a kind of affective journey that brings them in direct contact with the latter's daily realities. This can have unpredictable outcomes. Bornstein describes the encounter of a young Canadian with his sponsored child in Zimbabwe, which was full of awkwardness, dismay and even disappointment, as the structural complexities in which child sponsorship is situated revealed themselves during his trip.[17] Only gifts could bridge the gap between them. Such initial disappointment can have a happy ending, too. The national director of World Vision Zimbabwe recounted how an Australian man who had come on such a visit was bitterly disappointed when his child could not be located right away.

> We sat here with this chap. I cried, literally cried, and he cried … Now to me as a Zimbabwean who is here, that this man who had come all the way, [and] was moved to the extent of shedding tears for his sponsored child – I mean it did something to me. Now when we are talking about transformation, that's what it is, the love that so moves you to that extent.
>
> *(cited in Bornstein, 2003, p. 70)*

Both the sponsor and the NGO director were deeply affected by this temporary loss, pointing to intersubjective relations that extend beyond sponsors and children. Love, of the human and religious kind, is a central trope in this sponsorship discourse. Sometimes this is hard to understand for sponsored children, as one of them expressed: "they never met me, yet they are saying how much they love me. It was a bit difficult to believe" (quoted in Bornstein, 2003, pp. 85–86).

The effects of affective objects and journeys on sponsors often are intensely emotional and can lead to personal transformations. On one end of the spectrum is the simple satisfaction of having made a difference in the life of one person, a feeling that is nurtured by NGOs. A World Vision Canada appeal proclaimed that "you can rewrite the story of a needy child's life" (cited in Suski, 2009, p. 216). Similarly, World Vision Zimbabwe's sponsorship coordinator mused that

> it seems that the people we get the funding from can't relate to a big problem and feel like they can have some kind of import. Whereas if you give them one child they think, yes, I could make a difference in that one child's life.
>
> *(quoted in Bornstein, 2003, p. 82)*

As I analyzed in arguing for the financialization of poverty, making the problem of poverty and development small and manageable incites action, rendering its positive impact imaginable. On the other end of the spectrum are promises of salvation and redemption for sponsors, who become better Christians through witnessing the squalor and danger of their sponsored children's lives and sometimes end up rejecting their own wealth (O'Neill, 2013). Such emotional experiences are the result of carefully calibrated marketing campaigns. Mail flyers full of lone child photos and sponsor testimonials, telethons displaying crying television hosts, celebrities and sponsors who have met their children and mass emails show that child sponsorship remains one of the most important revenue streams for NGOs engaged in this activity (Jefferess, 2002; Suski, 2009). The emphasis in these appeals is always on the emotional experience of the sponsor, to which grateful, smiling children provide the background.

Child sponsorship has inspired related models, such as sponsoring a Kiva entrepreneur, which is the focus of the next chapter. Kiva's co-founders grew up sponsoring children through their families and churches, but Kiva has shifted the sponsorship model into the realm of the Internet: solicitation no longer takes place in shopping malls or by mail, but electronically; donations are made with a click of a mouse and handwritten letters have been replaced with electronic email updates. Nevertheless, the caring connection between two individuals, made easily consumable for Northern sponsors, remains the bedrock of the relationship. This has also allowed old-style organizations such as World Vision to move into the Kiva space; World Vision New Zealand launched its own Kiva-clone called *Micro* in 2013. At the price of a daily cup of coffee, sponsorship provides financial, social and emotional avenues for affective engagements, one individual at a time.

Consumption

Intimately linked to the campaigns that opened this chapter, consumption is another mode of affective engagement with roots in the early days of everyday humanitarianism. From the sugar boycotts that accompanied the abolition movement to fair trade to the (RED) campaign, consumption focuses directly on Western individuals to affect action through their buying decision.

Abolitionist Sugar Boycott

In 1791 Richard Fox published his *Address to the People of Great Britain on the Propriety of Abstaining from Sugar*. With a record print run in the hundred thousands and 26 editions in 2 years, the tract was spectacularly successful at mobilizing British sentiment and reason (Laqueur, 2009). Morally decent British subjects were to combine sympathy for slaves and disgust at the slave trade with an understanding of its causes and action toward its abolishment. The basis of this early consumer boycott was the framing of sugar consumption as a form of literal and symbolic contamination between the bodies of British consumers and Caribbean slaves, particularly an exchange of bodily liquids in the form of sweat and blood (Sussman, 1994). This embodied link stoked consumers' physical revulsion and fear of disease, their shock at the cruelties of slavery and their sympathy for slaves. Together, these sentiments translated into disgust toward the realities of the slave trade and thereby sought to mobilize British support for abolition. To eat slave-produced sugar in one's own home not only brought one into contact with a dirty, immoral industry, but also meant that one directly participated in it.

The sugar boycott gained momentum when the British parliament rejected an abolition bill in 1792. William Cooper, an abolitionist, enumerated that

> a family that uses five pounds of sugar per week, with the same proportion of Rum, will, by abstaining from the consumption 21 months, prevent the slavery, or murder, of one fellow creature; eight such families in nineteen years and a

> half, would prevent the slavery, or murder, of 100; and 38,000 would totally prevent the Slave Trade, by removing the occasion to supply our island.
>
> *(cited in Sheller, 2011, p. 179)*

Through a politics of detailed numbers, action, mediated by market mechanisms, was presented as possible and effective. Cold calculation established the link of cause and effect that is necessary for humanitarian sentiments to be translated into action, and about 300,000 people heeded the call to action.[18]

In encouraging British consumers to boycott slave-produced sugar and rum, campaigners brought Smithian notions of morality and responsibility into the realm of economy and thereby began to imagine a new politics of consumption. In *An Address*, Fox stressed the capacity of British consumers to make ethical choices in order to influence the affairs of geographically distant individuals and corporations (Sussman, 1994). In other words, he argued that consumers could be active political agents and that everyday acts of consumption could be reimagined as public mobilizations of humanitarian affect. This was an embodied practice, as "common consumer goods (primarily sugar, tea and cotton) formed the lens for ordinary people to understand tangibly (see, feel, taste and wear) how their daily lives were connected with and responsible for slavery" (Micheletti, 2007, p. 127). Everyday household items linked to this intimate consumption, such as cups and sugar bowls, further put the abolitionist cause on the dinner tables of British homes. Emerging humanitarian affects here worked through British bodies in producing both positive and negative sentiments that abolitionists were able to harness into concrete action against the slave trade, which was made illegal by the British parliament in 1807, a decade after the sugar boycott began.

A number of scholars have drawn historical connections between this boycott and current ethical consumption campaigns, such as the anti-sweatshop movement, fair trade and cause-related marketing (Micheletti, 2007; Sheller, 2011). Some of these appeal to the shared characteristics of producers and consumers, while others frame consumption as an act of political resistance. Many movements circulate their ideas, often in a simplified form, through promotional media like posters, cards, online videos and stickers, making it easy for hurried consumers to get and spread the message that shopping well can save the world.

At the same time, contemporary consumption-based movements are mobilizing different kinds of sentiment than the abolitionist boycotts. Ethical consumption is increasingly marketed as a practice that can benefit not only producers, but consumers as well, which is accompanied by a partial shift of focus from distant others to Northern selves (Cameron & Haanstra, 2008). As I have shown for other modes as well, contemporary humanitarianism is not only articulated through other-directed sentiments of compassion, but also through self-centered feelings of pride, self-worth and attraction. But even these are built on affective connections. The ways in which distant others are represented also varies, ranging from producers in a global economy in fair trade campaigns to victims of political and economic exploitation in anti-sweatshop campaigns to commodities through which humanitarian aims can be consumed in cause-related marketing (Bell, 2011). Many of these campaigns appeal to ideas of a common humanity that subsume individual stories in favor of recognizable narratives of global neoliberal power and domination. At the same time, they often maintain existing hierarchical relationships of dependency and thereby reinscribe boundaries between producers and consumers.

Fair Trade

Fair trade promotional materials present a good example. A poster for the fair trade coffee brand Cafédirect simply displays the face of Leonardo Navarro Bustinza together with the caption "Coffee Grower/Cocla, Peru." The close-up photo shows "every line and pore of his skin, . . . his tanned and weathered face suggesting a hard-working life" (Wright, 2004, p. 669). Where previously the work of people like Bustinza might have gone unseen, now the consumer is confronted with the face of coffee production. Unlike the unnamed and stereotyped slave in Wedgwood's *Am I Not a Man*, the poster does not portray Bustinza as a sufferer; he is named and gazes directly at the viewer, displaying dignity and promising the consumer a direct emotional connection to coffee growers like him. Clearly, this connection is illusory, and the poster challenges consumers to better understand the relations of production that link them to Bustinza. At the bottom of the image, a caption presents viewers with the abstract invitation to "Think it," shifting the realm of action to reflective buying and promising cultural capital (Wright, 2004).

At first glance, fair trade, as manifest in Cafédirect's poster, seems to appeal not to sentiments of pity or sympathy, but to a moral sense of responsibility and obligation. Fair trade engages consumers not on the basis of an "ad hoc sentimentality" but on the grounds that, since they are already causally linked to Third World producers, they have a moral duty to help them (Festa, 2010, p. 4). As with abolitionist calls for consumer boycotts 300 years earlier, fair trade is built on ideas of the market as a system that creates direct relationships of moral obligation between producers and consumers. It thereby obscures the political economy in which these relationships are embedded (Doane, 2010). Moreover, sentimentalized relationships between consumers and producers persist in the stylized and emotional content of fair trade adverts. Their products are associated with "pleasant emotions and deeply desired states, such as happiness, love, friendship" (Doane, 2010, p. 238). In doing so, fair trade marketing often attributes agency to Northern consumers who become agents *through* their feelings for Southern producers. Much fair trade is linked to pleasurable primary products such as coffee, tea and chocolate, so that "whenever the ethical dimensions of Fair Trade come to the fore, the attention of potential consumers is immediately turned to self-reward" (Wright, 2004, p. 669). Consumers in the global North can help producers in the global South through perpetuating consumer lifestyles that prioritize self-gratification.

(RED)

This emphasis is most forcefully expressed in the Product (RED) campaign, which entices consumers to buy specially branded products from companies that donate a percentage of their profits to the Global Fund, which provides HIV/AIDS services to several African countries (Richey & Ponte, 2011). According to its website, "(RED) is fighting to help deliver an AIDS-free generation by 2015."[19] While this generation refers to African AIDS victims, (RED)'s attention is squarely focused on Northern consumers, who are invited to enhance their status, affluence and conspicuous consumption through links with iconic brands such as Apple, Armani and Converse. Above all else, (RED) aims to "bring some sex appeal to the idea of wanting to change the world," in the words of its co-founder Bono (cited in Cameron & Haanstra, 2008, p. 1475). The campaign is thus a prime expression of development-made-sexy, whereby aid agencies engage Northern publics through sex appeal.

Still, even (RED) does not fully dispense with evoking conventional humanitarian sentiments of pity and sympathy. One of the key elements of its marketing campaign is *The Lazarus Effect*, consisting of photos in a 2007 *Vanity Fair* Special Africa issue guest-edited by Bono and two later videos that show before and after images of African AIDS patients taking the antiretroviral pills that (RED) finances. The images are unusual in "their obvious allusion to suffering" (Richey & Ponte, 2011, p. 73). While the before pictures evoke death through sick bodies and despair through tears and apathy, the after images convey health and hope. Much like the parable of the Good Samaritan often invoked by humanitarians, here another Biblical story, of Jesus raising Lazarus from the dead, provides a frame in which contemporary humanitarian action is situated. Bono himself becomes the "good-looking Samaritan who has brought to the cause a candid emotionalism – with a strong religious sensibility – that shapes his sense of public purpose" (Cooper, 2008, p. 37, cited in Richey & Ponte, 2011, p. 39). Relatedly, his creation, (RED), is presented as "a divine hand" that continues the Christian mission to save Africa (Bell, 2011, p. 168).

The faces of salvation are Silvia, Nancy and Elimas, whose photos compel the viewer to act with urgency. While their before images are "intimate and pleading to illicit [*sic*] pity from the readers" (Richey & Ponte, 2011, p. 73), their after photos "implore the viewer to engage via the affinity created by the smiling direct address to the viewer" (Bell, 2011, p. 167). In both cases, the viewer is engaged through affect. However, while seemingly telling the stories of individuals to aid affective investments, *The Lazarus Effect* presents an abstract form of suffering. The statement that "4,400 people die every day of AIDS in Sub-Saharan Africa. Treatment exists," which appears early on in the videos, shows that the experience of the three AIDS patients is not particular to them, but is something that can be aggregated with other experiences in order to represent the African AIDS epidemic as a whole. This results in "a one-world commonality that appeals to Western consumers" (Bell, 2011, p. 168). This removal of singularity is further reinforced when, in keeping with the (RED) logo, their names are displayed in parentheses, so that

(Silvia), (Nancy) and (Elimas) become part of the (RED) brand. They are located somewhere between the anonymous slave of the abolitionist campaign and the named coffee producer of fair trade campaigns. As a brand, they also contribute to Bono's explicit aim to "rebrand Africa ... as an opportunity, as an adventure, not a burden" (Bono, 2007). However, as much as Africa might get a makeover, it also becomes a place where, according to Bono, "we might actually find our own soul.... Something about serving the poor that you rediscover your reason to be" (quoted in Mathers, 2010, p. 177). Once again, Africa and its suffering inhabitants become a place where Northern publics can find meaning and salvation.

There is a disconnect between consumers' feelings and the actions (RED) asks them to take. The sentiments that are generated have little to do with purchasing a pair of Converse shoes or an Apple iPhone, so that the act of consumption has become distanced from the humanitarian act it is meant to enable. Consumers are only informed how many antiretroviral drugs their purchase will afford for the Global Fund, but not about how their actions fit into the broader political economy of HIV and AIDS in Africa (Bell, 2011). A simple graphic displayed on (RED)'s homepage explains how the campaign works: starting and ending with a Northern individual, the difference between before and after consisting of the red shopping bag that gets added on, arrows link money and the Global Fund to two pills and a schematic African continent, denuded of any reference to people, politics or power. This is the humanitarian cause and effect chain at its most pure and most problematic. In spite, or because, of this simplification, (RED) has raised millions of dollars for the Global Fund. It is effective because images of suffering have become part of the Northern collective consciousness, and no longer need to be referenced (Cameron & Haanstra, 2008). This allows white superstar models, be it in blackface, dressed in (RED) T-shirts or in provocative attire, to stand in for black women dying from sex in Africa. (RED)'s glitz and glamour glosses over the politics of HIV/AIDS and international development. Development has indeed become sexy and in turn allows its supporters to feel "sexy, affluent and sophisticated" (Cameron & Haanstra, 2008, p. 1476).

More generally, the consumption mode "exists through the mobilization of affect to produce certain kinds of donors who care" (Richey & Ponte, 2011, p. 52). Everyday humanitarian sentiments have now become key to the public construction of ethical consumers, allowing the latter to refashion their own selves as caring and sharing. Conversely, supporting ethical consumption campaigns has become publicly recognized as a signifier of consumers' compassion and moral awareness. In the consumption mode more than in any other, humanitarian sentiments and actions are absorbed into the everyday. Anyone, it seems, can be a humanitarian.

This transformation is actively fostered by development organizations. In the current era of increased competition for their funds, development supporters are becoming valued constituents in their own right, and organizations are paying more attention to their so-called giving experiences. Realizing that a generic donor does not exist, such organizations are adapting market segmentation exercises from the business world, together with the use of professional advertising and marketing companies, which in turn are contributing to making development sexy. While the identity of Northern donors and supporters has always been implicitly present in development representations, now "active and attractive Northern selves" are moving to the center of attention (Cameron & Haanstra, 2008, p. 1477). In the process, "Africans are [becoming] props in the West's fantasy of itself" (Ngozi Okonjo-Iweala quoted in Cameron & Haanstra, 2008, p. 1483) and critical discussion of the representation of the global South are elided altogether. The challenge, then, is to show the intimate connections between self and other representations and their effects on the politics of international development.

This brief history of affective engagements has shown the ways in which, over the last 300 years, Anglo-American Northern publics have increasingly been mobilized as constituencies of compassion in order to alleviate the suffering and poverty of distant others. How has this "celebrity – consumption – compassion complex" been operating (Goodman & Barnes, 2011, p. 72)? Diverse technologies of communication and commerce have played a key role in establishing connections that have allowed Northern publics to see the ways in which they are related to distant others and in which their actions can help them. The result is a "market in [humanitarian] emotions" (Goodman & Barnes, 2011, p. 81) that has been inciting its Northern consumers to care for slaves, victims of disasters, starving babies, lone children and AIDS patients. In what ways have these objects of concern been constituted as individuals? Ranging from generic and stereotyped to branded and named, the shifting category of victim on which humanitarian engagements relies is itself manufactured by the humanitarian industry. Furthermore, the neo-colonial representations of these categorical subjects, while conjuring a common humanity, re-establish hierarchies between passive and grateful recipients of care and active, generous givers. In the end, the distant other has come to serve as a backdrop that allows Northern publics to fulfill their ambitions of saving the world, in a generation, one person at a time.

Notes

1 Retrieved July 15, 2013, from http://news.bbc.co.uk/2/hi/uk_news/politics/4232603.stm.
2 GCAAP was established by the World Social Forum and brought together 84 national coalitions (Biccum, 2007).
3 Demands for debt relief continued the efforts of the Jubilee 2000 campaign, which had called for a cancellation of Third World debt by 2000, coinciding with the Great Jubilee celebration of the Catholic Church.
4 The video's virality surpassed all videos in all domains, including video games and music videos (retrieved November 2, 2013, from www.visiblemeasures.com).
5 The video makers were invited to a private signing ceremony with Obama.
6 I thank Sarah Pellett for drawing my attention to these numbers.
7 The Richter scale did not exist at the time, but Sliwinski (2009) summarizes reports showing that the tremors were felt from Finland to Africa.
8 I thank Paul Braund for pointing this date out to me.
9 Retrieved November 18, 2013, from www.youtube.com/watch?v=XYOj_6OYuJc.
10 MSF was expelled in December 1985 because it claimed that food aid was misused (Müller, 2013).

11 Retrieved August 13, 2013, from www.one.org/c/international/actnow/4137/?.
12 This amount is put into perspective by the total of US$7.3 billion given in bilateral aid by international governments (Brauman, 2009).
13 This circulation was helped by the good communication infrastructures in popular tourist spots like Thailand and Sri Lanka, which sidelined coverage from places that were not as connected.
14 Geldof was not an uncontroversial figure in the UK, especially because of his Irish origins. Widespread antipathy toward people of Irish origin in the UK was caused by the activities of the IRA, which in the 1980s carried out bombing attacks in England and, in October 1984, an assassination attempt on Margaret Thatcher in Brighton, which left five people dead.
15 The ad was banned by Ofcom, the UK media regulator, in September 2005 for being "too political" (Nash, 2008, p. 173).
16 There are two kinds of programs, one where individual children are the recipients, and one where the funds support community development, and the shift is toward the latter. However, the emotional appeal of children is the same for both.
17 While new relationships and bonds of belonging are forged between sponsors and "their" children, existing relations between children and their parents and wider communities are sometimes frayed in the process (Bornstein, 2003).
18 This also presented a boon to East Indian sugar imports that were explicitly marketed as "not made by slaves" (Sheller, 2011).
19 Retrieved November 25, 2013, from www.theglobalfund.org/en/partners/private sector/red.

Bibliography

Agamben, G. (1998). *Homo sacer: Sovereign power and bare life.* Palo Alto, CA: Stanford University Press.
Aitken, S. (2001). Global crisis of childhood: Rights, justice and the unchildlike child. *Area, 33*(2), 119–127.
Araujo, A. C. (2006). The Lisbon earthquake of 1755: Public distress and political propaganda. *e-JPH, 4*(1), 1–11.
Bell, K. (2011). "A delicious way to help save lives": Race, commodification, and celebrity in product (RED). *Journal of International and Intercultural Communication, 4*(3), 163–180.
Biccum, A. (2007). Marketing development: Live 8 and the production of the global citizen. *Development and Change, 38*(6), 1111–1126.
Boltanski, L. (1999). *Distant suffering: Morality, media and politics.* Cambridge: Cambridge University Press.
Bono. (2007, July). Guest editor's letter. *Vanity Fair.*
Bornstein, E. (2003). *The spirit of development: Protestant NGOs, morality and economics in Zimbabwe.* London: Routledge.
Bornstein, E. (2012). *Disquieting gifts: Humanitarianism in New Delhi.* Palo Alto, CA: Stanford University Press.
Brauman, R. (2009). Global media and the myths of humanitarian relief: The case of the 2004 tsunami. In R. A. Wilson & R. D. Brown (Eds.), *Humanitarianism and suffering: The mobilization of empathy* (pp. 108–117). Cambridge: Cambridge University Press.
Brockington, D. (2014). *Celebrity advocacy and international development.* Abingdon: Routledge.
Calhoun, C. (2010). *The idea of emergency: Humanitarian action and global (dis)order.* New York: Zone Books.
Cameron, J. & Haanstra, A. (2008). Development made sexy: How it happened and what it means. *Third World Quarterly, 29*(8), 1475–1489.

Chouliaraki, L. (2010). Post-humanitarianism: Humanitarian communication beyond a politics of pity. *International Journal of Cultural Studies, 13*(2), 107–126.

Chouliaraki, L. (2012). The theatricality of humanitarianism: A critique of celebrity advocacy. *Communication and Critical/Cultural Studies, 9*(1), 1–21.

Cohen, S. (2001). *States of denial: Knowing about atrocities and suffering*. Cambridge: Polity.

Coleman, D. (1994). Conspicuous consumption: White abolitionism and English women's protest writing in the 1790s. *English Literary History, 61*(2), 341–362.

Cooper, A. (2008). *Celebrity diplomacy*. Boulder, CO: Paradigm Publishers.

DATA. (2007). *The Data Report 2008: "Keep the G8 Promise to Africa."* Retrieved March 17, 2012, from http://one-org.s3.amazonaws.com/us/wp-content/uploads/2012/11/dr2008.pdf.

De Waal, A. (1997). *Famine crimes: Politics and the disaster relief industry in Africa*. Oxford: James Currey Publishers.

Doane, M. (2010). Relationship coffees: Structure and agency in the fair trade system. In M. Moberg (Ed.), *Fair trade and social justice: Global ethnographies* (pp. 229–257). New York: New York University Press.

Easterly, W. (2006). *The white man's burden: Why the West's efforts to aid the rest have done so much ill and so little good*. New York: Penguin.

Elavsky, M. (2009). United as ONE: Live 8 and the politics of the global music media spectacle. *Journal of Popular Music Studies, 21*(4), 384–410.

Fassin, D. (2010). Heart of humaneness: The moral economy of humanitarian intervention. In D. Fassin & M. Pandolfi (Eds.), *Contemporary states of emergency: The politics of military and humanitarian interventions* (pp. 269–294). New York: Zone Books.

Feldman, I. (2010). The humanitarian circuit: Relief work, development assistance, and CARE in Gaza, 1955–67. In E. Bornstein & P. Redfield (Eds.), *Forces of compassion: Humanitarianism between ethics and politics* (pp. 203–226). Santa Fe, NM: SAR Press.

Festa, L. (2010). Humanity without feathers. *Humanity: An International Journal of Human Rights, Humanitarianism and Development, 1*(1), 3–27.

Forstorp, P.-A. (2005). *Representing "the Other" in tsunami fundraising discourse: A Levenasian interpretation*. University of Stockholm.

Geldof, B. (1986). *Is that it?* London: Sidgwick & Jackson.

Gomberg-Muñoz, R. (2013). Year in review: Public anthropology. *American Anthropologist, 115*(2), 285–296.

Goodman, M. & Barnes, C. (2011). Star/poverty space: The making of the "development celebrity." *Celebrity Studies, 2*(1), 69–85.

Goodwin, J., Jasper, J. & Polletta, F. (2001). *Passionate politics: Emotions and social movements*. Chicago: University of Chicago Press.

Hague, S., Street, J. & Savigny, H. (2008). The voice of the people? Musicians as popular actors. *Cultural Politics, 4*(1), 5–24.

Haskell, T. (1985a). Capitalism and the origins of humanitarian sensibilities. *American Historical Review, 90*(2), 339–361.

Haskell, T. (1985b). Capitalism and the origins of humanitarian sensibility, part 2. *American Historical Review, 90*(3), 547–566.

Jefferess, D. (2002). For sale – Peace of mind: (Neo)colonial discourses and the commodification of Third World poverty in World Vision telethons. *Critical Arts, 16*(1), 1–12.

Juris, J. (2008). *Networking futures: The movements against corporate globalizations*. Durham, NC: Duke University Press.

Karlin, B. & Matthew, A. (2012). Kony2012 and the mediatization of child soldiers. *Peace Review, 24*(3), 255–261.

Laqueur, T. (1989). Bodies, details and the humanitarian narrative. In L. Hunt & A. Biersack (Eds.), *The new cultural history* (pp. 176–204). Berkeley: University of California Press.

Laqueur, T. (2009). Mourning, pity, and the work of narrative in the making of "humanity." In R. A. Wilson & R. D. Brown (Eds.), *Humanitarianism and suffering: The mobilization of empathy* (pp. 31–57). Cambridge: Cambridge University Press.

Lidchi, H. (1999). Finding the right image: British development NGOs and the regulation of imagery. In T. Skelton & T. Allen (Eds.), *Culture and global change* (pp. 88–104). London: Routledge.

Madianou, M. (2013). Humanitarian campaigns in social media. *Journalism Studies, 14*(2), 249–266.

Malkki, L. (1996). Speechless emissaries: Refugees, humanitarianism and dehistoricization. *Cultural Anthropology, 11*(3), 377–404.

Manzo, K. (2008). Imaging humanitarianism: NGO identity and the iconography of childhood. *Antipode, 40*(4), 632–657.

Mathers, K. (2010). *Travel, humanitarianism, and becoming American in Africa*. New York: Palgrave Macmillan.

Mazzarella, W. (2009). Affect: What is it good for? In S. Dube (Ed.), *Enchantments of modernity: Empire, nation, globalization* (pp. 291–309). London: Routledge.

Micheletti, M. (2007). The moral force of consumption and capitalism: Anti-slavery and anti-sweatshop. In K. Soper & F. Trentmann (Eds.), *Citizenship and consumption* (pp. 121–136). Basingstoke: Palgrave Macmillan.

Mittelman, R. & Leighann, C. (2011). Development porn? Child sponsorship advertisement in the 1970s. *Journal of Historical Research in Marketing, 3*(3), 370–401.

Mostafanezhad, M. (2013a). The geography of compassion in volunteer tourism. *Tourism Geographies, 15*(2), 318–337.

Mostafanezhad, M. (2013b). "Getting in touch with your inner Angelina": Celebrity humanitarianism and the cultural politics of gendered generosity in volunteer tourism. *Third World Quarterly, 34*(3), 485–499.

Moyo, D. (2009). *Dead Aid: Why aid is not working and how there is a better way for Africa*. New York: Macmillan.

Müller, T. (2013). The long shadow of Band Aid humanitarianism: Revisiting the dynamics between famine and celebrity. *Third World Quarterly, 34*(3), 470–484.

Nash, K. (2008). Global citizenship as show business: The cultural politics of Make Poverty History. *Media, Culture and Society, 30*(2), 167–181.

Ogden, T. (2009, October 19). *Kiva, a cautionary tale for social entrepreneurs?* Retrieved December 3, 2009, from http://blogs.hbr.org/2009/10/kivaorg-role-model-or-cautiona.

O'Neill, K. L. (2013). Left behind: Security, salvation, and the subject of prevention. *Cultural Anthropology, 28*(2), 204–226.

Pieterse, J. (1995). *White on black: Images of Africa and blacks in Western popular culture*. New Haven, CT: Yale University Press.

Pupuvac, V. (2001). Misanthropy without borders: The international children's rights regime. *Disasters, 25*(1), 95–112.

Redfield, P. (2008). Sacrifice, triage and global humanitarianism. In M. Barnett & T. Weiss (Eds.), *Humanitarianism in question: Politics, power, ethics* (pp. 196–214). Ithaca, NY: Cornell University Press.

Redfield, P. & Bornstein, E. (2010). An introduction to the anthropology of humanitarianism. In E. Bornstein & P. Redfield (Eds.), *Forces of compassion: Humanitarianism between ethics and politics* (pp. 3–30). Santa Fe, NM: SAR Press.

Richey, L. A. & Ponte, S. (2011). *Brand aid: Shopping well to save the world*. Minneapolis: University of Minnesota Press.

Rozario, K. (2003). "Delicious horrors": Mass culture, the Red Cross, and the appeal of modern American humanitarianism. *American Quarterly, 55*(3), 417–455.

Sheller, M. (2011). Bleeding humanity and gendered embodiments: From antislavery sugar boycotts to ethical consumers. *Humanity: An International Journal of Human Rights, Humanitarianism and Development, 2*(2), 171–192.

Sliwinski, S. (2009). The aesthetics of human rights. *Culture, Theory and Critique, 50*(1), 23–39.

Stewart, K. (2007). *Ordinary affects.* Durham, NC: Duke University Press.

Suski, L. (2009). Children, suffering, and the humanitarian appeal. In R. A. Wilson & R. D. Brown (Eds.), *Humanitarianism and suffering: The mobilization of empathy* (pp. 202–222). Cambridge: Cambridge University Press.

Sussman, C. (1994). Women and the politics of sugar, 1792. *Representations, 48,* 48–69.

Tatarchevskiy, T. (2011). The "popular" culture of internet activism. *New Media and Society, 13*(2), 297–313.

Waldorf, L. (2012). White noise: Hearing the disaster. *Journal of Human Rights Practice, 4*(3), 469–474.

Westley, F. (1991). Bob Geldof and Live Aid: The affective side of global social innovation. *Human Relations, 44*(10), 1011–1036.

White, M. (2010, August 12). Clicktivism is ruining the leftist activism. *Guardian.*

Wilson, R. A. & Brown, R. D. (Eds.). (2009). *Humanitarianism and suffering: The mobilization of empathy.* Cambridge: Cambridge University Press.

Wright, C. (2004). Consuming lives, consuming landscapes: Interpreting advertisements for Cafédirect coffees. *Journal of International Development, 16*(5), 665–680.

Zelizer, V. (1985). *Pricing the priceless child: The changing social value of children.* Princeton, NJ: Princeton University Press.

PART II
Mediations

3
VIRTUAL STORIES*

Bob Harris is a Kiva executive's dream. Since becoming a lender in January 2009, he has made 6,625 loans totaling more than US$300,000 (as of February 2014). He has his own eponymous lending team, which unites over 1,500 members who have chosen to link their loans to Bob Harris and which has lent over US$4 million. The team consistently ranks among the top 10 lending teams for new members recruited and loans made. Bob has traveled the world to visit many of his lenders, and, most importantly, he has written a book about it all. *The International Bank of Bob* capitalizes on the ubiquity of the name Bob given to ordinary, middle-class characters in American television, film and commercials to imply that anybody could enjoy being a Kiva lender (Harris, 2013). The book's opening scene, which sees Bob standing in the garage of a bicycle repairman named Mohammed in Rabat, Morocco, sets the tone for the next 400 pages: Bob is "flying on instinct" most of the time, the garage is "a work of love" that allows Bob to talk about the love of his own dad for his children and mutual feelings are conveyed through facial expressions without a need for words. This affective encounter and many others like it tell Bob, and the readers of his book, that effort and love must come together to give one's life meaning.

One of Bob's first loans was to a borrower at INM, an Indonesian microfinance institute (MFI) where I also conducted research. She was a wood carver whose Kiva profile showed Bob that the borrower

> had a workable business model, a track record of repaying previous loans, and a skill firmly rooted in local tradition – everything I could hope to support, even if she lived down the street. But [the borrower] was in Indonesia. Her profits would keep her children in school. I remember what I saw in the street there when young people ran out of better options. There was no way I couldn't chip in on her loan.
>
> *(Harris, 2013, p. 67)*

How does Kiva compel Bob's care for the Indonesian woman? How does it mobilize the affective investments of over 1 million lenders from dozens of countries across the globe, to the extent that even in its eighth year, when the novelty effect that propelled its early growth surely has worn off, an office worker from Australia makes 1,660 loans in 2 months because

> I believe it is the right thing to do and a 'help up' is not the same as a 'hand out'. Everyone should have the same opportunities in life regardless of where they are born and what they believe. This is a great way to help so many, over and over.[1]

In this chapter, I show that Kiva's affective effectiveness lies in its fit into the daily lives of its users, thereby providing ordinary recipes for and capitalizing on the ordinary affects of everyday humanitarians (Haskell, 1985; Stewart, 2007).

Like more traditional humanitarian organizations, Kiva "provides a mechanism for people to concretize and channel compassion; they also make a demand that people feel such compassion, seeking to create it where it may not already exist" (Feldman, 2010, p. 210). Kiva is also a literal channel through which hundreds of thousands of US dollars, in the form of virtually aggregated microloans, criss-cross the globe every month. In a Kiva promotional video, these are represented as "interconnected ballistic" points of light firing across a cybernetic globe moving people to make Kiva love and loans, not war.[2] Because Kiva works through forging intimate human connections, it is a prime location to study the mobilization of affective investments. Key to this mobilization is a particular kind of humanitarian "micronarrative" (Black, 2013, p. 108) that operates in the space created by classic humanitarian stories over 200 years ago. However, while the latter may be "sad and sentimental" (Rorty, 1993, pp. 118–119), Kiva's are narratives of empowerment, agency and hope because they capitalize on newer technologies of assistance and communication. First among these is microfinance, which "more than almost any other approach to helping the world's poor has this power to generate stories that resonate with potential supporters" (Roodman, 2011, p. 3). I will explore the visual aspect of these stories in the next chapter and here focus on their text. Second, micronarratives are shaped by the diminutive linguistic frames of new media technologies, exemplified by Twitter's 140 character limit, whose simplifications obscure what could stand in the way of microfinance's obligatory success story. In other words, Kiva's micronarratives are situated at the confluence of financial inclusion and virtual technologies – a sure recipe for affective appeal.

My analysis of Kiva is based on informally following the site's development from 2006 to the present and on formal research beginning in 2009. The latter consisted of fieldwork with Kiva partner MFIs in Central America and Indonesia, as well as interviews with Kiva staff, Fellows and lenders. I have also been a Kiva lender since 2007 and in this way conducted participant-observation on the Kiva website. This site is itself a treasure trove of information, just as it is for other scholars who often rely on it as the sole source of information.[3] In particular, I have drawn on the virtual conversations in the INM lending team and on the blog posts written by Kiva Fellows, which are the focus of Chapter 6.

In the first section of this chapter I analyze Kiva's "irresistible narratability" (Black, 2009, p. 276) and the way it mobilizes Northern publics' affective investments in distant borrowers by examining a range of narrative sites, from the origin stories told by the organization's co-founders to the actual website to the profiles of Kiva borrowers displayed there. The second section focuses on a number of affective socialities forged via micronarratives, manifesting in the Kiva community at large, in virtual connections between lenders and borrowers and in lending teams. Love, for Kiva and its cause, is the predominant sentiment emerging from this analysis and asks us to seriously consider "a political concept of love [with] the power to create bonds that are at once intimate and social" (Hardt, 2011, pp. 676–677).

Stories from the Kiva Factory

The claim that "story telling is central to humanitarian action" (Wilson & Brown, 2009, p. 25) becomes enacted in Kiva's business model, where stories of its borrowers have been made into "the heart of Kiva's goals and strategy" (Flannery, 2007, p. 31). They work as a marketing device, as the differentiator from other online lending platforms and as the emotional glue of the site. Stories are also the currency in which lenders are paid, thereby becoming transformed into a kind of narrative capital. Kiva's origin story tells of the organization's founding by a young Silicon Valley husband-and-wife team who wedded the region's technological and business innovations, giving birth to the Kiva website as the place where all Kiva users meet.

A Labor of Love

Kiva is a quintessential Silicon Valley social enterprise, and its co-founders embody the marriage of Silicon Valley technology – Matt Flannery was a computer programmer at Tivo – and business – Jessica Jackley has an MBA from the Stanford Business School. Flannery grew up in Oregon, holds a BS in symbolic systems and an MA in analytical philosophy from Stanford University. It was him who brought Jackley, who had grown up in Pennsylvania in a Christian household and holds a BA in philosophy and political science from Bucknell University, to the West Coast. As Kiva's first marketing officer, Jackley was the more outgoing and personable of the two, with an easy smile and conviction in her voice. She got her first taste of social change while being active in student government at Bucknell. By comparison, Flannery was always more reserved and methodical, fitting with his technology background. Their respective origin stories (Flannery, 2007, 2009; Jackley, 2010) are partial narratives that chronicle the rise of Kiva as an affective journey, literally and metaphorically.

When Jackley was working at Stanford University's Center for Social Innovation, she took Flannery to hear Mohammad Yunus talk about microfinance. While for Flannery it was "a great story from an inspiring person" (Flannery, 2007, p. 32), the talk was a transformational experience for Jackley. She recounted that

> I reacted with both my head and my heart. My head said: Microfinance is effective. It's powerful. It works. But the most important part was what my heart said. The way he talked about the poor was beautiful, respectful and dignified. I didn't have feelings of guilt and shame like I did after a lot of non-profit messaging. Instead, I wanted to be there, listening to people's stories and talking with clients face to face.
>
> *(quoted in Coates & Saloner, 2009, p. 69)*

For Jackley, Yunus' stories "perform[ed] the vital function of generating appropriate feelings" (Butt, 2002, p. 6). Pegging Kiva's genesis to Yunus also gave the fledgling organization early legitimacy, especially following his award of the 2006 Nobel Peace Prize. After Yunus' talk, Jackley quit her job and went to East Africa to work with the Village Enterprise Fund, which disbursed microloans to small businesses. In her phone calls from Africa — "the place where Americans can be good Americans" (Mathers, 2010, p. 184) — she told Flannery about these businesses and their owners. Eventually Flannery visited Jackley to collect their stories for a short documentary. He was surprised that a place he had imagined to be full of disease and starvation was actually "infused with a spirit of entrepreneurship" (Flannery, 2007, p. 40). The challenges faced by the people he interviewed included a lack of access to capital to start a small store, to get a bus ticket to buy supplies directly from the source rather than from middlemen, or to purchase new inventory. Out of these encounters grew the idea of sponsoring such budding entrepreneurs through loans, which tapped into the co-founders' personal beliefs and histories. Both had grown up sponsoring children in Africa through their families and churches, and in many ways, Kiva is built on these traditional philanthropic models, bringing them into the realm of the Internet and shifting their focus to microentrepreneurs.

Back in California, the co-founders spent a number of months trying to sort out financial and legal issues, without much success, until they reached "a point where we didn't live and breathe this concept [of Kiva] anymore. It was no longer rewarding and we had lost touch with the reasons we had started at all" (Flannery, 2007, p. 39). When they realized that the emotional drivers of the project had fallen victim to bureaucratic maneuvers, they decided to reconnect with what "we had dreamed up on our long bus rides across East Africa" and just started building the site, which led to many late-night coding sessions in San Francisco coffee shops (Flannery, 2007, p. 40). Creating Kiva had become a personal mission in which Flannery and Jackley had become invested, not only with their time and energy, but also with their emotional and physical lives.

Kiva's beta site went up in early 2005 with seven loans posted in collaboration with Moses Onyango, a pastor in Tororo, Uganda, whom Jackley had met during her time there. Emails to 300 people on the co-founders' wedding list resulted in

US$3,500 being raised to fund all seven businesses in one weekend. When Onyango started blogging about their intimate business challenges and successes, these updates became a constant topic of conversation among the co-founders' friends and relatives who had funded the loans. It was then that the former realized that "people cared about the progress of an entrepreneur half-way across the planet. There was, to some degree, a sustained mental and emotional connection" (Flannery, 2007, p. 43). Financial, social and emotional commitments became articulated through the stories of distant others, and "retelling the story of the poor" became central to the Kiva business model (Jackley, 2010). Later it emerged that some of Onyango's stories were fictional, as he had created a fraudulent organization and fictitious borrowers to enrich himself, realizing that "you could make a pretty penny, all you had to do was tell a good story" (Flannery, 2009, p. 42). Shining light on a central lesson of humanitarian fundraising, Onyango's actions also reveal the constructed nature of humanitarian narratives (Wilson & Brown, 2009; Sandvik, 2009).

In October 2005 the *Daily Kos*, a popular political blog, featured Kiva on its homepage in a post called "Microcredit – Be a Venture Capitalist." The post led to a sell-out of all loans in a matter of hours. Shortly thereafter, Flannery became "consumed by an overwhelming feeling: pain. For the first time, I connected with how much it actually hurt to not fully pursue a passion that had been ignited a year and a half earlier in Africa" (Flannery, 2007, p. 45). Just like for many young US travelers before him, Africa "create[d] the intimate and embodied love affair that is consummated by the returned traveler's determination to seek succor for the ills of this continent" (Mathers & Hubbard, 2006, p. 83). This was an intensely embodied experience and led Flannery to quit his job to become Kiva's CEO. It was the culmination of a professional and emotional journey that came not without sacrifice, as it eventually led to the divorce of the co-founders and Jackley's departure from Kiva in 2009. This has not stopped her, however, from continuing to describe Kiva as a "love story" materializing people's desire "to really be meaningful and useful" in other people's lives (Jackley, 2010).

The co-founders' affectively charged language fits the current moment of humanitarianism. Kiva became a *coup de coeur*, to borrow the term used by French humanitarian organizations for "projects close to the heart" (Rubenstein, 2008, p. 229). Showing the co-founders' commitment not only in professional but also in emotional terms makes their labor of love all the more appealing. In the process of creating Kiva, both Flannery and Jackley became transformed, taking "a risk in which we abandon some of our attachments to this world in the hope of creating another, better one" (Hardt, 2011, p. 678). Such change is one of the qualities of a love with political aspirations, in which political interests and affective lives become united.

The co-founders' origin stories also establish Kiva's narrative foundation in a double sense, telling of its birth and putting stories at its center. They produce narrative authority and engender sentiments of trust in the co-founders and their creation, the Kiva website.

The Heart of Kiva

According to Flannery, when you come to the Kiva site, "the first thing you notice are faces" (2007, p. 40). Indeed, looking back at the visitor to the Kiva homepage are 33, mainly non-white, faces of women, men, couples and groups, arranged in identical 2×2 cm small squares. The effect is striking. Although, not unlike in the Cafédirect poster of Bustinza, the emphasis is on the individual, because "individual victims' narratives seem to be a necessary component in the mobilization of empathy" (Wilson & Brown, 2009, p. 20), the Kiva borrowers' representation as a wall of faces turns them into a mass of Third World entrepreneurs. Their visual standardization denies their uniqueness: "through a process of repetition and accumulation of images, an overwhelming sense of 'the South' as a single, though endlessly diverse, place where poor women are constantly, diligently and happily engaged in small-scale but productive labor for the market" is created (Wilson, 2011, p. 323). The homepage's technical design and interface also "mainstream" borrowers' voices and neutralize any subversive potential their portrayal might have (Gajjala & Birzescu, 2011, p. 100). Moving the cursor over the pictures of hopeful borrowers will break the individual out into a larger text box that provides additional information. This information is dwarfed by a large orange *Lend Now* button, which signals that action is only one click away and of primary importance.

The people in the pictures clearly pose for the camera, often in their place of work. In contrast to claims that borrowers are not making direct eye contact with the camera, which has been interpreted as a lack of agency and objectification (Gajjala et al., 2011), what strikes the visitor to the Kiva homepage is the frankness with which borrowers are looking into the camera. This is in itself the result of the interaction of the borrower with the photographer, who is often a Kiva Fellow, a volunteer placed with partner MFIs to help their integration into the Kiva system.

According to an INM Kiva Fellow I interviewed, during their weeklong training at Kiva's headquarters, Fellows are given specific guidelines for taking borrower pictures: faces should be clearly seen, borrowers should ideally be in their places of work and above all, they should be smiling. Even in places where smiling is not part of appropriate conduct, especially in front of a camera, Fellows usually try to get borrowers to smile. This is because most Kiva lenders come from countries where smiling is taken as an indication of a person's openness and honesty, so smiling borrowers in colorful and evocative photos are funded the fastest. Fellows frequently blog about borrowers' initial resistance, for a variety of reasons ranging from spiritual to suspicious, to having their picture taken, which usually fades when the Fellows explain that the photo will lead to a loan. Borrowers' gazes from the Kiva website invite the viewer to establish a relationship with them through making this financial commitment. This invitation works through affect, as perceiving the face of another (human) being creates an ethical demand that is not understandable through language (Parreñas, 2012, drawing on Levinas & Butler). Materializing the social dimension of affective investments, the images and stories of borrowers are mediated in multiple ways so as to represent them as deserving recipients of microloans. Furthermore, the snapshot-like quality of borrower photos aims to minimize the perception of difference between borrowers and lenders, aiding in establishing familiarity rather than alterity and thereby affective identification (Black, 2009).

Underneath hopeful borrowers' faces on the homepage are numbers, impact counters and social network plug-ins, firmly situating Kiva within the social entrepreneurial business and technology milieu of the San Francisco Bay Area where it is still headquartered. This is reinforced by Kiva's characterization as a "self-regulating lending marketplace where microfinance institutions can raise loan capital online" (Flannery, 2007, p. 34). Following the organization's phenomenal growth, its executives have been celebrated as social entrepreneurs by organizations such as the Clinton Global Initiative and the World Economic Forum. As online microfinance evangelists, they share Silicon Valley's dream of making the world a better place through its technology. Kiva's original goal to become "the world's hub for alleviating poverty" through raising US\$1 billion for 2 million entrepreneurs by 2014 was overly ambitious, but made for good marketing. Equally hyperbolic, Flannery has claimed that with the help of the Internet's efficiency, Kiva could "become one of the most highly-leveraged philanthropic opportunities in all of history" (2009, p. 42).[4] While such fantasies are part and parcel of legitimizing oneself in Silicon Valley, they also confirm that new media technologies are allowing humanitarian stories to reach wider audiences more quickly (Laqueur, 2009).

As a technology platform that enables individual lenders' financial commitments, Kiva pools and channels these funds to its field partners, which are MFIs located in dozens of countries around the world. These in turn distribute the loans to their clients. On a superficial level, Kiva money to the MFIs is free because partner organizations are not charged fees or interest for these funds. There are, however, costs associated with fulfilling the requirements of being a Kiva partner, such as getting borrower profiles and pictures on the website and writing regular updates on their progress, which sustain the social and emotional commitments of Kiva lenders. This task is carried out by specially trained MFI staff, often assisted by Kiva Fellows. Partner MFIs range from small, less-established organizations to major quasi-banks; their visibility on the Kiva website makes all of them amenable to lender support. Kiva calls this a form of "democratic capital" that readies especially small MFIs for mainstream investors and eventual entry into the global financial marketplace emerging around microfinance (Flannery, 2007).

The director of INM, the Indonesian MFI where I conducted field research, recounted how he received a letter from Flannery in 2006, inviting him to become a Kiva partner. He was initially reluctant to join because the money was disbursed in US dollars, but changed his mind a year later when he realized that Kiva could serve his organization as a marketing tool: it would allow INM to build an international reputation through good performance on the Kiva website. Over the years, Kiva has established a sophisticated verification system aimed at establishing trust in its MFI partners, consisting of a set of minimum requirements to become a partner, a star-rating system that shows the risk investing in partner MFIs poses to lenders, and auditing procedures donated by Ernst & Young. INM itself was down-graded from 4 to 2.5 stars in September 2011. All INM lenders were told through a message on INM's Kiva page was that information gathered as part of Kiva's general risk rating overhaul "led us to revise INM's risk rating." I sent an email to Kiva asking for more specific information, which was answered with similarly vague language. From my own research at INM I knew that there were some concerns about INM governance structures and financial management, but these were not shared with Kiva users who had to accept INM's significant downgrade at face value. In the hypercompetitive environment on the Kiva site, where hundreds of MFIs vie for loans, such action can limit MFIs' fundraising abilities.

Lender trust needs to be established not only in partner MFIs, but also in Kiva itself, which happens in the *About Us* section of the website. This page is dominated by a photo of all its San Francisco headquarters employees and represents Kiva as a quintessential hi-tech start-up workplace – informal, hip, fun – with obligatory dog and Flannery and Shah, Kiva's President, tucked away among their T-shirt-and-jeans-clad employees. The picture changes regularly as the number of Kiva's paid employees grows. Kiva's mission statement – "we are a non-profit organization with a mission to connect people through lending to alleviate poverty" – makes one of the few mentions of poverty on the entire website.[5] This is in keeping with an early decision by the co-founders to focus on "progress rather than poverty" (Flannery, 2007, p. 36). This semantic sleight of hand sanitizes borrowers' lives. Furthermore, progress is firmly framed by the financialization of poverty when the webpage states that "safe, affordable access to capital to those in need helps people create better lives for themselves and their families." Lending through Kiva provides this capital, and the webpage emphasizes that 100 percent of the loans made go directly to the field partners to be disbursed to borrowers. This appeals to a generation of everyday humanitarians who have become wary of traditional charities with large overhead costs and opaque finances. Kiva itself is funded by optional donations from lenders, philanthropic grants as well as financial and in-kind donations and pro-bono work by technology, legal and financial companies. All of these contributions are made possible by Kiva's 501(c)3 non-profit status, which also fosters lender trust, as 50 percent of lenders would not use the site if Kiva was a for-profit organization (Flannery, 2007). As a non-profit, Kiva must make its financial statements available on the website, which further reinforces its quest for transparency. The webpage concludes with an organizational timeline, which reveals that in spite of its new technology focus, traditional media – an appearance on the *Oprah Winfrey Show*, a PBS *Frontline* documentary,[6] numerous newspaper and magazine articles – have been crucial for the growth of the organization. In short, Kiva presents itself as an efficient, focused, transparent and widely celebrated organization.

For many potential Kiva supporters, a visit to the Kiva site will be their first introduction to microfinance, which makes the *About Microfinance* webpage, which works as an introduction to microfinance, especially significant.[7] It is here that Kiva legitimizes its cause by establishing microfinance as a superior, albeit not stand-alone, poverty-alleviation tool. Ubiquitous references to the Consultative Group for the

Advancement of the Poor (CGAP) align Kiva with that organization's minimalist, finance-only, commercial approach. A heat map of the globe showing the percentage of people living on less than $1/day, without any explanation as to why that would be relevant and how it is connected to microfinance, also corresponds to a financialized view of poverty. This is followed by a number of sections providing more information about various aspects of microfinance. Each of these begins with a photo and story of a Kiva borrower, making Kiva's approach paradigmatic for financial inclusion. In the section titled "Costs, Interest Rates and Sustainability," for example, Sikiratou Salami from Togo is headlined, "[who] took a loan out to purchase supplies for her cosmetics business and plans to use part of her profits to finance the schooling of her three children." Such references to profits reinforce that microfinance works. Microfinance's controversially high interest rates are explained with a reference from CGAP, a microfinance think tank housed at the World Bank, to the various high costs incurred by MFIs. As CGAP is the main advocate of the ongoing commercialization of microfinance, which drives the need for high interest rates so that MFIs can be financially sustainable and increasingly profitable, the absence of a more critical perspective on the interest rate debate, or microfinance at large, is not surprising.

Last but not least, readers can learn about the impact of microfinance, which is essential in turning them into Kiva lenders. Empirical evidence and CGAP's "comprehensive impact studies" are drawn on to authoritatively show a number of positive impacts that can be summarized as improvements in living conditions, "household economic welfare," resilience and risk protection. In general, a shift from daily survival to a future-oriented attitude that allows the poor to plan business, educational and health-related activities enables them to be more proactive and fiscally prudent. Among these impacts, women's empowerment is singled out and reinforced with a quotation from Rose Athieno, a produce reseller from Uganda, who states that "thanks to the loan I received ... you have made me a champion out of nobody." This first-person narrative and direct address to the reader powerfully frames the subsequent invitation to become a lender to Rose and others like her by joining Kiva, at the same time as it ignores the ongoing debates over the contested impact of microfinance in poor women's lives. Rose's story thus serves as an example of how information on the Kiva website, which is itself shaped by microfinance's obligatory success story, become Kiva-truths about microfinance and the poor. Establishing trust in these truths is one of the preconditions of mobilizing affective investments, and "Kiva is about creating thousands of mini-moments of trust," according to one of its Fellows. It is Kiva's micronarratives about the poor that extend this trust to distant borrowers reconstituted as "Kiva entrepreneurs."

Profiling the Poor

In early 2010, we made a loan to Deti and three other women in an INM lending group. To fill the US$1,125 loan, we were joined by 29 other lenders. Over half of us came from North America, with more than a quarter from California,

20 percent from Europe, four from Australia and New Zealand and one from Indonesia. Our ages were fairly evenly distributed between early 20s and late 60s, about half of us were women and most of us were occupied in education, business/finance or creative professions. While only two of us had made a handful of loans, 15 had made several hundred, a third had made several thousands and one, a secretary from France, had made close to 15,000 loans since she joined Kiva in March 2007.[8]

Deti was presented to us on the Kiva website in the following way:

> a 35-year-old female … married and has four school-aged children. She owns and operates a general store, selling daily-use products such as shampoo, soap and toothpaste in the local community. She has been engaged in this business for over a year and earns approximately 1,000,000 IDR a month.[9] In 2010, [she] joined INM to gain access to financial services to help improve her living situation and her ability to engage in business activities. She is now requesting a loan of 2,500,000 IDR which will be used to purchase additional inventory and used as working capital.

Deti's so-called "borrower profile" is the standard story found on Kiva, replicated thousands of times on the site. There are exceptions; some MFIs post more colorful and detailed narratives than others. However, because MFI's Kiva coordinators use questionnaires to compose these profiles, standardized, generic and "monophonic" accounts are the norm (Gajjala & Birzescu, 2011, p. 100).

Profiles give the gender and age of the borrower, the number of children and other family circumstances, as well as type of business to be supported. Sometimes there are allusions to personal tragedy; as one Kiva Fellow wrote in his post on the Kiva Fellows' blog, "a touching story of sorrow endured is also part of an attractive profile."[10] In addition, there is usually information about what borrowers hope to do with the money they gain from investing the loan in their business. The assumption is that such elementary information, in conjunction with the detailed financial information about the MFI that runs alongside the story, is all that potential Kiva supporters need to make their lending choices. This makes the way in which these stories are told even more significant. Another Kiva Fellow's blog post summarized the borrower profile page as "Kiva's face: when you look the photo in the eye, the borrower's story below smiles back at you. Freckles of financial data accents the overall visage: a tidy, friendly invitation to the lending community." By combining touching yet superficial personal information with financial data, profiles appeal to lenders' heads and hearts. The ubiquity of numbers on the site also serves as a constant reminder that Kiva is first and foremost a financial platform moving thousands of dollars every day. The financial, legal and technological infrastructures that make these transactions possible are completely invisible on the site however. Instead, the emphasis is on the borrowers.

Their profile stories are not neutral representations of their lives on the Internet, but social constructions created through borrowers' unequal interactions with the various Kiva agents who are part of profiling them. Representations must be appealing to lenders who can chose among hundreds of online profiles. In this competition for virtual attention and hard cash, faces need to come across as honest and their owners as responsible, in need and deserving. In general, lenders and borrowers map onto the global North and South divide, but there are lenders who live outside the G8 countries and in 2009 Kiva began making loans to borrowers in the United States.[11] To fit into Kiva's diminutive narrative frame, borrowers' stories need to be straightforward, short and simple (Black, 2009). As a result, they become "condensed and powerless" and local experiences assume mere ornamental value (Butt, 2002, p. 6). In addition, Kiva's micronarratives fill the current categories of international development narratives (Suski, 2009), in this case of financially needy and morally worthy poor individuals constituted as always already entrepreneurs. Through this transformation, development narratives become the basis on which global poverty-alleviation interventions such as financial inclusion are enacted. Because of microfinance's focus on empowered entrepreneurs, Kiva's stories do not reproduce the passive suffering victim versus active benefactor chasm of classical humanitarian narratives. Nevertheless, the real extent to which Northern donors and Southern recipients are entangled in each other's lives, which goes far beyond $25, is necessarily obscured by Kiva's narrative simplification.

Kiva stories do not mobilize affective investments in and of themselves, but because today, after 200 years of humanitarian narratives, people expect to be presented with moral claims in the form of stories (Butt, 2002; Rorty, 1993). For these to be translated into action, humanitarian narratives must "expose the lineaments of causality and of human agency: ameliorative action is represented as possible, effective and therefore morally imperative" (Laqueur, 1989, p. 178). In other words:

> Drawing on a view of humanitarian communication as performative, enacting paradigmatic forms of feeling and acting towards suffering, ... such communication does not simply address the public as a pre-existing collectivity that awaits to engage in action but that it has the power to constitute this collectivity as a body of action in the process of visualizing and narrating its cause ... [through] a series of subtle proposals as to how we should feel and act towards suffering.
>
> *(Chouliaraki, 2010, p. 110)*

Everyday humanitarian action is not guaranteed, but only engendered under certain circumstances. Kiva's stories translate into loans due to the contemporary financialization of poverty and the popularization of development, both of which implicate everyday people in the projects of poverty alleviation, through lending on Kiva. And even then, "narratives ... do not come with built-in moral gyroscopes" (Laqueur, 2009, p. 35). While they can produce pleasure, blindness, exclusion or oppression, most often they lead to "facile empathy ... from afar" (Butt, 2002, p. 7). According to Premal Shah, Kiva's President (2008), only a small percentage of visits to the Kiva site translate into loans, showing that for every lender, countless others do not see in Kiva a convincing enough recipe for practice. Still, Kiva entices enough people to be a significant force in everyday humanitarianism through microfinance.

While Kiva lenders can post their own stories directly on their lender profile pages on the Kiva website, borrowers are spoken for by MFI Kiva coordinators, Kiva Fellows and volunteer translators. Their stories are multiply mediated, in part because borrowers frequently lack technological skills or access to the Internet. This gap only gets obscured when new media technologies, in contrast to more static representations through print, film or television, deploy "a rhetoric of interactivity and participation" wrongly promising that subjects are able to represent themselves (Gajjala & Birzescu, 2011, p. 95). In addition, borrowers' stories are appropriated for the larger cause of financial inclusion via Kiva. Here, the questions of rights, ownership and authority that result from the use of an individual's story by somebody else become compounded by the instrumental nature of the appropriation: to raise money (Shuman, 2005). Because of humanitarian narratives' seemingly unmediated access to "what really happened," they are frequently deployed to lend credibility or make truth claims. Even when appropriating intermediaries contend to speak in the interest of the people represented and to tell stories that otherwise would not be told, the voices of those spoken for are silenced. The latter are also not in a position to stop their stories from becoming spectacles to be witnessed or from resulting in "complacent neo-imperial voyeurism" (Black, 2009, p. 284; Suski, 2009).

As part of our research at INM, we decided to visit Deti, to whom we had made a Kiva loan earlier. Wayan, who was in his 30s and had become INM's Kiva coordinator a year earlier, showed us the way on his motorbike. En route, we stopped at INM's local office to pick up its manager and Deti's loan officer. By the time we turned off the main road and drove down a dirt path to Deti's small house, the size of our entourage took Deti by surprise, even though she had been told that we were coming. Hastily, she procured more plastic chairs from behind her house and arranged them around a table in front of her house. At some point during the interview, my partner Paul showed Deti a printout of her Kiva profile page, which also contained a photo of her and the other three women in her lending group. Never having seen the page before, she was surprised at the sight of her picture, not knowing why it was there or where exactly it was displayed. This was not a unique occurrence.

When a *New York Times* reporter went to visit his borrower in Afghanistan, he found out that the baker did not know anything about him or Kiva (Kristof, 2007). Kiva Fellows also blog about the awkwardness that can ensue when borrowers see their profile for the first time. In these accounts, borrowers are often shy, then embarrassed, but always seem to end up proudly showing the pictures to family members and friends who are invariably present. Some of these blog posts are accompanied by Fellows' requests for lenders to post pictures of themselves on their own profile page, which allows borrowers to see who has contributed to filling their loan, reinforcing the two-way connection that Kiva sells.

Facing Deti, all we could do was ask if she liked her picture, which elicited a non-enthusiastic smile. Wayan, INM's Kiva coordinator, was sitting next to us and confirmed that Deti indeed did not know about her Kiva profile and had not been told anything about Kiva. Back in the office, he elaborated that there was a purpose to this omission, as it was not in INM's interest to tell its borrowers that their loans are coming from abroad. He explained that this was to prevent borrowers from thinking of them as international charity that does not have to be repaid, although it might also have reduced the esteem in which borrowers held INM if it was revealed that INM was not the original source of the money.

Kiva's loans are thus situated within a larger political economy of aid and its established dependency relationships, even though Kiva is trying to work against this with its business–not–charity philosophy. However, the organization does not operate outside the aid apparatus, which itself has stretched its boundaries to include social enterprises like Kiva and the companies and foundations supporting it. Moreover, in lenders' minds Kiva's micronarratives rub against traditional development representations, producing juxtapositions that are expressed in ambivalent lender profiles (Black, 2013).

When any of the lenders want to take out a loan, it is a confidential matter between them and their financial institutions, while Kiva borrowers' personal and financial information are openly displayed on the website, universally searchable and often making individuals and their cash holdings easily identifiable. This means that what is also at stake in Kiva's micronarratives are issues of privacy and security. One astute Kiva Fellow pointed out in one of his blog posts that some borrowers might reject being labeled as poor, which for him was an issue of "cultural imperialism" that was not sufficiently addressed by Kiva. In response to such concerns, in 2010 Kiva adopted a "do no harm"[12] policy and made it mandatory for all MFIs to use a standardized client waiver to ensure borrowers' consent to have their information published on the Internet. Borrowers can choose to delete their name and location from their profile, but must agree to have their story made public.[13] In sensitive locations such as Iraq, borrowers' faces are often obscured for security reasons. However, detailed financial transactions, such as when loans were disbursed and installments repaid, including exact amounts, are always posted on a subpage of the borrower's profile. While this might satisfy lenders' need for risk assessment and organizational transparency, it does not protect borrowers from the demands of relatives or the threat of robbery. Indeed, Shah (2008) recounted how in Tororo, Uganda, where Kiva started, the site had become an unofficial credit bureau serving as a "a bulletin of creditworthiness" where neighbors can check up on each other.

At INM, the waiver was implemented by Heike, INM's Kiva Fellow at the time of my research, who explained to us that to the many INM borrowers who had never been on the Internet, it was explained as "a public space where the information can be seen by people around the world." However, because it is up to the MFI to decide how it wants to explain Kiva to its clients, INM's waiver still does not mention Kiva or Kiva lenders. Heike's explanation for this absence echoed Wayan's words about established expectations of international money being charity that does not need to be repaid, which she attributed to a "dependency mentality."

Kiva's client waiver does not address any of these issues, but only presents a bureaucratic solution to larger questions of informed consent and unequal international development relations perpetuated by Kiva.

Foremost among these are the different obligations lenders and borrowers have to make themselves visible on the Kiva site (Black, 2009). Of the 30 people who lent to Deti's group, 17 posted a picture of themselves in their personal profiles, but only 3 gave detailed personal information; 12 others provided some information and 8 chose to remain anonymous. This shows the various extents to which lenders are willing to share information about themselves. For Kiva executives, however, technical solutions are sufficient to a problem they do not recognize as such.

During his keynote address at a social finance conference in San Francisco in 2010, Flannery joked about the difficulty of explaining to a borrower that her loan had been made by a cat, which elicited much laughter from the audience. That lenders can post pictures of their pets to represent themselves, or even establish Kiva accounts in their pets' names, while borrowers have no such liberties, shows the latter's inability to participate as equals in conversations about their lives. It draws attention to Kiva's location within an emerging "infopolitics" (Coopman, 2014). At this intersection of information and politics sits the "informational person [who] politically and culturally [is] increasingly defined through an array of information architectures." Kiva forms part of this architecture for its users, some of whom enter it more knowingly than others. For the latter, infopolitics morphs into an "informatics of domination" (Haraway, 1985).

Virtual Socialities

In keeping with its location in the social-entrepreneurial culture of the San Francisco Bay Area, where "technological benevolence" is harnessed to make the world a better place (Gajjala & Birzescu, 2011, p. 99), Kiva wants to appeal not to lenders' guilt or compassion, but to their interests in and sense of respect for others (Flannery, 2007). To achieve this, Kiva constitutes borrowers on the site as "unusually vibrant and resilient investment opportunities," thereby instrumentalizing human lives in another instance of the financialization of poverty (Flannery, 2009, p. 49). Likewise, business is presented as "a universal language that can appeal to people of almost every background," creating bonds that tie the poor and the affluent together across virtual space (Flannery, 2007, p. 40). The focus on financially enabling Kiva entrepreneurs becomes the basis for creating a community, both on- and offline, where lenders and borrowers become connected through shared entrepreneurial interests. However, everyday humanitarianism's financial, legal and entrepreneurial dimensions cannot be separated from its moral and emotional ones (Wilson & Brown, 2009). Kiva has been characterized as a "matrix of intimate mediation" (Roy, 2012, p. 151), and although the dream of a technology-enabled affective space that includes both lenders and borrowers is still marketed by Kiva, what has materialized is an arena for lender connections produced through token borrower presence.

A Community of Kivans

According to Flannery, over the years Kiva has put much effort into constituting itself as "an emerging community, [since] we are all here because of the shared belief that ordinary people can actually make a difference in lessening the world's poverty."[14] His statement shows that lenders are the primary recipients of Kiva's attention, as they are the main constituency on which Kiva's growth depends.[15] Many new features on the Kiva site are aimed at either attracting new lenders or getting current ones to lend more. Gift certificates make Kiva loans and their borrowers easily consumable, especially at Christmas and other occasions when certificates are marketed as a responsible giving choice to loved ones (Black, 2009). They have been the most basic form of growing lender numbers, together with offers of a free loan for each new lender who is recruited. More recently, lenders have been able to dedicate their loans to others, who are then featured on the lender's personal page, which fosters sentimental ties between lenders. A partnership with TripAdvisor that gave Kiva gift certificates to people writing travel reviews on the TripAdvisor site capitalized on people's frequent desire to do something good for the people and places they have just visited.

Nevertheless, borrowers continue to be presented as crucial members of this community, not least of all because they are the precondition for Kiva's "connected capital" (Flannery, 2009, p. 40). Besides being "patient, catalytic and accountable," this capital is seen to be "democratic," because after 8 years, over 1 million lenders have given loans to over 1 million borrowers. These numbers show that Kiva does bring together a great number of people from all parts of the globe, with the aim to empower them with a $25 loan. While such empowerment is usually aimed at poor borrowers, Kiva is also empowering lenders in the global North, who feel that their small contributions are making a visible difference in other, less fortunate, people's lives. This power of giving is reinforced by books like former US President Bill Clinton's *Giving*, which presents Kiva as "enabling citizens of modest means who share a common concern to amass huge sums of money" (Clinton, 2007, p. 27). In the process, lenders come to see themselves as micro-venture capitalists who are funding small businesses all around the world. Bob Harris, whose story opened this chapter, feels that he is running a mini-foundation every time he goes to the Kiva site to reinvest his money. Here, financial calculations are articulated with affective sentiments to become affective investments that are part of a "compassionate capitalism" espoused by philanthrocapitalists like Bill Gates (Schwittay, 2011). In other words, Kiva capitalizes on the "dual meaning of being invested in somebody," and it is precisely its ability to harness people's economic self-interest to their desire to feel connected to a larger purpose that has contributed much to Kiva's popularity (Black, 2009, p. 285).

There is pleasure in this participation. One Kiva lender-cum-Fellow described his feelings when making a loan, and a few hours later getting an update that a dozen other lenders have helped to fully fund the loan: "it's a beautiful moment, where elegant software design harnessed people power. There is something elated and wondrous about it. It restores my faith in the world, in humanity." Kiva also aims to create an environment where "philanthropy can actually become addictive" (Flannery, 2007, p. 40). Almost real-time updates on available loans, which can be tailored to one's lending preferences, as well as blogs and tweets, keep Kiva fans glued to the site, which is anchored in people's everyday electronic consumption. Scoring a loan in a coveted and popular location creates virtual gratification. The capitalist dictum that "the continuous production of newness generates continuous consumption" is now sped up by the Internet and its technological affordances (Gajjala & Birzescu, 2011, p. 96). These also include the forging of human connections between lenders and borrowers, which are seen as the most important ingredient in the mobilization of affective investments via Kiva.

Affective Investments

According to Jackley (2010), "loans are a very interesting tool for connectivity" because of their two-way nature. On Kiva, through the process of making a loan and receiving repayments and updates, money becomes transformed into a kind of emotional capital, imagined to be more financially and socially sustaining than a mere donation would be. Flannery describes the relationships that are forged in this way between lenders and borrowers as "dignified, intellectual and equitable," as they aim to raise awareness of the lives of distant others and loans to support them (Flannery, 2007, p. 32). For Jackley (2010), they are a

> partner relationship, not a relationship that's based on the traditional sort of donor beneficiary weirdness that can happen. But instead a relationship that can promote respect and hope ... and blur the lines between the traditional rich and poor categories that we are taught to see in the world, this false dichotomy of us and them, have and have not.

In these words of the co-founders, two-way loan relationships create entrepreneurial partnerships that dispense with paternalistic charity impulses. Credit relations are also debt relations, however, with corresponding risks for lenders and borrowers. Highlighting the first, as Kiva does on its homepage, and ignoring the second, which is nowhere articulated, is part of Kiva's affective sleight of hand.

The "feelingful ties" (Moodie, 2013, p. 280) on which Kiva relationships are based begin when a potential lender comes to the site to choose a borrower from hundreds of profiles. In general, lenders are motivated by altruism, a sense of social responsibility and often reciprocity and their belief in microfinance as an effective development tool (Liu et al., 2012). Their choices of borrowers are often informed by personal reasons, based on identifications with particular parts of life stories, similarities in occupations, travel experiences or personal preferences. In her reply to a blog post by an INM Kiva Fellow, one lender to INM described becoming very upset when she found out that the loan she thought she had made to a rice-growing group actually went to a pig-raising group. As a devout vegetarian, she did not care about the centrality of raising pigs in local women's lives and livelihoods. Similarly, another lender-cum-Fellow blogged that initially he did not make loans to people in the charcoal trade because he considered this a dirty business in conflict with his environmental sensibilities. He did change his mind, however, when in the course of his Kiva Fellowship he realized how important charcoal was to some of his MFI's clients. At one point, Kiva experimented with posting loan requests in their original language, rather than translating them into English. The loans filled just as quickly, which one Kiva Fellow interpreted in her blog as lenders choosing loans because of their emotional reactions to borrowers' photos. She for her part made a loan to a Vietnamese woman because she had the eyes of her adopted sister.

Lenders make their choices with clear preferences: "Africans first, women first, and agriculture first" (Flannery, 2007, p. 50). These preferences are constituted by post-colonial development discourses, where rural female Africans represent the most stereotypical notions of poverty, backwardness and vulnerability that permeate representations of poverty and development. Conversely, loans to Eastern European countries are the hardest to fill because their borrowers do not correspond to mediatized images of poverty. A Kiva Fellow posted to the Ukraine mused that "perhaps it's the well-stocked shelves or maybe the often unsmiling, warmly dressed men and women, that do not illicit [sic] immediate sympathy or the thoughts of poverty that lenders often associate with Kiva borrowers?" Although decreasingly so, the majority of Kiva borrowers are still female, in keeping with microfinance's general emphasis on women, but also with women's particular appeal to lenders based on their construction as vulnerable, caring, responsible and hence deserving. It was partly to counter such sentimental lending preferences that Flannery wanted to institute interest payments to lenders.[16]

Once the loan has been made, the relationship continues when lenders receive regular updates from their borrowers. In spite of an early promotional video showing an African Kiva borrower sitting in front of a computer sending an email to her lender in San Francisco, borrowers' updates, called journals, are written by MFI Kiva coordinators or Kiva Fellows. One of the updates I received for Deti, written by Heike on the Kiva website after a visit to Deti's house, stated that

> It was amazing to see Deti, who operates a warung (a small store) in her house and talking to her about her business I could see how important it is for her ... The [Kiva] loan made it possible to purchase additional inventory for her store like rice and pig feed to sell in her neighborhood. With this business she earns now about 800,000 Rupiah (about 80 Dollars) a month. The interest per month on her individual 100$ loan is about 2,5$ so in her case the loan supports her business without troubles through repayments. ... The loan helps the group members to support the daily needs of their families and gives the perspective to reach financial self-sufficiency on a higher scale of their businesses which can lead to a higher standard of living for their whole family. But the social, non-financial aspect which is very prominent in

women's groups shouldn't be neglected. . . . The spirit of the community supports the empowerment of the women who are now more independent from their husbands. They simply have more perspectives since they formed a group and take loans.

When I visited Deti a couple of days after Heike, I found her shop closed and looking rather abandoned. All we could see were a few empty bottles standing in front of a boarded-up window in the front room of her house. When I asked Deti why her store was closed, she told me that she had not operated it for a while because her husband had been in the hospital. In fact, he had just come home that morning and was sitting in a corner of the house, away from our party, seeming downcast and frail. We were all disappointed, but none more than my kids whom I had promised some sweets to boost Deti's business. I felt that she could use all the sales she could get, since her house was located along a narrow dirt lane at some remove from the main street with its numerous similar kiosks. There were not too many other houses in close proximity and when I asked Deti where the customers for her wares came from, she said that there were lots more houses further down the track. Like all women in Bali, Deti also raised pigs to supplement the (probably meager) income from her store.

While I came away from meeting "my" Kiva borrower with a sense of excitement, which nevertheless was troubled by my critical stance toward microfinance and Kiva, I was bothered by the discrepancy between Heike's story and what I had just seen and heard. Neither Heike nor Wayan wanted to engage my questions about it. However, when I reread the above blog post carefully, I realized that Heike had actually never written that she saw Deti operating her store at the time of her visit. It was just an assumption that I, and probably most other readers of her post, had made. Her careful language thus allowed Heike to keep up microfinance's, and Kiva's, obligatory success story. Part of that story is glorifying poor people's survival strategies as entrepreneurial activities.

According to Wayan's last journal update for Deti, her group was not seeking another loan "because they already have enough capital from their business profits." Given that repeat loans are encouraged by Kiva and its MFI partners since they ensure organizational growth and are also seen as an indication of a loan's positive impact, it is unusual for a borrower not to climb the loan ladder. Deti's refusal to do so thus casts further doubt on Heike's success story. Other researchers of microfinance have found that loans are often used for consumption smoothing or to pay for emergency expenses (Brett, 2006), and there is a possibility that Deti, who only joined INM earlier in 2010, might have done so because she knew that a large hospital bill would be coming her family's way. Using loans to cover such expenses is risky business, since no income is generated to make interest and installment payments.

Kiva is able to distance itself and its lenders from this risk by enveloping creditor–debtor relationships in virtual social and emotional connections that neutralize their financial aspects (Moodie, 2013). Furthermore, borrowers' riskscapes, while tied to global financial networks, are shaped by local gendered codes, such as honor and shame in Bangladesh (Karim, 2008) or status and reputation in Bolivia (Maclean, 2013). Not many of Kiva's users, employees or even Fellows are aware of these norms, and Kiva's micronarratives are not able to capture them. Instead, on Kiva risk is turned into another way to foster lender–borrower connections, by having lenders assume the risk for their loans (Flannery, 2009). Small letters at the bottom of Kiva's homepage inform potential lenders of "the risk of principal loss," although until recently MFIs were able to cover delinquent payments to keep their good standing on Kiva. This is also a safeguard for Kiva, which only reimburses lenders when MFIs have engaged in fraudulent activities, which happens rarely due to Kiva's extensive and growing due diligence apparatus.

Last but not least, the official Kiva Fellows blog, called *Stories from the Field*, is yet another means by which the connection between lenders and borrowers is maintained. As I show in Chapter 6, while there are occasional reports of hardship that invariably focus on personal misfortunes, the great majority of blog posts replicate microfinance's obligatory success story, as Heike did above. Some of the blog posts talk about Fellows showing borrowers the profiles of their lenders, which usually elicits borrowers' surprise, interest and gratitude. One Fellow collected the responses of borrowers at her Kenyan MFI. These included:

> I'm very grateful and actually feel that there is love outside there for people … to lend money to people they have never met and don't know apart from just reading their profiles on the internet. It makes me encouraged. Because I feel at least someone outside also thinks about me…

> [T]hrough support, I think even me I want to work hard to be among the people who are lending also, because me I have been supported.

> [T]hese people, may God bless them, and if I could just see them with my own eyes, the embracement I would give them, no one would be able to imagine. I'm unable to express my gratitude. I am very happy.

These rare examples of borrowers' sentiments make the powerful potential of Kiva as a more inclusive humanitarian communication space visible. They show that affect circulates and that the discourse of love is not confined to Kiva lenders. If a political concept of love "should have to operate in a field of multiplicity and function not through unification but the encounter and interaction of differences" (Hardt, 2011, p. 678), then bringing lenders and borrowers together in ways that matter personally and politically could present a step toward such a promise. As it stands, the token presence of borrowers on the Kiva site and their instrumentalization to generate more loans presents a significant hurdle.

Still, over the years Kiva has experimented with various ways of creating more mutual lender–borrower relationships. An option of having lenders email questions for a particular borrower to a Fellow about to visit that borrower elicited only a standard exchange between INM lenders and borrowers (Q: "What will the borrower do with the money from her business?" A: "Pay school fees"). While it was quickly abandoned at INM, it seemed to have been more successful at other MFIs. A Fellow at an MFI in Togo blogged that a woman named Paula from Spokane in the United States wanted to know what Félicité's, one of her borrowers, challenges as a working mother were. Félicité answered that her biggest challenge was being the sole provider for her 10-year-old daughter and younger sister. The Fellow concluded:

> this exchange is remarkable because it's a relevant question to a woman like Félicité from Lomé *and* a woman like Paula from Spokane. This new tool by which lenders can ask their borrowers questions levels the playing field and highlights the fact that on both ends of the Kiva lending process are real people who are probably not so different from one another as they might think. Kiva is special and relevant precisely because it makes poverty alleviation personal. As people like Paula are personally touched by what they've learned, they're going to continue to make small contributions that amount to large life changes for the thousands upon thousands of borrowers who have themselves been touched by Kiva. In turn, people like Félicité not only receive financial support from Kiva lenders, they are also *personally* empowered by the realization that some*one* is cheering them on!
>
> *(original italics)*

This Fellow's articulation of financial, social and emotional commitments is not as equal as the above passage makes it seem. While both women are named, only the borrower has her full name made public, together with a hyperlink to her Kiva profile page that provided more of her personal information as well as loan details. Had the Fellow done the same for Paula in the United States, Kiva might have had to contend with a complaint about privacy violations. Once again, borrower and lender were differently positioned informational subjects (Coopman, 2014). In addition, there was no question asking why the borrower has to care for her younger sister, which might have highlighted broader circumstances under which African women must labor.

The blog post was written in response to revelations that Kiva's person-to-person connection was an illusion, which created much debate in the blogosphere (Roodman, 2009). In 2009, David Roodman showed that most loans do not go directly to the borrower chosen by the lender on the site, but are used to backfill the loans of the MFI that had already given a loan to the borrower displayed on the website.[17] Most importantly, most lenders were probably not aware of this information, which ran directly counter to claims on Kiva's homepage at the time.[18] Although some lenders felt betrayed, declaring that they could no longer use Kiva because they had been too heavily invested in the personal connections it had promised, the larger tenor of the discussion was that in light of Kiva's overall impact, the transgression could be forgiven. Other lenders remain attached to the person-to-person illusion, to the point where they do not want to lend to borrower groups because that would negate the individual connection. What became obvious in the debate was that lenders had not only made affective investments in Kiva borrowers, but also in the organization itself and in its cause of poverty alleviation and empowerment through microfinance. Ironically, the fiction of the direct connection between lenders and borrowers can only be maintained by making organizational intermediaries, such as Kiva and its partner MFIs, invisible.

Affective Collectives

To cater to lenders' needs for community, connection and caring, in 2008 Kiva created lending teams that allow lenders to pool their loans with like-minded individuals. According to their announcement on the official Kiva blog, the aim was to manifest the Kiva community and to make it easier for existing lenders to broadcast Kiva in "their own communities," in order to recruit new lenders.[19] At the time, Flannery was a guest blogger on Social Edge, the blog of the Skoll Foundation, which is the foremost social entrepreneurship organization in the San Francisco Bay Area and had just awarded US$1 million to Flannery and Shah. In his blog post, Flannery wrote that the lending teams were not meant to be "a dating site or a Facebook ripoff," but that "socializing on Kiva … within the context of making loans [aims to] leverage the basic human need to socialize for the higher cause of serving the working poor in this world."[20] Capitalizing on the popularity of social networking sites like Facebook, lending groups are nevertheless firmly situated within the larger Kiva purpose of raising money.

As of February 2014, according to the Kiva website, there were close to 27,800 lending teams, grouped into 17 categories ranging from families to business, common interest, local areas to educational and religious institutions. From the early days, the largest lending team by loan amount has been the *Kiva Atheists, Agnostics, Skeptics, Freethinkers, Secular Humanists and the Non-Religious*, who lend because "we care about the suffering of human beings."[21] This situates its more than 28,400 members, who describe themselves as "those of us who know we are one human family," squarely within the common humanity ethos. The team also hosts a search engine for secular MFIs on Kiva to facilitate loans to non-religious institutions. By contrast, the second largest team are the *Kiva Christians*, who draw directly on religious tenets, such as helping widows and orphans, to explain their lending activity. In different ways, both teams make the usually implicit religious undertones of Kiva manifest. Besides religion, technology is another major draw for lenders, and the largest team by member numbers are the *Nerdfighters*, gathering close to 44,500 lenders who profess to "fight against suck." Most MFI Kiva partners also have their own dedicated lending team. In November 2013, the *Friends of INM* team had 75 members, whose geographical origins were fairly evenly distributed between the global North, Indonesia itself and undisclosed locations.

A digital word map of the lending motivations of 170 teams shows that "world" was the most commonly used word, "revealing the emotional investment many lending teams place in the idea of their own worldliness" (Black, 2013, p. 111). An ethics of care speaks through the next set of prominent words such as "help," "want" and "make." "Entrepreneur," "other" and "people" show a particular conception of those whom lenders see themselves as helping.

A leader board ranks team performances by loan amount and new members, on a monthly and all-time basis, reinforcing Kiva's almost game-like character.[22] As one Kiva lender noted, a bit of friendly competition goes a long way; it also echoes the general competitive tone of the site. Such competition can also give rise to playful irony, when for example the *New York Giants Fan* team lends because "Dallas fans won't" or when the *Ohio Wittman Family* team declares that "we are going to beat the Wittman Colorado team" (all cited in Black, 2013, pp. 113–114). Shameem Black argues that such constructions of non-borrower others point to a post-humanitarian irony emerging on Kiva, where grand emotions of pity and gratitude are abandoned for more contingent and ambivalent sentiments that "reflect a critical self-consciousness that recognizes that doing good in the world is often filled with unexpected pitfalls" (Black, 2013, p. 114, drawing on Chouliaraki, 2010). This raises the question of whether the rejection of empathy for the other reflected in such statements opens up the possibility of a more critical engagement with the larger giving project and with some of the problems of microfinance. For Chouliaraki, the self-centered turn such irony takes does not allow for this to happen, and Black herself argues instead for a "protective indemnification" that shields ironic lenders from the possible realization of microfinance's more negative impacts (2013, p. 116). In other words, critical awareness might exist but is sublimated rather than acted upon.

Kiva lending teams are an example of "affective collectivities" (Richard & Rudnyckyj, 2009, p. 66) brought together by shared other-concern and self-identification. Teams allow lenders to express themselves and their identities through joining particular groups, reinforcing personal positioning by way of lending to distant others. On Kiva, affect aligns individuals with virtual collectivities "through the very intensity of their attachments" (Ahmed, 2004, p. 119), which are reinforced through offline events that have become an important part of the Kiva community at large. Kiva birthdays are celebrated with events in San Francisco, there are regular open houses at the headquarters, and meet-ups, marathons, fashion shows and other events are organized in the many large cities that have Kiva chapters. While US Kiva borrowers attend such events in the United States as well, it is predominantly lenders that come together to revel in their common cause. This is secondary, however, to making new loans and recruiting new adherents, which is always the stated goal of these events. What Kiva creates, then, is a form of financio-sociality where groups form around financial practices (cf. Rabinow, 1992, on bio-socialities).

As a collective space enabled by new media technologies, Kiva "gives form to communities of sentiment, affect-charged groups with the potential for transnational movement from shared imagination to collective action" (Dechaine, 2002, citing Appadurai, 1996). Such collective action has not yet materialized beyond the lending groups that aggregate individual loans. Flannery speculates that maybe one day "Kiva might find itself wading into advocacy [based on] a large list of highly engaged, socially conscious users with the ability to rally support behind certain causes" (2009, p. 48). The potential of mobilizing great numbers of people who have already shown an interest, however superficial, in poverty alleviation, and who are starting to organize in lending teams on the basis of mutual interests, as a political force is certainly great. As Boltanski (1999) has argued, not only donations, but also donors need to be aggregated to form the groups on which political action depends. However, transforming lending teams into such groups would take a more concerted effort by Kiva leadership than has happened to date.

When Jackley was asked during an event in 2009 about the potential negative consequences of microfinance,[23] she answered "I've only seen positive things happen" (quoted in Moodie, 2013, p. 300). Talking about her own personal, positive experiences with microfinance with the authority of being Kiva's co-founder allowed her to evade the question. Her answer also points to the privatization of microfinance at play in Kiva. From Kiva's person-to-person fiction to the accounts of its co-founders to the individual borrower and lender stories on the site to the groups that bring together individual Kiva lenders to support individual Kiva entrepreneurs, it is a focus on the individual that gives the organization its appeal. Similar to the personalization of humanitarian narratives to compel care, Kiva operates one borrower at a time. Its impressive number of financial contributions to distant borrowers is enabled by social connections that generate emotional returns for those who make these contributions. It is in this way that Kiva becomes a prime site for the mobilization of affective investments, where stories fuel a continuous virtual-virtuous cycle. Almost a decade after its creation, the site continues to sign up thousands of new lenders each week, who continue to choose from 33 faces on the homepage and hundreds more found on a page simply called *Lend*.

Most academic critiques of Kiva have focused on its commodification of borrowers' perilous lives and the way in which it both accommodates and promotes middle-class values (Black, 2009; Gajjala & Birzescu, 2011; Gajjala et al., 2011; Moodie, 2013). In the words of Shameem Black,

> Kiva might be seen to contribute toward a larger cultural project of repression since its ability to spark vivid feelings of responsibility potentially allows lenders to forget how large-scale development aid has worked to produce the uneven topographies of capitalism across the world that microfinance ostensibly seeks to alter.
>
> *(2013, p. 108)*

Such criticism is an indictment of global capitalism, of the development apparatus that is entangled in it and of Kiva, which is embedded in both. These critiques are important and accurate, but what if after we have made them we moved to a more immanent form of critique by taking seriously what Kiva is offering?

The question then becomes whether Kiva's humanitarian micronarratives and the sentiments of aid to which they give rise can generate an affective politics. I argue in the Conclusion that such a politics would be different from classical prescriptions of collective action. Maybe a political concept of love offers a solution? As I have shown throughout this chapter, Kiva does exhibit the three qualities of such a concept: it creates bonds that are both intimate and social, it accommodates difference and it transforms individuals (Hardt, 2011). But is that sufficient? Or is Kiva's potential terminally blocked by its clicktivist action, which does not ask lenders to question their banal and historic complicity or to leave their zones of comfort? A detailed engagement with these questions will have to wait for the book's conclusion. First, I complement this chapter's analysis of the narrative dimension of microfinance and everyday humanitarianism with an examination of their visual character.

Notes

* Parts of this chapter are based on analysis and writing undertaken jointly with Paul Braund, which resulted in two unpublished working papers in 2010. Especially the section on Profiling the Poor and in particular the exchange with Deti around her Kiva page are based on an interview and writing by Paul analyzing privacy and surveillance on the internet. I am thankful for his permission to use this material.
1 Retrieved July 11, 2013, from www.kiva.org/lender/michelle77908454.
2 Retrieved July 11, 2013, from www.youtube.com/watch?v=n1V9jVtssfw. My interpretation also hints at the 1960s counterculture in the Bay Area, from which Kiva might also have drawn some inspiration.
3 Although I have not undertaken quantitative analyses of website data, the way in which the extensive information about lenders and borrowers on the site lends itself to "big data analysis" is worth mentioning (Boellstorff, 2013). Because Kiva gives interested and technologically inclined researchers backdoor access to its datasets, computer scientists have analyzed lending preferences, lending team behavior and relationships between the two.
4 The leverage ratio is a measurement of the amount of money sent to borrowers as a factor of Kiva's cost.
5 Retrieved June 20, 2012, from www.kiva.org/about.
6 PBS – Public Broadcasting Service – is the most prominent provider of content to US public television stations and *Frontline* is its highly acclaimed public affairs program. After the documentary, Kiva's website crashed because of high demand, and such system failure became part of the success story.
7 Retrieved July 11, 2011, from www.kiva.org/about/microfinance.
8 This refers to the number of loans made as of October 2013.
9 About US$110 as of September 2010.
10 All Kiva Fellows' quotations in this chapter are taken from blog posts.
11 This was met with much initial criticism, even leading to the formation of a *Pissed-off Kiva Lenders* lending team. Besides the feeling that Kiva was straying from its mission to alleviate poverty, the fear was that the much larger US loans would take money away from international loans. As Kiva has shifted to larger loans to keep up its growth, the number of unfilled loans has indeed increased from next to nothing to 5 percent in 2012, according to Kiva's 2012 annual report.
12 The similarity to Google's infamous motto is perhaps not incidental. I thank Paul Braund for this observation as well as his astute analysis of issues around Kiva's privacy and surveillance, on which my thinking is based.
13 If they do not want to appear on the Internet, they are still guaranteed a non-Kiva loan from the MFI, as part of the Kiva–MFI contract.

14 Retrieved April 2010, from www.kiva.org/blog/2008/08/28/two-big-steps-for-kiva-website.html.
15 Growth is a paramount objective for Kiva, which had branched out from business loans into student loans and sustainable energy loans and is also partnering with non-MFI organizations in order to increase its loan volume.
16 Because of rules by the US Securities and Exchange Commission on securitization required for interest-paying institutions, a complex area Kiva chose to avoid, it cannot pay interest to lenders (Flannery, 2009).
17 One commentator drew parallels to child sponsorship's fall from grace in the 1990s (Ogden, 2009).
18 Kiva did change its misleading tagline and representation of the lending process immediately and redesigned its entire website by early 2011.
19 Retrieved February 13, 2012, from http://kivanews.blogspot.co.nz/2008/08/new-lending-teams-feature.html.
20 Retrieved February 13, 2012, from www.socialedge.org/blogs/kiva-chronicles/archive/2008/08/26/liquidity-and-community.
21 Retrieved July 11, 2013, from www.kiva.org/team/atheists.
22 I thank Paul Braund for pointing this out to me.
23 At this point, Jackley had already left Kiva and founded a new company called ProFounder.

Bibliography

Ahmed, S. (2004). Affective economies. *Social Text, 22*(2), 117–139.
Appadurai, A. (1996). *Modernity at large: Cultural dimensions of globalization.* Minneapolis: University of Minnesota Press.
Black, S. (2009). Microloans and micronarratives: Sentiments for a small world. *Public Culture, 21*(2), 269–291.
Black, S. (2013). Fictions of humanitarian responsibility: Narrating microfinance. *Journal of Human Rights, 12*(1), 103–120.
Boellstorff, T. (2013). Making big data, in theory. *First Monday, 18*(10).
Boltanski, L. (1999). *Distant suffering: Morality, media and politics.* Cambridge: Cambridge University Press.
Bornstein, E. (2012). *Disquieting gifts: Humanitarianism in New Delhi.* Palo Alto, CA: Stanford University Press.
Brett, J. (2006). "We sacrifice and eat less": The structural complexities of microfinance participation. *Human Organization, 65*(1), 8–19.
Butt, L. (2002). The suffering stranger: Medical anthropology and international morality. *Medical Anthropology, 21*(1), 1–24.
Chouliaraki, L. (2010). Post-humanitarianism: Humanitarian communication beyond a politics of pity. *International Journal of Cultural Studies, 13*(2), 107–126.
Clinton, B. (2007). *Giving: How each of us can change the world.* New York: Knopf.
Coates, B. & Saloner, G. (2009). The profit in nonprofit. *Stanford Social Innovation Review,* Summer, 68–71.
Coopman, C. (2014, January 26). The age of "infopolitics." *New York Times.*
Dechaine, R. (2002). Humanitarian space and the social imaginary: Medicins Sans Frontieres/Doctors without Borders and the rhetoric of global community. *Journal of Communication Inquiry, 26,* 354–369.
Feldman, I. (2010). The humanitarian circuit: Relief work, development assistance, and CARE in Gaza, 1955–67. In E. Bornstein & P. Redfield (Eds.), *Forces of compassion: Humanitarianism between ethics and politics* (pp. 203–226). Santa Fe, NM: SAR Press.

Flannery, M. (2007). Kiva and the birth of person-to-person microfinance. *Innovations: Technology, Governance, Globalization, 1*(1), 31–56.

Flannery, M. (2009). Kiva at four. *Innovations: Technology, Governance, Globalization, 4*(2), 31–49.

Gajjala, R. & Birzescu, A. (2011). Digital imperialism through online social/financial networks. *Economic and Political Weekly, 66*(13), 95–102.

Gajjala, V., Gajjala, R., Birzescu, A. & Anarbaeva, S. (2011). Microfinance in online space: A visual analysis of Kiva.org. *Development in Practice, 21*(6), 880–893.

Haraway, D. (1985). *A manifesto for cyborgs: Science, technology, and socialist feminism in the 1980s.* Center for Social Research and Education.

Hardt, M. (2011). For love or money. *Cultural Anthropology, 26*(4), 676–682.

Harris, B. (2013). *The International Bank of Bob: Connecting our world one $25 Kiva loan at a time.* New York: Walker & Company.

Haskell, T. (1985). Capitalism and the origins of humanitarian sensibilities. *American Historical Review, 90*(2), 339–361.

Heim, K. (2006, December 18). Web of giving. *Seattle Times.*

Jackley, J. (2010). *Poverty, money and love.* TED talk. Retrieved October 10, 2012, from www.ted.com/talks/jessica_jackley_poverty_money_and_love.

Karim, L. (2008). Demystifying micro-credit: The Grameen Bank, NGOs, and neoliberalism in Bangladesh. *Cultural Dynamics, 20*(5), 5–30.

Karim, L. (2011). *Microfinance and its discontents: Women in debt in Bangladesh.* Minneapolis: University of Minnesota Press.

Kristof, N. (2007, March 27). You, too, can be a banker to the poor. *New York Times.*

Laqueur, T. (1989). Bodies, details and the humanitarian narrative. In L. Hunt & A. Biersack (Eds.), *The new cultural history* (pp. 176–204). Berkeley: University of California Press.

Laqueur, T. (2009). Mourning, pity, and the work of narrative in the making of "humanity." In R. A. Wilson & R. D. Brown (Eds.), *Humanitarianism and suffering: The mobilization of empathy* (pp. 31–57). Cambridge: Cambridge University Press.

Liu, Y., Chen, R., Chen, Y., Mei, Q. & Salob, S. (2012). *"I loan because..." Understanding motivations for pro-social lending.* Paper presented at the Proceedings at 5th ACM International Conference, New York.

Maclean, K. (2013). Gender, risk and micro-financial subjectivities. *Antipode, 45*(2), 455–473.

Mathers, K. (2010). *Travel, humanitarianism, and becoming American in Africa.* New York: Palgrave Macmillan.

Mathers, K. & Hubbard, L. (2006). Doing Africa: Travelers, adventurers and American conquest of Africa. In L. Vivanco & R. Gordon (Eds.), *Tarzan was an eco-tourist: Reflections on the anthropology of adventure* (pp. 197–216). New York and Oxford: Berghahn Press.

Moodie, M. (2013). Microfinance and the gender of risk: The case of Kiva.org. *Signs, 38*(2), 279–302.

Ogden, T. (2009, October 19). *Kiva, a cautionary tale for social entrepreneurs?* Retrieved November 3, 2009, from http://blogs.hbr.org/2009/10/kivaorg-role-model-or-cautiona.

Parreñas, R. (2012). Producing affect: Transnational volunteerism in a Malaysian orangutan rehabilitation center. *American Ethnologist, 39*(4), 673–687.

Rabinow, P. (1992). Artificiality and enlightenment: From sociobiology to biosociality. In X. Inda (Ed.), *Anthropologies of modernity: Foucault, governmentality and life politics* (pp. 179–193). Oxford: Blackwell.

Richard, A. & Rudnyckyj, D. (2009). Economies of affect. *Journal of the Royal Anthropological Institute* (N.S.), 15, 57–77.

Roodman, D. (2009, October 2). Kiva is not quite what it seems. Retrieved November 3, 2009, from www.cgdev.org/blog/kiva-not-quite-what-it-seems.

Roodman, D. (2011). *Due diligence: An impertinent inquiry into microfinance.* Washington, DC: Center for Global Development.

Rorty, R. (1993). Human rights, rationality, and sentimentality. In S. Shute & S. Hurley (Eds.), *On human rights: The Oxford Amnesty lectures* (pp. 111–134). New York: Basic Books.

Roy, A. (2010). *Poverty capital: Microfinance and the making of development.* New York and London: Routledge.

Roy, A. (2012). Subjects of risk: Technologies of gender in the making of millennial modernity. *Public Culture, 24*(1), 131–155.

Rubenstein, J. (2008). The distributive commitments of international NGOs. In M. Barnett & T. Weiss (Eds.), *Humanitarianism in question: Politics, power, ethics* (pp. 215–234). Ithaca, NY: Cornell University Press.

Sandvik, K. B. (2009). The physicality of legal consciousness: Suffering and the production of credibility in refugee settlement. In R. A. Wilson & R. D. Brown (Eds.), *Humanitarianism and suffering: The mobilization of empathy* (pp. 223–244). Cambridge: Cambridge University Press.

Schwittay, A. (2011). The marketization of poverty. *Current Anthropology, 52*(S3), 71–82.

Schwittay, A. (2014). Making poverty into a financial problem: From global poverty lines to Kiva.org. *Journal of International Development, 26*(4), 508–519.

Shah, P. (2008). Going beyond Web 2.0. Talk delivered at PARC, Palo Alto, CA, February 28.

Shuman, A. (2005). *Other people's stories: Entitlement claims and the critique of empathy.* Urbana and Chicago: University of Illinois Press.

Stewart, K. (2007). *Ordinary affects.* Durham, NC: Duke University Press.

Suski, L. (2009). Children, suffering, and the humanitarian appeal. In R. A. Wilson & R. D. Brown (Eds.), *Humanitarianism and suffering: The mobilization of empathy* (pp. 202–222). Cambridge: Cambridge University Press.

Wilson, K. (2011). "Race," gender and neoliberalism: Changing visual representations in development. *Third World Quarterly, 32*(2), 315–331.

Wilson, R. A. & Brown, R. D. (2009). Introduction. In R. A. Wilson & R. D. Brown (Eds.), *Humanitarianism and suffering: The mobilization of empathy* (pp. 1–28). Cambridge: Cambridge University Press.

4

REPRESENTING MICROFINANCE*

According to a senior advisor at the Consultative Group for the Advancement of the Poor (CGAP), microfinance has been very successful at "pulling on heartstrings" with the help of "heart-warming images of poor people" (quoted in Roy, 2010, p. 27). He thereby acknowledged the central, but often overlooked, role of representations in the constitution of microfinance as a popular cause, which is reinforced by CGAP's Microfinance Photo Contest. Since its establishment in 2006, the contest has been aiming to "raise awareness of the range of microfinance going on around the world" as well as its impact on recipients' lives, according the Jeanette Thomas, the competition's founder and organizer. It has grown from a few hundred to over 2,000 entries from 70 countries in 2011.[1] Each year, a panel of microfinance and photography expert judges selects 3 winners and 20 finalists, who include both professional and amateur photographers, predominantly from the countries where the picture has been taken. Their photos are shown on the CGAP website and in exhibits organized by partner organizations, where they bring public exposure not only to the photographers, but also to CGAP's version of microfinance.

CGAP is an independent microfinance policy and research center housed at the World Bank and supported by over 30 development agencies and private foundations. Its website states that it "provides market intelligence, promotes standards, develops innovative solutions and offers advisory services." The organization was established in 1995 by Ismail Serageldin at the World Bank, who was inspired by the work of Mohammad Yunus. Yunus himself served as the first chair of CGAP's Policy Advisory Board and contributed to CGAP being a "counter-establishment institution" in its early days (Roy, 2010, p. 74). Over the years, this role has changed,[2] as CGAP has come to advocate a minimalist, finance-driven and commercialized version of microfinance focused on the financial sustainability of microfinance institutions (MFIs) and on the scaling of financial services to the over 2 billion poor people who do not have access to them at the moment. By translating this absence into their need for financial services, financial inclusion advocates are able to call for scalable models to serve these vast numbers, which can only be achieved by tapping mainstream financial markets. In other words, the creation of needs, in this case for microloans, becomes a means of justifying continuing demand for resources, and for legitimizing particular agendas. Vincanne Adams has similarly argued for the "fiscal potential" inherent in affect and "its ability to generate new business investments" (2012, p. 211).

The need for poor-appropriate financial services has resulted in recent mutations of microfinance, by which I mean the fraught juxtaposition of various instantiations of microfinance, resulting from the influx of commercial investors and their calls for financial sustainability, and in some cases profitability. Borrower suicides exist alongside public offerings of MFIs in India, leading to accusations of financial apartheid on the one hand and of financial exploitation on the other. In Bangladesh, Yunus, whose 2006 Nobel Peace Prize contributed much to microfinance, popular visibility, is painting institutions that aim to bring the benefits of his creation to larger numbers of people as greedy loan sharks. Meanwhile, politicians, journalists and scholars in his own country refer to MFIs there as foreign, itinerant and untrustworthy moneylenders (Roy, 2010); they also have given rise to Muslim women moneylenders making a living from the indebtedness of their neighbors (Karim, 2008). Microfinance increasingly uses benchmarks and indicators from the very banking industry it was supposed to challenge, and "financial norms [have] come to supersede social norms" in this pre-eminent global poverty-alleviation strategy (Roy, 2010, p. 47). And last but not least, images of smiling women microentrepreneurs sit alongside haunted figures of despair and death, which points to the gendered nature of the mutations of microfinance and their representation.

The result of these mutations is a fierce ideological and practical struggle over two different models of financial inclusion: Yunus' model of microfinance as a poverty-alleviation tool and CGAP's model of microfinance as a commercial opportunity. The CGAP photo competition and its role in the constitution of microfinance supporters take on particular meaning in this context. The contest was launched in 2005, the UN Year of Microcredit,[3] and its first winners were announced in 2006, the year in which Yunus received the Nobel Peace Prize.[4] These two events not only brought microfinance further into the public spotlight but also legitimized "the Bangladesh consensus on microfinance"; they allowed Yunus to proclaim that "the era of showing profits is over.... We will measure our success not on the rate of return on investment but by the number of people coming out of poverty" (quoted in Roy, 2010, p. 90). While these words were a direct attack on CGAP's market-driven model, they also implicitly acknowledged that CGAP is currently controlling the truth about microfinance. Being in the business of knowledge management through its authoritative benchmarks, guidelines, indicators and best practices not only has meant that even Yunus admits that Bangladeshi practitioners need to have their knowledge validated by CGAP, but has also contributed to the theoretical and abstract nature of CGAP's work.

According to Thomas, one of the objectives of the photo contest has been to ground CGAP's model of microfinance more firmly in reality. By representing poor women and men in developing countries, its winning photos tell a particular story about microfinance and the need to expand its reach. They aim to foster institutional and public support for the growth of microfinance through establishing affective connections that are grounded in a history of development representations. This chapter makes these broader connections, beginning with an overview of theories of representation, and then focuses on CGAP's distinctive representations of deserving microfinance clients.

Theories of Representation

Photos derive much of their power from a "seductive belief that what we see in a photograph is an authentic representation of the world" (Bleiker & Kay, 2007, p. 142). Correspondingly, photographers are often assumed to be objective witnesses, able to show truthful realities in neutral and value-free ways. Scholars of photographic representations, by contrast, have highlighted the ways in which photographs construct particular images of the world, whose meanings depend on multiple processes of mediation (Berger, 1972; Sontag, 2002).

They show that photographs are produced, disseminated and viewed through "a set of cultural filters" often informed by stereotypes about particular places and the people living there (Parvez, 2011, p. 688). In other words, photography is "a technology used to construct certain kinds of truths about certain categories of persons" (King & Lidchi, 1998, p. 13). This imaging of the world and its inhabitants is enabled by photographs' threefold decontextualization: first, photos do not show how what they depict came to be; second, they do not reveal the contexts of their own making; and third, because they are so easily transportable, they can be viewed as completely separate from their original context of creation (Lidchi, 1999). While this decontextualization contributes to the constructed nature of photographs, their claims to veracity are even further undermined in the current age of digital manipulation (Gürsel, 2012). As a result, photos obtain much of their authority from the reputation of photographers, channels of distribution and places of exposition.

A photograph's constructed representation of the world begins with the aesthetic, visual and technical choices made by the photographer. Subsequently, it is the context of its use that gives a photo its meaning. Lastly are the viewers' interpretations of the photo, shaped by their personal and social contexts. These subjective interpretations, which also depend on the context of the viewing, are neither stable nor guaranteed. In sum, regarding photography as a practice of constructing particular views of the world affords us

> insights into the institutions and actions and episodes through which the real has been fashioned, a fashioning that has not been so much a matter of immediate acts of consciousness by persons in everyday life as it has been a historically

developing kind of imposition, now largely institutionalized in the prevailing kinds of meanings deeply inscribed on things, persons and structures.

(Saphiro, 1988, p. xii)

I regard the CGAP photos as "formative fictions", defined as "constructed representations that reflect current events yet simultaneously shape ways of imagining the world and political possibilities within it" (Gürsel, 2010, p. 38). Calling them fictions does not imply that these photos deceive, but rather draws attention to their creation of particular stories about microfinance. They are fictions because they are not objective depictions of the realities of microfinance, but are constructions of such realities informed by personal and institutional agendas. In addition, the CGAP photos are formative because they shape, at the same time as their interpretations are shaped by, viewers' attitudes, affects and actions. These photos (in)form particular views about microfinance, give rise to a host of emotions and can move people to action (Parvez, 2011). It is in this way that photos constitute microfinance supporters and mobilize their affective investments.

This is not a neutral process, because microfinance representations as formative fictions are inherently political, just as photography is a political process of representation, rife with power relations and often motivated by political – in the broadest sense of the word – agendas. However, "what makes photographs unusually powerful – and at times problematic – is that their analogically perfect representation of a visual image masks the political values that such representations embody" (Bleiker & Kay, 2007, p. 143). This means that CGAP photos act as a form of "ideological currency, [with] the ability to strengthen and reinforce existing narratives" about the CGAP model of microfinance (Parvez, 2011, p. 689). Control over microfinance representations brings with it the authority to shape particular discourses and practices of it, which in turn has material effects on the lives of the financially included poor. Many of these are women, who still receive 80 percent of all microloans (Visvanathan et al., 2011).

This chapter is based on a content analysis of the 10 winning CGAP photos from 2006 to 2011, as well as email conversations and a Skype interview with Jeanette Thomas, the contest organizer at CGAP, in March 2012. While I have examined the top 60 images to establish a broad, quantitative sample, I have analyzed in detail the five winning entries of each year. My foremost interest lies in the ways in which they represent the world of financial inclusion and legitimize particular models of it. This necessitates an intertextual reading (Dogra, 2011), which puts the photos in relation to other messages conveyed mainly in their titles, captions and in the judges' comments. I also distinguish between the photos' denoted messages – their literal meanings – and their connoted messages – their symbolic meanings.[5]

The Public Face of Microfinance

The public face of microfinance is the Third World woman entrepreneur, who has recently been joined by female borrowers giving "testimonials of death and despair" resulting from unbearable debt burdens (Roy, 2012, p. 135). Their frequent imagings are embedded within broader historical trajectories of developmental representations, and in spite of CGAP's claims that its contest photos are "timeless images of aspiration," (Roy, 2012, p. 135) they and other microfinance representations have to be considered within this larger history.

Traditional Women Entrepreneurs

Lisa Malkki, in her work on Rwandan refugees, has shown the existence of a "global visual field of often quite standardized representational practices" (1996, p. 386). This certainly holds true for microfinance. An Internet image search produces pages and pages of women, often in groups, usually dressed in colorful, exotic clothes and frequently smiling, at their places of work or at loan group meetings. Such photos also grace the websites of major microfinance organizations, such as Opportunity International, Finca and Accion.

The winning entries from the early years of the CGAP contest resonate with these images. The first-ever winner in 2006 shows a woman in a red sari sitting under a tree weaving a basket. She is turning her head to look into the camera and smiles. There is an undertone of allure and attractiveness, generally found in images of exotically dressed women, even when such depictions are not overtly sexualized or seductive (Wilson, 2011). Furthermore, like the great majority of women depicted in the CGAP photos, the basket weaver is young; pictures of older women are rare, which ignores the active roles they play in supporting their families. The second place photo in 2008, titled *Spinning*, shows a woman in a sari sitting on her own inside an almost bare room behind a charka, a traditional Indian spinning wheel. She is raising one arm in the air to pull up some thread. Her face points upwards toward her hand, and in that posture she evokes images of Hindu goddesses (see Figure 4.1).

The caption confirms that the woman is spinning yarn in the traditional way. This is the way that was advocated by Gandhi, which not only recalls India's struggle for independence, but also spinning as a spiritual practice in the service of others. The photo is devoid of any traces of modernity and in that emanates a sense of "chronic backwardness ... poverty and neediness that presents [the developing] world in a state of retarded development" (Abraham, 2007, p. 158). Such absences, of modern activities and artifacts, are a recurrent way in which CGAP photos image diverse needs – the need for development that legitimizes interventions, the need for technology that calls for technocratic solutions, and ultimately the need for financial inclusion that leads to the constitution of microfinance supporters.

Furthermore, photography "freezes a moment which has ceased to be" (Lidchi, 1999, p. 89), producing both a temporal dislocation and a denial of coevalness that places those depicted in development representations in a different time from that of the representations' producers (Fabian, 1983). The former are situated in the there and then, which through the act of taking a picture becomes transformed into the here and now, but only symbolically. Especially through their attire and

FIGURE 4.1   *Spinning* (source: Kushal Gangopadhyay/CGAP).

activities, poor women remain firmly fixed as the exotic other and the guardians of authenticity and tradition (Dogra, 2011). It is in this way that they allow Western viewers' romantic fantasies about escaping the pressures of their modern lives. The photos provide an opportunity to support, by way of microloans and donations to the organizations dispensing them, an idealized, pastoral way of life no longer available in the industrialized West. The vast majority of the top 60 CGAP photos that depict women do indeed show them in traditional clothing pursuing customary roles, such as crafts, farming and food preparation. The captions give these pictures an entrepreneurial frame of reference through phrases such as "a Muslim woman prepares newly harvested corn grain to sell at market in the Philippines" or "the owner of this [food making] workshop was jobless until small enterprise financing helped her to establish her business." Such images also "demonstrate important continuities with representations of 'productive and contented' workers in colonial enterprises" (Wilson, 2011, p. 316). The global South becomes a place where women are happy and hyper-industrious, empowered to enterprise themselves out of poverty with microloans and other help from Northern lender-donors. Such representations did, and still do, erase relations of exploitation and oppression that continue under neoliberal capitalism.

Orthodox depictions of women microloan recipients are frequently used to mobilize affective investments in the form of financial donations based on social and sentimental identifications with those depicted. By showing them as providers and nurturers, photos render poor women worthy of Western aid (Dogra, 2011). This worthiness becomes especially visible when compared to representations of poor women in the West – the so-called welfare queens (Metha, 2010). In contrast to the latter, diligent and honest Third World women are endowed with a work ethic that is shared by many Northern donors and that makes the women deserving of donor support. To raise funds, such images are often accompanied by narratives that forge a connection with middle-class aspirations of children's education and home improvement.

These representations must be compared to others that mobilize donations by highlighting women's vulnerabilities, especially in the context of emergencies. Indeed, it was in response to images of famine victims that debates over the representation of poverty, and its alleviation, came to the fore.

Negative Representations

What is frequently called "the pornography of poverty" refers to "the worst of the images that exploit the poor for little more than voyeuristic ends and where people are portrayed as helpless, passive objects" (Plewes & Stuart, 2007, p. 23). The 1984–1985 Ethiopian famine is commonly identified as a low point of such negative imagery, which "do[es] not reflect real human bodies but curiosities of the flesh that mobilize a pornographic spectatorial imagination between disgust and desire" (Chouliaraki, 2010, p. 110). Along with the reports and spectacles described in the previous chapter came a debate over the use of negative images for fundraising purposes. Such images rely on neo-colonial stereotypes that reinforce notions of poor people in developing countries as passive, helpless and dependent. They not only ignore local, indigenous development initiatives, but also neglect to show how people in the global North have been complicit, through consumption and political choices, in the relations of exploitation and inequality that contribute to the perpetuation of poverty (Plewes & Stuart, 2007). Because it is through such images, together with media portrayals that are often even more damaging, that many ordinary people in the global North learn about the global South, they ultimately feed a Southern negative self-image and Northern continued benevolence (Lidchi, 1999). A maximum hierarchical distance is established between suffering victims and Northern spectators, with an attendant "affective regime of guilt, shame and indignation" (Chouliaraki, 2010, p. 111).

Negative images shock, especially when viewed from a perspective of Northern affluence. They "coax, cajole and bludgeon donations from guilt-ridden Northern Publics" (Smillie, 1995, p. 136). Donors can be shamed into action, made to feel guilty about their wealth or pity for helpless others (Cameron & Haanstra, 2008; Lidchi, 1999). The result is "a sentiment of collective guilt" based on a sense of historical complicity (Chouliaraki, 2010, quoting Le Sueur & Bourdieu, 2001, p. 148). Shame, on the other hand, stems from the "banal complicity" of Northern publics' everyday awareness of suffering without taking commensurate action (Chouliaraki, 2010, p. 111).

Negative images have also been connected to compassion fatigue (Moeller, 1999), described as "the exhaustion of our sympathies in the face of persistently painful realities, [which] make so many demands on our emotions that we eventually stop feeling" (Cameron & Haanstra, 2008, p. 1479). Such desensitization stems from the increasing familiarity of pictures of suffering, which lose their emotional charge. By contrast, images of starving babies can overwhelm viewers who take them for all there is and will be, often feeling powerless because they don't know any better. Anger at the images and those who send them can be another reaction (Cohen, 2001). When the inward-facing sentiments of guilt and shame become "the more extrovert and assertive emotion of indignation, ... social relations of complicity become political" (Chouliaraki, 2010, p. 111). The consequent shift of attention from individual persecutors to generalized structures of power can lead to action for social justice (Boltanski, 1999). However, such action is not free from the tension inherent in Northern spectators as both accomplice and benefactor.

The critique of negative representations of development led to more positive imagery, albeit images often contain both negative and positive elements, whose readings furthermore depend on the audience (Dogra, 2007). It has resulted in the adoption of guidelines and codes of conduct by a number of countries and organizations, even though it remains debatable how far these are being followed (Plewes & Stuart, 2007; Wilson, 2011). Positive imagery has also been connected to nongovernmental organizations' (NGOs) increasing emphasis on education and advocacy (Dogra, 2007), and their growing role in the government of the poor (Wilson, 2011). However, the legacy of negative representations lingers (VSO, 2002), in part because of their fundraising appeal. More damagingly, the stereotyped images of helpless poor people have become part of "our collective societal consciousness," which contributes to their persistence, on the one hand, and on the other has allowed for the consumption mode of affective engagements to emerge (Plewes & Stuart, 2007, p. 33; Cameron & Haanstra, 2008). Positive images exhibit a complex "emotional connectivity" (Chouliaraki, 2010, p. 109) that does not invoke hierarchical distance, but a shared humanity. Attendant sentiments of empathy and gratitude are ambivalent, however, as they are anchored in "the social logic of the gift without reciprocity between unequal parties" and "unite donors in a community of virtue that discovers in its own fellow-feeling for distant others a narcissistic self-contentment" (Chouliaraki, 2010, p. 113). To what extent does microfinance, both its empowering representations and its exchange practice, disrupt this perpetuation of the problematic relationships of international development?

While most of the negative development images have come out of Africa, reinforcing the continent's imagined status as a diseased, war-torn and famine-plagued place (Richey & Ponte, 2011), nearly 80 percent of CGAP winners and finalists are from South and Southeast Asia. One third of the top 60 photos is from India, followed by Bangladesh, China, Vietnam and the Philippines. According to Thomas, it should not be surprising that South Asia, as the cradle of microfinance, would be over-represented; however, it was when a photo club in West Bengal informed its members about the contest that many high-quality images started flooding in from India and somewhat "distorted" the geographical focus of the winning entries. Consequently, the contest organizers have put much effort into broadening the geographical coverage of the entries; it grew from 50 countries in 2010 to over 70 a year later. In 2011 regional winners were announced for the first time, in part to allow images from Africa, Latin America, the Middle East and Eastern Europe to be celebrated.

There is, however, one picture that strongly resonates with the portrayals of helpless, passive victims of poverty (see Figure 4.2). The photo, which was a finalist in 2006, shows a woman, completely covered by a large black cloak, sitting by the side of a road, with a blur of bicycle tires behind her. Two handles of a plastic bag are sticking out from the edge of the cloth, but otherwise the woman is one black, harrowing figure. The viewer is not told anything about her. Why is she huddling there? Is she begging, grieving, waiting? The picture does not evoke compassion, but a sense of unease, even fear. The sepia color of the original photo contributes to its mysterious, haunting, almost creepy nature, in keeping with the usual coding of negative images (Lidchi, 1999).

The caption tells us that "across the world, two-thirds of microfinance clients are women. In South Asia, it's as high as 98 percent, offering them opportunities to help themselves." For the (Western) photographer, the image is one of the world passing the woman by and speaks to microfinance as an alternative to begging.[6] However, a different reading of the photo, informed by scholarly critiques of microfinance, is also possible. While it agrees that the woman under the cloak seems to be completely robbed of opportunity, ignored and written off by the

FIGURE 4.2 *Untitled* (source: Dave and Kendra Larson/CGAP).

world around her, almost to the point where her humanity is denied, in the second reading the reproduction of microfinance's standard story in the caption reinforces the negative image that actually contradicts the caption's hopeful message. The woman is faceless, voiceless, powerless, and in that she is reflective of critiques that microfinance can push poor women borrowers into over-indebtedness and potentially deeper poverty or even suicide (Karim, 2011).

In late 2010, a "suicide epidemic" swept through the Southern Indian state of Andhra Pradesh, where more than a third of its 30 million households carry microfinance debt (Biswas, 2010). This has given rise to a new public face of microfinance, of "shrunken and shriveled women, their aged faces lined with worry … no smile adorns [them], no bustle of microenterprise surrounds [them]" (Roy, 2012, p. 135). As a result, local politicians told borrowers to hold repayment, threatening the Indian microfinance market, which is the largest in the world, with an "Indian version of the US subprime mortgage debacle" (Polgreen & Bajaj, 2010). Because it is not poor people's productivity gains but the assumption that "the poor always pay back" (Dowla & Barua, 2006) that shores up microfinance's commercial edifice; once they stop paying, as they also did in Bolivia in 1999, the mutations of microfinance emerge ever more sharply (Roy, 2010). Thus, only 3 months earlier, SKS, India's largest for-profit lender, had gone public. Following in the footsteps of Compartamos, SKS's revenues and profits have grown at an annual rate of 100 percent, and its founder, Vikram Akula, became personally wealthy in the public offering. While Akula argued that "destroying [microfinance] would result in nothing less than financial apartheid" (quoted in Polgreen & Bajaj, 2010), others have characterized microfinance as a necropolitics dealing in death (Roy, 2012). It is these mutations of microfinance, which go unmentioned in its obligatory success story, that stand in the way of the equalizing potential of microfinance exchanges between Northern lenders and Southern borrowers. The debt relations created and perpetuated by microfinance result in their own set of hierarchies based on financial risk embedded in local and global socio-economic and financio-political relations.

In the face of such debates, legitimizing CGAP's commercially driven model of microfinance, in order to achieve the institutional and financial support necessary to reach the scale of financial inclusion envisioned by the organization, becomes increasingly important. The photo contest plays an important role in this process, which raises the question of the contest's multiple audiences. On the one hand, the photographers are aiming to win over the judges, who until recently have been US-based photojournalists, photo editors, academics, art curators and microfinance practitioners. In 2013, for the first time, a Bangladeshi photographer, who has been among the finalists several times, joined the judges. According to Thomas, they are told to evaluate entries first and foremost on their photographic merits, although the stories they tell about microfinance, and the balance they achieve between technical skill and narrative, are often what makes a photo a winner in the end.

Since the beginning of the contest, one of the judges has been from Citigroup, a multinational bank that has a large microfinance operation. Bob Annibale, the global director of Citi Microfinance, sits on CGAP's board and, according to Thomas, has been supportive of the contest from its early days. Winning photos prominently grace Citi Microfinance's homepage and exhibiting them on the company head-quarters' executive floor has allowed Annibale to engage Citi's senior executives in conversations about microfinance. Citi Microfinance occupies an ambiguous posi-tion in the financial inclusion assemblage, sponsoring events such as the Financial Inclusion Track at the 2012 World Economic Forum[7] and the 2011 Microfinance USA Conference, some of whose speakers decried the financial giant as representa-tive of the reckless high finance that caused the 2008 global financial crisis (Roy, 2012). In keeping with Annibale's claims of microfinance as "resilient finance" espoused during the opening session of the conference, Citi Microfinance is taking the lead in creating a "microcredit securitization market." This has encompassed setting up a local currency structured bond for Compartamos and a local currency securitization for BRAC, a prominent Bangladeshi NGO. That deal was celebrated as bringing "the global financial markets to the doorstep of nearly 1.2 million house-holds in Bangladesh" (all quoted in Roy, 2012, p. 135), moving one step closer to the large-scale financial inclusion envisioned by CGAP. However, microfinance in Yunus' home country has not been free from controversy, in the country's own press and in scholarly accounts (Karim, 2011; Rahman, 1999). The latter focus on the ways in which Bangladeshi NGOs, which are the country's most prominent microfinance actors, use social codes of honor and shame to govern the conduct of female borrowers and to further an agenda of capitalist expansion (Karim, 2008).

At CGAP's home at the World Bank, winning photos are displayed on the floor of the President's office during the Annual Meetings, so that country leaders visit-ing the Bank President are exposed to them. Therefore, high-level decision makers, from the global North and South, are a second audience of the photo contest; their abilities to shape microfinance practices at a policy and corporate level accords extra significance to the photos and the stories they tell about microfinance. It is in this way that national and international institutional support for CGAP's microfinance model is generated.

Most important for everyday humanitarian support of microfinance, the contest also aims to inform the general public. In contrast to many microfinance novices who find their way to the Kiva website, the contest website, which is a subpage of the CGAP website, usually attracts visitors who are knowledgeable about micro-finance to varying degrees; they predominantly hail from the United States, Europe and English-speaking developing countries. Citigroup helps to exhibit the photos in London and New York each year, and they have also been shown in Spain, China, Mexico and India. What visitors of these exhibits have seen in recent years are beautifully composed and technically sophisticated images that reinforce Walter Benjamin's 1934 observation that "the camera has succeeded in turning abject poverty itself, by handling it in a modish, technically perfect way, into an object of enjoyment" (quoted in Sontag, 2002, p. 107). How can such depictions do justice to livelihood struggles in the global South and garner support for their improve-ments? Do they correspond to a post-humanitarian mode of communication, where photorealism no longer functions as an authentic witness, but "as yet another aesthetic choice by which suffering can be represented" (Chouliaraki, 2010, p. 116)? The resulting de-emotionalization turns images from direct inspirations for action into objects to be contemplated. This shift is indeed visible in more recent CGAP finalists, which offer complex gendered representations that move beyond orthodox images of traditional women entrepreneurs.

Beyond Smiling Women

One of these photos is *Little Tofu Shop next to Job Site* by Kexin Zheng, one of the few female photographers among the top 60. A finalist in 2010, the photo shows a young Chinese woman in a thick red and gray jacket and blue apron standing behind several tables holding large, thick blocks of tofu (see Figure 4.3). The whiteness of the tofu contrasts sharply with the black clouds and the dark earthy ground that fill out most of the picture, giving it an ominous feeling.

The woman is holding a knife in one hand and a plastic bag in the other, obviously just in the process of cutting a piece of tofu for the man whose hand is visible at the very edge of the picture, giving her a coin in exchange. The woman is saying something, but because she is looking into the camera, probably at the photographer's prompt, it is not certain who she is speaking to. The background is dominated by a large digger, parked between two mounds of earth on which two dark silhouettes of men in hard hats can be seen. There is also a dirt-brown motorbike on the left side of the picture; through its color it seems to belong to the masculine world of heavy construction that emanates from the image.

FIGURE 4.3 *Little Tofu Shop next to Job Site* (source: Kexin Zheng/CGAP).

Within this clearly male environment, the woman's position is ambiguous, as she is engaged in food provision, a female activity, but clearly not in a traditional, unpaid home setting. Framed by the dark landscape and two male figures, she comes across as assertive and strong. The caption states that she obtained a loan to open her stall after migrating to the city. Urban migration is the story of millions of people in China, although women are more often imagined to work in factories mass-producing consumer goods than setting up shop, on their own, at a construction site. This photo therefore both disrupts and reinforces several standard narratives, about microfinance, China's socialist market system and women's role in it.

There are other, similarly unorthodox images: an older Indian woman in a sari standing smiling high atop an oxcart, reins in hands; another woman wading ankle-deep in a large body of water and swinging an oversized fishing net over her head; and a third photo of a Pakistani milk collector measuring the fat content of the milk she is about to buy. Such non-standard depictions of women, especially in relation to masculine work worlds, do reflect and reassert microfinance's narrative of women's improvement. Far from straightforward, however, these pictures are ambiguous, at the same time challenging orthodox images of women in traditional roles and reinforcing some parts of them, either through attire or activity. Similarly to Dogra's analysis of British NGO representations of women, "their messages contradictorily valorize individual MW [majority world] women as 'heroines' while keeping their portrayals strictly within what is expected of MW women as a group" (2011, p. 338). Complementing these depictions are the large numbers of men portrayed by CGAP finalists.

Bringing Men Back into the Picture

Among the top 60 photos, 26 show men, 21 women and 5 mixed gender (the rest is made up by children and scenery). This is remarkable because of the strong emphasis on women not only in microfinance, but also in development representations. Here, the flipside to women's "ubiquit[y] across all representational sites of disaster, development and advocacy" (Dogra, 2011, p. 335) has been the absence of men. If they are present, then they are usually in negative roles, such as corrupt leaders or violent rebels, that constitute men as yet another of poor women's problems. Such images often rely on the binary construction of responsible women and absent men that rarely connect with patriarchal divisions of labor or male labor migration. They also reinforce "essentialised constructions of men in the global South as inherently 'lazy,' irresponsible and preoccupied with sensual pleasure" (Wilson, 2011, p. 318). In addition, the neediness and vulnerability of women without male providers can invoke paternalistic responses that drive fundraising appeals (Dogra, 2011). It allows (male) Kiva lenders or other everyday humanitarians to step into the space left by absent men. The predominance of men in the CGAP photos must therefore be connected to their potential valorization as deserving microfinance recipients.

Family Business

Among the top 10 photos in 2009, two show older, male tailors at work in make-shift urban street shops. In the second of these, the man is accompanied by his wife, who is crouching on the floor and looking up at her husband, as he stands hunched over an old, manual sewing machine stitching a piece of cloth (see Figure 4.4). This is one of the few images that show older people, as well as a couple.

In the press release announcing the 2009 winners, judge Suzanne Lemakis, Citi's art curator, commented that

> the sewing machine is such a totemic image for microfinance. But there's a kick in the tail on this one: he is doing the ironing, while she is giving the orders – it captures the way that microfinance turns traditional gender roles upside down.
>
> *(Blassys Microenterprise eMagazine, 2010)*

Interestingly, while in the press release the photo is called *Busy at Work*, which was the original caption suggested by the photographer, it has been changed to *The Family Business*. This shows the "light editing" of titles and captions, which are supplied by photographers as part of their entry, that is occasionally, and always with permission from the photographer, undertaken by CGAP staff, according to Thomas.

The final caption reinforces the message of gender equality that CGAP wanted the photo to convey. However, Lemakis claims that a gender reversal has taken

FIGURE 4.4 *The Family Business* (source: Sourav Karmakar/CGAP).

place, and the body language of the couple – the woman with her legs open and hands held strongly in front of her body in a confident, almost male pose and the man in an archetypal female pose, bent over a sewing machine and his bare arms and feet conveying a sense of vulnerability – seems to agree with this reading.[8] However, the sight of male tailors is a frequent one in Indian cities and speaks to a specific cultural division of labor. In addition, claims of women's empowerment through microloans are contested and need to be situated in complex family and kinship dynamics that shape women's ability to negotiate microfinance obligations and opportunities.

It has long been an open secret that many of the loans that are officially disbursed to women are used by their male kin (Goetz & Sengupta, 1996). It is the latter's ability to exert patriarchal control over women that constitutes them as "conduits through which capital is exchanged between the [Bangladeshi] NGOs and rural men" (Karim, 2011, p. 86). Now, however, men are becoming microfinance recipients in their own right, which necessitates a change in their representation.

Worthy Men

While the large number of men in the CGAP photos might be explained by the fact that over 95 percent of finalists are male photographers, it also reflects the growing inclusion of men into microfinance activities. This shift is partly driven by CGAP's insistence on MFIs' financial sustainability and by the demands of commercial microfinance investors for growth and profits. One way to achieve these is by increasing the number of microfinance clients through the incorporation of men.[9] This has several effects, such as an increase in the size of loans, where larger loans are less resource- and labor-intensive and usually go to men. In parallel, there has been a growth of individual loans, in keeping with efforts to make access to credit less onerous for the poor. However, along with individual loans comes the introduction of mainstream risk-assessment technologies such as credit bureaus and credit scoring; traditional forms of lending group pressure to cross-guarantee loans work less efficiently on men who are not embedded in the same cultural codes as women. Last but not least, given the previously described negative stereotypes of irresponsible men, their financial inclusion necessitates the transformation of men from "formerly non-performing assets" into promising, worthy borrowers (Roy, 2010, p. 72).

Depictions of men can also contribute to constituting Western men as microfinance supporters, leading to personal identifications based on shared concerns to provide for one's families. Indeed, the CGAP photos show men as hardworking rickshaw drivers, porters, fishermen, small merchants, agricultural laborers, tailors and artisans, carrying out gender-appropriate activities as responsible breadwinners. This is reinforced by captions such as "He now earns enough to sustain his family and look after his parents" or "He pulls his [rickshaw] van all day. He is paying off his loan, and bringing in a little extra money to help the family." *The Transporter*, whose photographer was a contest judge in 2013, is exemplary of these images (see

Figure 4.5). In this original black-and-white photo, a man in typical Bangladeshi clothing is pulling a cart piled high with empty oil drums. Dwarfed by his load, he is confined to a small corner of the photo. As the transporter, he is also marked by his strenuous activity, which shows in his taut arms and lowered head. By representing the man akin to a pack animal, the photo manifests his need for a loan to purchase a real beast of burden to lighten his load.

Some images constitute men as innovators, such as the one titled *Tradition Meets Modern Technology*, which received a special mention in 2008 (see Figure 4.6). The photo shows the profile of a man with a turban and scarf over his shoulder holding a mobile phone to his ear, with a group of camels in the background in a desert landscape. The caption states that "every winter, people from all over Rajasthan travel to the Great Pushkar Fair, known as the cattle fair, to buy and sell camels, horses and bulls." There is a growing scholarship on the use of mobile phones to increase poor people's bargaining power in market transactions (Donner & Escobari, 2010). More importantly, with the emergence of mobile and electronic money, mobile phones are seen as essential to achieving large-scale financial inclusion (Maurer, 2012). Based on the phenomenal uptake of M-Pesa, an SMS-based money transfer system launched in Kenya in 2007 by a Vodafone subsidiary, multinational technology and telecommunication companies are joining global financial corporations in scaling financial inclusion. Such corporate efforts are frequently framed as Bottom-of-the-Pyramid or BoP strategies, in reference to C. K. Prahalad's vision to eradicate poverty through profits (Schwittay, 2011). They also contribute to the mutations of microfinance through capitalizing on its "trade in debt" by marketing consumer goods to the poor (Roy, 2012, p. 133).

FIGURE 4.5 *The Transporter* (source: Mohammad Rakibul Hasan/CGAP).

FIGURE 4.6 *Tradition Meets Modern Technology* (source: Sandipan Majumdar/CGAP).

Tradition Meets Modern Technology, then, imag(in)es the promises of new technologies, but keeps them firmly embedded in traditional contexts, as if signaling
that microfinance strengthens rather than disrupts authentic, often romanticized,
ways of life. This framing also aligns with arguments that "images of too much
modernity in the majority world make the relationship between 'us' and 'them'
difficult both economically and psychologically" (Clark, 2004, p. 696). The great
majority of CGAP photos do show people working with their hands or using basic,
manual tools such as rickshaws, bicycles, fishing nets and craft tools. This reinforces
the backwardness and hardship of lives in developing countries; it also reflects a
traditional-versus-modernity frame materializing in a techno-evolutionary scale
that marks developing countries by the absence of modern technical and scientific
equipment (Abraham, 2007). Even in the rare depiction of modern artifacts such as
the mobile phone above, the CGAP photos produce a distance that reinforces conventional understandings of lives and livelihoods in the global South. This reinforces
the need for more support from Western spectator-donors, which can improve
livelihoods via the provision of microloans. *Jute Monster*, the second place winner
in 2010, echoes this reading.

This black-and-white photo shows the face of a Bangladeshi man sticking out
from underneath enormous piles of jute draped over his head and around his shoul-
ders. The expression of the man, who wears a headband and is looking straight into
the camera, is hard to read. Is he smiling or straining under the seemingly enormous
weight of the jute? The photo is reminiscent of ethnographic pictures of dark-
skinned men with tribal masks, evoking a sense of the mysterious, exotic, wild. The
photo's title feeds that sentiment: Who is the monster, the man or the jute that

becomes his naturalized burden through seeming like untamed, out-of-control hair? Why is he or it monstrous? And why is he carrying such an enormous weight? The caption only informs us that "a man carries jute to market. Because of its eco-friendly nature, the jute industry in Bangladesh is seeing a revival." While aiming to establish a link between microfinance and environmental concerns, the emphasis in the caption, as in the photo, is on the jute and not its carrier, who, similar to the transporter, seems engulfed by it. Its load connotes the poor's daily struggle for survival. It also implies the man's need for a microfinance loan to purchase a trans-portation device.

The visualization of this need not only constitutes the jute carrier as a deserving microfinance client, but also brings the need for large-scale financial inclusion into the picture. Showing poor people in the global South earning their living with bare hands and a few basic tools reinforces CGAP's argument about the need for commercial capital to scale microfinance to such proportions that all of the world's deserving poor can be financially included to purchase the means to a better livelihood. It brings us back to the initial need created by the absence of formal financial services, a need that is a product of the financial inclusion assemblage and a precondition of its existence. Marilyn Strathern's argument that "new needs are created to promote the need for new debts" holds as true for microfinance as for the subprime mortgage crisis to which it has sometimes been compared (quoted in Peebles, 2010, p. 227). Imaging hard-working poor people's need for more loans is also the way in which the CGAP Microfinance Photo Contest mobilizes support for its model of microfinance.

In exploring how different modes of representation embody ideologies, Bleiker and Kay (2007) have advanced a notion of pluralist photography that aims to vali-date local photography and thereby multiple sites for representation of, in their case, HIV/AIDS. Such pluralism can "disrupt hierarchies and power relationships – for instance the ability of Western photographers and media representations to frame the suffering of others" (Bleiker & Kay, 2007, p. 151). This is especially important in light of the continued dominance of the "international image economy" and the ways in which its demands shape the style and content of rep-resentations of the global South (Clark, 2004, p. 693). This economy is still mostly dominated by white male photographers; if pictures by native photographers are used, they are often stock photos of slums and poverty that feed the stereotypical imaginations of Western viewers (Alam, 2007).

Seen in this light, the shift from the first 2 years, when Euro-Americans submit-ted over half of the winning CGAP pictures, to the last 3 years, when 95 percent of the winning images were by amateur and professional photographers from the countries where the picture was taken, is significant. These local photographers are not "natives," because they are of a different social standing, and often gender, than the people in their pictures. Still, their linguistic, cultural and political knowledge of their home countries translates into complex images of microfinance, and the diversity of these images, their distinctiveness from orthodox depictions and their aesthetic beauty and technical sophistication speaks to the power and quality of local photography.

At the same time, these photos, legitimized by the judges as authoritative representations of CGAP's commercially driven model of microfinance, only create awareness of a simplified, uncritical story of microfinance that does not convey its complexities and contradictions. The images themselves often have only tentative connections to microfinance, and not a single caption mentions any of the controversies surrounding it. Where the CGAP photos succeed is in disrupting stereotypical representations of poverty and development and in moving viewers to reflect on their portrayals of lives and livelihoods in the global South. As formative fictions, these images appeal to their spectators aesthetically and affectively, and in the process constitute microfinance supporters as new political subjects of development.

If photographic representations are not able to convey the complexities and contradiction of microfinance, how can Northern publics learn about its mutations? Do we need to move from virtually mediated forms of affective engagement, in this case through Kiva and CGAP, to personal encounters with financial inclusion and its providers and recipients? The two chapters in the next part of the book examine such encounters through microfinance tourism in India and volunteering for Kiva. They ask whether the shift from electronic to embodied connections and the affective intensification it entails can not only mobilize affective investments, but moreover enable a more critical engagement with microfinance?

Notes

* An abridged version of this chapter was previously published in *Anthropology Today*, 29(5) (October 2013).
1 The contest is open to anybody over the age of 18 without strong ties to CGAP.
2 The renaming of CGAP from Consultative Group to Assist the Poorest to Consultative Group to Assist the Poor was a manifestation of this change.
3 The credit in "year of microcredit" was a nod to Yunus, who established Grameen around microloans, although in later years its activities have expanded far beyond these.
4 According to Thomas, this timing was coincidental; she launched the contest upon her arrival at CGAP in late 2004 (Jeannette Thomas, personal interview, March 2012).
5 The focus of this chapter is on the images rather than their photographers. This limits my reading of them, as it does not allow me to situate their CGAP photos within the photographers' larger body of work. I do know that many top-placed photographers participate regularly in international photo competitions.
6 Email conversation with Dave Larson, March 2011.
7 The CGAP photos were exhibited there too.
8 I thank Susanna Trnka for this astute reading.
9 When Yunus started the Grameen Bank, the majority of borrowers were men. However, he soon found that women made more responsible clients who were also easier to discipline, and subsequently focused on recruiting women.

Bibliography

Abraham, C. (2007). *Images of Third World women: Difference and disjuncture in development representations*. Doctoral dissertation, McGill University, Montreal. Retrieved January 12, 2011, from http://digitool.library.mcgill.ca/R/?func=dbin-jump-full&object_id=18780& local_base=GEN01-MCG02.

Adams, V. (2012). The other road to serfdom: Recovery by the market and the affect economy in New Orleans. *Public Culture, 24*(1), 185–216.

Alam, S. (2007). The visual representation of developing countries by developmental agencies and the Western media. *Policy and Practice: A Development Education Review, 5,* 59–65.

Berger, J. (1972). *Ways of seeing.* London: Penguin Books.

Biswas, S. (2010, December 16). India's micro-finance suicide pandemic. *BBC News.*

Bleiker, R. & Kay, A. (2007). Representing HIV/AIDS in Africa: Pluralist photography and local empowerment. *International Studies Quarterly, 51*(1), 139–163.

Boltanski, L. (1999). *Distant suffering: Morality, media and politics.* Cambridge: Cambridge University Press.

Blassys Microenterprise eMagazine (2010). "Magic of Microfinance" wins the 2009 photography contest. Retrieved August 22, 2014, from http://blassys.com/component/content/article/12-people/top-entrepreneurs/270-winners-of-the-2009-citi-micro-entrepreneur-awards10.

Cameron, J. & Haanstra, A. (2008). Development made sexy: How it happened and what it means. *Third World Quarterly, 29*(8), 1475–1489.

Chouliaraki, L. (2010). Post-humanitarianism: Humanitarian communication beyond a politics of pity. *International Journal of Cultural Studies, 13*(2), 107–126.

Clark, D. J. (2004). The production of a contemporary famine image: The image economy, indigenous photographers and the case of Mekanic Philipos. *Journal of International Development, 16*(5), 693–704.

Cohen, S. (2001). *States of denial: Knowing about atrocities and suffering.* Cambridge: Polity.

Dogra, N. (2007). "Reading NGOs visually": Implications of visual images for NGO management. *Journal of International Development, 19*(2), 161–171.

Dogra, N. (2011). The mixed metaphor of "Third World woman": Gendered representations by international development NGOs. *Third World Quarterly, 32*(2), 333–348.

Donner, J. & Escobari, M. (2010). A review of evidence on mobile use by micro and small enterprises in developing countries. *Journal of International Development, 22*(5), 641–658.

Dowla, A. & Barua, D. (2006). *The poor always pay back: The Grameen II story.* Bloomfield, CT: Kumarian Press, Inc.

Fabian, J. (1983). *Time and the other: How anthropology makes its objects.* New York: Columbia University Press.

Goetz, A. M. & Sengupta, R. (1996). Who takes the credit? Gender, power, and control over loan use in rural credit programmes in Bangladesh. *World Development, 24*(1), 45–63.

Gürsel, Z. D. (2010). The rule of text: Everyday practices of editing the world. In E. Bird (Ed.), *The anthropology of news and journalism: Global perspectives* (pp. 35–53). Bloomington, IN: Indiana University Press.

Gürsel, Z. D. (2012). The politics of wire service photography: Infrastructures of representation in a digital newsroom. *American Ethnologist, 39*(1), 71–89.

Karim, L. (2008). Demystifying micro-credit: The Grameen Bank, NGOs, and neoliberalism in Bangladesh. *Cultural Dynamics, 20*(5), 5–30.

Karim, L. (2011). *Microfinance and its discontents: Women in debt in Bangladesh.* Minneapolis: University of Minnesota Press.

King, J. C. H. & Lidchi, H. (1998). *Imaging the Arctic.* London: British Museum Press.

Lidchi, H. (1999). Finding the right image: British development NGOs and the regulation of imagery. In T. Skelton & T. Allen (Eds.), *Culture and global change* (pp. 88–104). London: Routledge.

Malkki, L. (1996). Speechless emissaries: Refugees, humanitarianism and dehistoricization. *Cultural Anthropology, 11*(3), 377–404.

Maurer, B. (2012). Mobile money: Communication, consumption and change in the payments space. *Journal of Development Studies, 48*(5), 589–604.

Metha, N. (2010). Opposing images: "Third World woman" and "welfare queen." *Women's Policy Journal of Harvard, 7*, 65–70.

Moeller, S. (1999). *Compassion fatigue: How the media sell misery, war and death.* New York: Routledge.

Parvez, N. (2011). Visual representations of poverty. *City, 15*(6), 686–695.

Peebles, G. (2010). The anthropology of credit and debt. *Annual Review of Anthropology, 39*(1), 225–240.

Plewes, B. & Stuart, R. (2007). The pornography of poverty: A cautionary fundraising tale. In D. Bell & J.-M. Coicaud (Eds.), *Ethics in action: The ethical challenges of international human rights nongovernmental organizations* (pp. 23–37). Cambridge: Cambridge University Press.

Polgreen, L. & Bajaj, V. (2010, November 17). India microcredit faces collapse from defaults. *New York Times*, p. 5.

Rahman, A. (1999). *Women and microcredit in rural Bangladesh: Anthropological study of the rhetoric and realities of Grameen Bank lending.* Boulder, CO: Westview Press.

Richey, L. A. & Ponte, S. (2011). *Brand aid: Shopping well to save the world.* Minneapolis: University of Minnesota Press.

Roy, A. (2010). *Poverty capital: Microfinance and the making of development.* New York and London: Routledge.

Roy, A. (2012). Subjects of risk: Technologies of gender in the making of millennial modernity. *Public Culture, 24*(1), 131–155.

Saphiro, M. (1988). *The politics of representation: Writing practices in biography, photography and policy analysis.* Madison, WI: University of Wisconsin Press.

Schwittay, A. (2011). The marketization of poverty. *Current Anthropology, 52*(S3), 71–82.

Smillie, I. (1995). *The alms bazaar: Altruism under fire: Non-profit organizations and international development.* Bourton, UK: Practical Action Publisher.

Sontag, S. (2002). *On photography.* New York: Farrar, Straus and Giroux.

Visvanathan, N., Duggan, L., Wiegersma, N. & Nisonoff, L. (2011). *The women, gender and development reader* (2nd ed.). London: Zed Books.

VSO (Voluntary Service Overseas) (2002). LiveAid legacy. Retrieved March 22, 2011, from www.eldis.org/vfile/upload/1/document/0708/DOC1830.pdf.

Wilson, K. (2011). "Race," gender and neoliberalism: Changing visual representations in development. *Third World Quarterly, 32*(2), 315–331.

PART III
Encounters

5

MICROFINANCE TOURISM*

August 2012. The second day of our Opportunity International Insight Trip** to Chennai, the capital of the Indian state of Tamil Nadu, started early. After a 7 a.m. breakfast meeting with two members of the local US consulate, we embarked on our journey to a small fishing hamlet close to the town of Pulicat on the Bay of Bengal. En route we visited two microfinance borrower groups, before arriving at our final destination in the early afternoon. Pulicat had been severely affected by the 2004 tsunami, and the hamlet consisted of several rows of newly built yet already derelict-looking government houses, with a larger school building nearby.[1] It was a gray, overcast day, and knowing about the giant waves that had swallowed up this stretch of land 6 and a half years earlier only heightened its forlorn, ominous atmosphere. The mountains of trash being blown around by the wind did not help, and neither did the warnings of our guides that we had to take care not to be mistaken for American missionaries. Only 3 weeks earlier, a Tamil Nadu fisherman had been killed by a US Navy patrol off the coast of Dubai, and anti-American sentiment ran high.[2] A group of 10 Americans, who had come to India for a week to learn first-hand about Opportunity's microfinance work, was definitely drawing attention. Hosted by Niti, Opportunity's local partner organization, our tour itinerary was filled with visits to numerous Niti borrower groups and branches, meetings with local organizations and tourist activities. No longer a virtual engagement with microfinance – such as offered by Kiva or CGAP – this was a visceral encounter with it that allowed me to explore how affective investments are produced when Northerners come face to face with the people entangled in microfinance as borrowers and microfinance institutions (MFI) staff.

Back in Pulicat, to keep a low profile we split into small groups and visited the houses of local fishing families, who told us how microfinance impacted their livelihoods and showed us the orange iceboxes they had received as part of the tsunami relief. Afterwards, we were greeted by members of Niti's local borrower group in the hamlet's community center, which also served as the local church and Niti's newest branch office. Twenty women had lined up to shake our hands, dot bindis on our foreheads, hang fragrant flower garlands around our necks and offer us rock candy. Then, seated on a row of plastic chairs at the back of the room, we witnessed the by now familiar opening rituals of Niti borrower group meetings: after their attendance was taken, the women recited the Niti pledge, prayed and listened to a talk by their loan officer. In a departure from the educational games and Q&A period with us that usually followed, we were paired with small groups of women and together cooked local seer fish over small kerosene stoves. Our efforts were then judged, Masterchef style, by two participants of our tour. There was much laughter and merriment as we were trying to cook the crispiest fish possible, using gestures, grimaces and sign language. After the prize giving, we gathered for the obligatory group photos. Then, despite our protests that we were tired, had a long drive back home and a dinner reservation waiting for us, we were shepherded to the nearby beach where a temporary shelter had been set up. We did get out of the planned soccer game and excused ourselves after a short walk along the beach. It must have seemed strange to Niti staff and borrowers that we had come all the way from the United States to Pulicat to meet them and then were rushing back to our hotel.

Our meetings in Pulicat provide a good entry to the central themes of this chapter: a direct, personal encounter with poor microfinance borrowers and the organizations serving them in their places of living and work; a desire for connection despite linguistic, cultural and material differences; and first-hand observations of financial inclusion in action. To what extent did these encounters mobilize affective investments, in the form of financial, social and emotional commitments to distant others, among tour participants? How was microfinance, Opportunity-style, represented during our journey and to what effects? In answering both questions, I argue that my fellow travelers and I were drawn into a performance of microfinance, centering on key rituals and individuals, especially Niti staff and borrowers. They were not classical Goffmanesque strategic actors, however. Instead, I draw on the concept of performativity, which "refers to the normative dimension of performance as the reiteration of norms which precede, constrain and exceed the performer and in this sense cannot be taken as the fabrication of the performer's 'will' or 'choice'" (Butler, 1993, p. 234, cited in Chouliaraki, 2012, p. 5). Because the performance was highly scripted, critical engagement with microfinance throughout the tour was limited.

A couple of weeks after our visit to Pulicat, a member of our tour group recounted our experiences in a post on the official Opportunity Blog. After explaining that Niti was providing financial opportunities and transformational training to poor, hard-working and joyful women, thereby helping them thrive in new ways, he compared our personal encounter with the borrowers to Jesus meeting people in their own circumstances, whatever their faith or wealth. He described Niti staff "as the hands and feet of Christ, serving the poor, who are chosen by God to be rich in faith and accepting in the face of harsh lives, even though they are not able to speak about him openly."[3] Both Opportunity and Niti are Christian microfinance organizations, and the religious inflection of our Insight Tour allows me to examine religion as an important element of affective investments.

In a welcoming letter to all tour participants, our Opportunity Tour guide Ananya had written that

> your experience will be very different from that of normal tourists ... [because] you will have the privilege of seeing a developing nation through the eyes of the poor. We will be exploring how financial services can have a great impact on not only entrepreneurs, but on entire communities. I hope that this is an educational, eye-opening trip for all of us.

I analyze this trip as an "affective journey" (Solomon, 2011) that brought 10 people from the United States to Chennai to witness the transformational nature of Opportunity's and Niti's microfinance work with poor women. Similar to the journeys undertaken by American and British patients to Indian hospitals, affect was fundamental to and constitutive of our microfinance tour, as it animated all of our encounters. Through the language of God's love that framed this tour, the tears flowing in the face of grateful recipients and the furtive touches by the women borrowers when taking pictures with us, affective connections were forged through which Opportunity generated renewed support for its work.

The active force of these sentiments materialized in the interactions of tour participants with each other and with Niti staff and borrowers, and was mediated through objects such as gifts, bank books and photographs. These exchanges took place in a variety of affective spaces (Navaro-Yashin, 2009). From the colorfully decorated outdoor areas surrounded by the women's mud brick and thatched roof houses, to branch offices whose walls were covered with tables and charts, to the living rooms of borrower group leaders where we caught glimpses into intimate family lives – a bunk bed hidden behind a sheet draped across a door, laundry hanging in the kitchen, photos of weddings and movie stars on the walls – these areas provided the stage on which our encounters in Chennai took place. Thinking of this tour as a "theatre [that] possesses a material and regulatory organization which may influence the kinds of performances that are enacted" (Edensor, 2000, p. 341) also draws attention to the performative aspects of microfinance tourism. The multiple ways in which financial inclusion was enacted in our meetings with Niti staff and borrowers rarely deviated from the obligatory success story of microfinance. I will show this by first elaborating on the connection between religion and development, and microfinance in particular. I will then examine the performance of microfinance, with particular attention to the embodied nature of our journey and its linguistic and emotional interactions. Lastly, photographic interactions with borrowers gave rise to moments of communitas that brought all actors together and cemented the mobilization of affective investments through this Insight Tour.

I was an integral part of this journey. After obtaining permission from Opportunity to participate in this tour as a researcher, and introducing myself as such to all other participants by email, in the Trip Guide everybody received from Opportunity before departure and then in person during the orientation breakfast meeting, I made all formal research interactions such as interviews official through completing ethics forms. There was a general sense of excitement about having a researcher come along and ask questions, and I was thanked several times for my interest in Opportunity's work. As a participant of the tour who shared its intensity with my fellow travelers, my participant-observation morphed into auto-ethnography as my own critical, academic positionality vis-à-vis microfinance and my experiences during the trip became an intimate component of the research (Barbieri et al., 2012). My questions and observations shaped my interlocutors' perceptions about microfinance, and thereby about what they encountered around them. This was also a form of mobile ethnographic research, which not only allowed me to access the "scenic intelligibility" provided by shared movement through space (Diekmann & Hannam, 2012, p. 1322), but also acknowledged the importance of moving and being moved, in an emotional sense, for the success of microfinance tourism's performance.

Religious Development

During my research with INM in Indonesia,[4] I had traveled to Kristen, a small Christian village in the western part of Bali, where one of INM's main offices is located.[5] As a parting gift, the local minister, who runs the only guest house in the village, gave me a book called *Don't Look Back: How an Abandoned Child Became a Champion of the Poor* (Tyndale, 2004). The book chronicles the story of David Bussau, an Australian businessman-cum-philanthropist, social entrepreneur and one of the co-founders of Opportunity, in the words of Philippa Tyndale. She had become interested in Opportunity when she met some of its clients during a holiday in Bali, and writing this book was her way of supporting the organization. Tyndale recounts how Bussau's ideas about giving loans to poor people for small business development emerged when he lived in Kristen to help rebuild the village's church, which had been destroyed in a 1976 tsunami that killed several hundred people in Bali. The new church is a splendid example of Balinese-Christian architectural syncretism, combining ornate Balinese carvings with a church-like structure crowned by a large cross, and remains Kristen's landmark to this day.

Bussau had become interested in development work in 1974, when he coordinated the rebuilding of Darwin in northern Australia after a cyclone. His construction and management skills, honed in the running of his own successful building company that would later provide the start-up capital for his philanthropic activities, landed him the job through connections at his local church. Taking his young family to Kristen, an isolated village, in the 1970s, was Bussau's "first real exercise in faith … and the training ground for much of [his] later work in development" (Tyndale, 2004, pp. 78, 88). During his year there, Bussau became concerned about the lack of economic opportunity in the village, and, as a businessman, he felt that small enterprises could create local jobs. He had also witnessed the debilitating effects of generational debt dependency on local money lenders, and therefore decided to use some of his personal funds to start a revolving loan fund for local people with business ideas. The ways in which these first loans improved the lives of their borrowers – allowing them to establish Bali's first travel agency or buying a truck and moving into wholesale coconut distribution – led Bussau and his wife to establish the Maranatha Trust in 1979 to give loans on a more systematic and sustained basis.[6]

Almost 10 years later, at the end of 1988, the Trust joined forces with the US-based Institute for International Development Incorporated (IIDI), which had started giving microloans to families in Colombia in 1971, to form Opportunity International (Tyndale, 2004). Maranatha itself ended up becoming Opportunity International Australia in 1996, around the time when Opportunity's global structure was put in place. According to its website, Opportunity "was one of the first nonprofit organizations to recognize the benefits of providing small business loans as capital to those working their way out of poverty. Today, we offer loans, savings, insurance and training to clients around the globe."[7] To date, Opportunity has established an international network of funding operations in the United States, United Kingdom, Canada, Germany and Australia. In 2012, it had a total charitable income of US$61 million, which served more than 3.9 million clients in 20 countries, predominantly in Africa, Asia and Latin America. The organization is "motivated by Jesus Christ's call to love and serve the poor," but works with people of all religions.[8] As a self-identified Christian organization, Opportunity is part of a growing group of religious organizations (ROs) that are working in the area of international development in general and microfinance in particular.[9]

Religious Organizations: A Link in the Chain around the Elephant's Neck

The emergence of ROs parallels the role that religion, faith and spirituality have been occupying in international development. For a long time marginal to official development research and practice because of their adherence to modernization and secularization narratives, religion, faith and spirituality have assumed a more central position over the last 2 decades, in line with their embrace by international development organizations.[10] No longer the "elephant in the living room" (McGehee & Andereck, 2008, p. 20), religion is emerging as "one more 'missing link' in development" (Jones & Petersen, 2011, p. 1302). Indeed, in the current political climate, a number of organizations are reconstituting themselves as ROs to access new funding streams (Tomalin, 2012). In this chapter, I focus on Opportunity and Niti as Christian organizations. Their work is guided by the Christian concept of brotherly love and the Parable of the Good Samaritan, according to which all suffering humans are equally deserving of care (Redfield & Bornstein, 2010). While the egalitarianism inherent in this concept could have radical potentials, "since its inception it was more often used in the service of reproducing social inequality" (Mühlebach, 2013, p. 457, drawing on Schneider, 1991).

This recent (re)engagement of religion and development builds on centuries of missionary activities. Christian missions have been part of colonial and imperial interventions, especially in the areas of health, education and emergency relief, and have contributed to the rise of humanitarian sentiments. The very word charity has its Latin origins in *caritas*, meaning authentic Christian love (Mühlebach, 2013). The 1550–1551 Valladolid debate between Bartolomé de las Casas, a Dominican Friar who argued that newly discovered Amerindians were free men, and Juan Ginés de Sepúlveda, a secular priest who saw them as natural slaves, is often regarded as "ancestral to a broad complex of cosmopolitan humanisms, as well as related assumptions that even unfamiliar peoples and their lives might hold equal worth to one's own kin" (Redfield & Bornstein, 2010, p. 13; Calhoun, 2010).

Religious activities inspired by such ideas of shared humanness have continued under current development regimes, especially in states considered too fragile to care for their own populations (Lunn, 2009). In addition, some of today's best-known secular organizations such as Oxfam and Amnesty International have Christian origins (Deneulin & Bano, 2009).[11] During the neoliberal wave of the 1980s, when governments rolled back social spending, ROs, much like their secular counterparts, grew in strategic importance. This has been especially prominent in the United States, concurrent with the rise of the Evangelical Christian Right and culminating in the doubling of funding for ROs during the presidency of George W. Bush (Tomalin, 2012). By contrast, more secular European countries have not embraced ROs to the same extent and many of them downplay their religious orientation there, as well as in developing countries where it might conflict with local belief systems. Other factors in the growth of ROs include the rise of public religion as part of identity politics and the centrality that religion, especially Islam, has assumed in foreign and security politics since 9/11 (Jones & Petersen, 2011). The Jubilee 2000 campaign showed the power of religious organizations united for good, in this case debt relief, and prompted the World Bank to rethink its policies on international debt (Lunn, 2009).

Already in 1998, the World Bank had held a Development Dialogue on Values and Ethics, under the auspices of then President James Wolfensohn and George Carey, then Archbishop of Canterbury, which subsequently became the World Faith Development Dialogue (Jones & Petersen, 2011). Similarly, a number of national funding agencies, from DFID in the United Kingdom to the Swiss and Swedish agencies, began to fund research and convene conferences to understand the current confluence of religion and development better. As a result of these activities, ROs are now seen by some to have a "comparative advantage" over secular NGOs, although systematic studies of their impact have not yet been carried out (Tomalin, 2012, p. 692). Nevertheless, religiously inspired development work, seen to be guided by compassion and respectfulness, is often regarded as more authentic, community-based and people-centered, resulting in more transformative and sustainable change (Jones & Petersen, 2011; Lunn, 2009).

Such celebratory accounts usually engage only cursorily with the oppressive practices that can and have been carried out in the name of religion. Especially critical development scholars caution against the current embrace of ROs, reminding their proponents of religion's links to colonialism, and the corresponding danger that ROs could contribute to a "neo-colonial process of underdevelopment" (Harper et al., 2008, p. 9). Religions have also been associated with long-standing discriminations around race and gender; in their most extreme forms they have led to violent intolerance. This also means that ROs are often seen in opposition to programs and policies related to AIDS/HIV, gender and reproductive health issues. Another fear is that, consciously or subconsciously, ROs might try to convert the poor; after the 2004 tsunami, humanitarian aid was "the guise for aggressive proselytism" in a number of countries (Lunn, 2009, p. 944).

Many practitioners and scholars agree that spirituality plays a central part in the lives of many poor people in the global South, shaping their attitudes, practices and engagements with development efforts (Deneulin & Rakodi, 2011). While the neat separation between the religious and the secular that guides ROs often does not correspond to the way religion and spirituality manifest themselves in the global South (Tomalin, 2012), religions have been recognized as an important reservoir of power and hope for the poor. This also means that much of the growing scholarship on religion and development has focused on the work of ROs or on the way in which poor people's spirituality and religion can be harnessed in the name of development (Ver Beek, 2000).

What is of interest to me, and almost absent from this literature, is how ROs present a vehicle for believers in the global North to manifest their worship of God and fulfill their religious obligations. According to Max Weber, "salvational religions define giving as a sacred act with other-worldly incentives" (quoted in Redfield & Bornstein, 2010, p. 8). Consequently, assistance to ROs, in the form of financial donations or volunteer time, is an essential part of being a faithful person and leading a good religious life (O'Neill, 2013). Opportunity, which frames its financial inclusion activities as an expression of God's love for the poor, is part of this emerging landscape of religious development. However, working in microfinance with its economic focus creates particular challenges.

Faith in Microfinance

As Max Weber, Marcel Mauss and Albert Hirschman have shown, faith and economic development can be closely linked (Brown, 2009; Rudnyckyj, 2010). In development, the ideas of Amartya Sen, Nobel Prize-winning economist, have opened economic-centered ideas of development to the inclusion of poor people's own values, including spiritual ones (Sen, 1999). Still, the tests for Christian microfinance organizations such as Opportunity have only grown in the current era of microfinance commercialization.

Most significantly, ROs' mandate, inspired by religious tenets to serve the poorest, stands in tension with the current emphasis on MFIs' financial sustainability (Harper et al., 2008). When ROs' focus on social outcomes comes in conflict with the demands of financial performance and its attendant effects, ROs often continue to focus on the former, to the point where Catholic Relief Services discontinued microlending in 2005 because "our explicit mission to serve the poor and marginalized may not receive the same attention as concerns for financial profit" (Wilson, 2007, p. 97). Such resistance to the dictates of international donors and agencies like CGAP is underwritten by a broader conception of humans. According to Bussau, rather than as the rational economic agents promoted by microfinance, borrowers are seen as spiritual and relational beings, and financial service provision and microenterprise development do not only focus on economic activities (Bussau & Mask, 2003).

Furthermore, Christian MFIs believe that it is ethically unacceptable to charge usurious interest rates, which translates into lower financial bottom lines than those of their secular counterparts (Mersland et al., 2012). A large study comparing the performance of Christian and secular MFIs also found relatively fewer female clients in Christian MFIs, which might seem at odds with the female empowerment agenda espoused by many MFIs. However, given the contested impact of microfinance on women and the general feminization of poverty and poverty-alleviation interventions (Chant, 2008), the researchers concluded that "considering the risk of feminizing families' debts, it might well be that the share of female clients in Christian MFIs are on healthier levels than in secular MFIs" (Mersland et al., 2012, p. 151). However, religion can also be used to exert pressure for repayment in God's name, thereby acting as a form of religious or spiritual collateral (Harper et al., 2008).[12] Similarly, when the provision of microfinance is made contingent on subscribing to certain beliefs or associated behaviors, exclusionary practices can be the result.

Opportunity serves clients of all faiths. According to its website, it only shares its Christian beliefs when "clients ask us why we care so much about helping them transform their lives."[13] It is no surprise then that religion cast a long, if diffuse and sometimes confusing, shadow over our Insight Trip.

Sacred Journey to India

Tourists have been described as "secular pilgrims searching for the authentic" (MacCannell, 1976, p. 42) and their pastime as "the modern equivalent for secular societies to the annual and lifelong sequences of festivals and pilgrimages found in more traditional, God-fearing societies" (Graburn, 2001, p. 43). Our tour can similarly be understood as "a modern-day sacred journey" (Sharpley & Sundaram, 2005, p. 162). Most of its participants were devout Christians who had come to India to see first-hand the religiously inspired work of a Christian microfinance organization they all supported. The Insight Tour was thus a pilgrimage of some sort to the homes of poor women to witness the transformations brought about by microfinance. Moreover, some tour members, most of whom were white middle-aged and middle-class men from the Midwestern United States, sought to reaffirm themselves as good Christians and strengthen both their religious dispositions and support for Opportunity. In their short bios that had been circulated in the Trip Guide, all had highlighted their involvement with their local churches and their charitable activities, ranging from working with criminals recovering from drug addiction to supporting organizations for people with developmental disabilities to leading community groups. The observation that tourists' "emotional and affective experiences with a given place depend as much upon the quality of their co-travelling social relations as upon the place itself" (Urry & Larsen, 2011, p. 201) held as true for this journey as for tourism in general.

Our group included Bill, a high-level executive at Opportunity, who came from a long career in managing professional sports teams to his current outreach and fundraising work for the organization. As part of his job, he regularly attended Insight Tours, although he had never been in India before. He was accompanied by his high-school-age son, who wanted to deepen his understanding of ancient cultures; both also wanted to spend some quality father–son time together. Another tour participant was Mike, who was a manager for his family's gunpowder company and also served on the boards of several of his family's charitable foundations. He had started to support Opportunity many years ago after receiving a mailer in his mailbox and now wanted to see "what it is like on the ground, on the other side." He had gone on an Inside Trip to Central America 6 years previously and in the interim had attended several of his church's mission trips to Guatemala. Then there was Paul, also a manager of his family business, who together with his wife has been supporting Opportunity for over 25 years. He was especially looking forward to visiting a new Niti branch that he had funded and to letting its staff know that "they are supported." Paul was the only member of the tour for whom religion was "not a huge deal"; on the contrary, he wanted to make sure that it was not getting in the way of what Opportunity was doing in India. As an atheist, I felt a certain affinity with him. Also in the group was Frank, who owned his own business that provided strategic advice to small and medium-sized enterprises. He loved traveling and this was his second Insight Trip in a year. Lastly, Robert was the president of a large, multinational transportation company and former chief of staff for the Governor of his home state, who later became a US Attorney General. As an active Opportunity supporter in his hometown, he had been instrumental in brokering several large funding deals for the organization. The only other woman besides me was Susan, a vivacious, recently divorced "military brat" from California, who was working as a consultant for a personalized clothing design company. Its foundation partnered with Opportunity and Susan had won the trip through her work. She was excited, if a little anxious, about being in India, also because of her own interest in jewelry design. Susan was very new to microfinance and soaked up all she could learn. By contrast, all the other group members had prior knowledge of microfinance; it was a case that was close to the hearts and heads of these businessmen, many of whom were self-employed. It is thus not surprising that all of them were Opportunity Governors, having committed themselves to raising funds for and awareness about Opportunity's work.[14] According to Frank, the honorary title of Governor was bestowed on major donors as a "motivating tool that makes us feel closer to the organization and gives us a greater sense of ownership and responsibility."

Our tour guide was Ananya, the Director for International Education at Opportunity, whose job it is to organize and participate in Insight Trips. In her short bio, Ananya had expressed her gratitude for her "dream job," as she described it to me, in the following words: "on a daily basis [I] thank God for this privilege and [am amazed] at how He works all things out for our good." Her mother had immigrated to the United States from the Indian state of Andhra Pradesh, and Ananya had been born and raised in the United States. She took care of all the logistics of the trip, serving as the liaison between tour members, hotel and restaurant staff and drivers, and keeping us on task, safe and healthy. She was guiding us in a literal sense, providing direction in an environment that was foreign to most of the tour participants, and a bit threatening to some like Susan. Ananya was also a key person in our interactions with Niti staff and borrowers, often advising us before meetings what to look out for. Her authoritative voice, amplified by her own Indian origin, and the fact that she had been on a tour to Chennai before, made her instrumental in our tour's "hegemonic meaning making" through scripting and monitoring our performance (Edensor, 2000, p. 323). Part of this performance were small religious rituals, such as daily prayers, morning devotions and grace before meals. Besides these, religion was discussed openly only during a few occasions, which revealed as much about individual tour participants as about the places we were visiting. One such site was a leper colony.

Before we disembarked from our bus, Susan had asked what we should expect to see, "so that we would not be too shocked." Ananya, after consultation with Niti staff, told us to look out for some deformities or small marks on people's eyes or hands. She also advised us "not to touch and not to ask people about leprosy." Susan admitted that she had been a bit nervous when she first found out that we were visiting a leper colony; her subsequent Internet research had revealed, to her relief, that leprosy is not contagious when treated. Still, Ananya explained, leprosy was heavily stigmatized in India, which is why the government had set land aside so that the lepers and their families could live away from mainstream society. Susan concurred that "even in the bible there is stigma attached to leprosy," whereupon Frank replied quite poignantly that the New Testament states that Jesus walked among the lepers. After Susan retorted testily that she was not Jesus, Frank concluded that "if you believe in Jesus you must have faith and cannot be afraid." Frank was one of the most devout members of our group, and in my interview with him he talked about the poor always being with us, which necessitates love, care and charity toward them.

That this brief religious discussion between Frank and Susan happened in the context of leprosy is not surprising, given its "imperative" status in India (Hutnyk, 1996, p. 104; see also Bornstein, 2012). Lepers are one of the country's most marginalized groups, and the visit to the leper colony featured on our schedule to highlight how Niti was fulfilling its own Christian calling, especially in contrast to the many commercial MFIs that are now populating the microfinance landscape in India.[15] According to its website, Niti is "inspired by the love of God . . . to alleviate poverty through motivation, training, counseling and microfinance, thereby enabling the poor to become self-reliant, attain dignity, transform holistically and become citizens of excellence." Striving to imbue a sense of citizenship in its poor clients was one way in which Niti was carving out a space as a Christian organization in India. As Raj, Niti's passionate CEO who had recently joined the organization after a long corporate career, had explained to us during his introductory presentation, the organization had to take care not to fall foul of the country's anti-conversion laws, which make it illegal to evangelize.

This raised many questions among tour participants: Did the borrowers know that Niti was a Christian organization and if so, how? How could we tell during borrower visits whether particular women were Christian, Hindu or Muslim? And was it at all possible to talk about Jesus with the women? Raj explained that while it was only possible to speak openly about Jesus if the women asked directly, there were more subtle signs of Niti's identity, such as staff addressing the women as sisters, which also fit into Niti's family image of itself. In turn, women who did not wear the Hindu bindi could be Christian, but this was not always the case. What emerged from this confusion was a picture of religious syncretism, where the prayers at the beginning of each borrower group meeting could be Christian, Muslim or Hindu, just like the church in the leper colony was used by Christians, Muslims and Hindus alike. What was most important, according to Raj, was that Niti practiced "transformational lending" that provided women of every faith not just with loans, but also with support in the form of business lessons and other education. The fact that there was a waiting list to join Niti, when the women could join numerous other MFIs operating in Chennai, was given as evidence that Niti's mission was recognized and appreciated by the women, who were always "looking forward to the visit of the Niti loan officer."

Religion and spirituality are also part of the stereotypical "perennial Western tourism representations of India" (Bandyopadhyay, 2009). The trope of timelessness presents the country as a "spiritual utopia of peace and premodernity" (p. 29), which is perpetuated by travel magazines and brochures, guide books and popular books and films such as *Eat, Pray, Love*. While the spiritual touristic experience began in the 1960s, international travel to India started a century earlier under British colonial rule (Sharpley & Sundaram, 2005). A central figure in this endeavor was Thomas Cook, a Baptist minister and social reformer; Cook also began mass tourism when in 1842 he organized an all-inclusive tour to a temperance meeting (Graburn, 1977). Our own Trip Guide, which served as a condensed guidebook, provided us with a very brief, selective history of India as one of "successive invasions." The growing population of the country and the strain it put on its natural resources was presented as "the fundamental social, economic and environmental problem," thereby providing a Malthusian view of contemporary India. On the other hand, the country's extensive poverty, which attracts a number of "charity tourists" to India "to encounter the 'other' as a form of postmodern pilgrimage" (Bornstein, 2012, p. 126; Hutnyk, 1996), was only mentioned in passing.

The Trip Guide also did not contain much information about microfinance, other than in the summaries of Niti's and Opportunity's activities. This information came in another book that was part of our pre-trip package. Titled *UnPoverty: Rich Lessons from the Working Poor* and written by Mark Lutz, senior Vice-President of Global Philanthropy at Opportunity, it "tells unforgettable stories about heroic people" who had transformed their lives through microfinance (Lutz, 2010, p. 17). Thin enough to take on the plane for pre-trip education (although none of my fellow trip participants had actually read it), the book set the tone for our encounters with microfinance by repeating and reinforcing its obligatory success story. Lutz's narrative was uniformly positive, transformative and life changing – not only of the poor's lives but, perhaps more importantly, of his own. The book was thus a prelude to the performance of microfinance that we, together with Niti staff and borrowers, enacted in Chennai.

Performing Microfinance

During one of our borrower group visits, we were treated to a dance performance by five beautifully adorned, nervous young girls. They gracefully moved to Bollywood music blaring from a box that was manned by a group of teenage boys, who were eyeing the whole scene, and particularly the girls and us, with much interest. At the end of their dance, the girls invited Susan and me to join them; I excused myself, too shy and also eager to watch and take pictures of Susan dancing. Her attempts to keep up with the girls' intricate hand and body movements elicited much good-natured laughter from everybody. Once the entertainment was over, the meeting proceeded with the more conventional microfinance rituals: attendance taking, incantation of the Niti pledge, a training session and then a question and answer period with us. The girls' literal performance provides an entry point into my analysis of microfinance, and by extension microfinance tourism, as a performance. Rather than subscribing to the negative connotations of the word as a form of deception (Larsen, 2005), I see the performativity of microfinance as a productive enactment of a number of rituals that make it recognizable. It generates encounters between microfinance tourists, poor women borrowers and loan officers, which in turn mobilize affective investments. Microfinance's performance also follows certain scripts, which limit tourists' critical engagement with it. These discussions must start, however, with the tourist journey that enables personal encounters with microfinance.

Embodied Journeys

Travel accounts are often infused with descriptions of, or more likely complaints about, malodorous heat, traffic congestion and stomach pains, and our trip was no exception. Because tourist sites "are made significant through the way we encounter them, and the encounter happens in an embodied way," sensory perceptions "are part of the tourist's competence of making sense" (Crouch et al., 2001, p. 259). Travel feeds the prediscursive, bodily aspects of affect. This is especially true for India, which is often presented as "an assault on your senses" (*Lonely Planet India Survival Kit*, cited in Bhattacharyya, 1997, p. 380).

Our own encounter with this sensory commotion was mediated by the large white air-conditioned bus that marked its cargo's travel through the crowded streets of Chennai. Modes of travel are not only a way in which tourists are physically moved, but also a focal point for sense-making, as roads can be too congested, too bumpy or not authentically rugged enough (Mathers, 2010). Our bus served as a second home where we chatted, napped, sometimes ate or, in my case, usually interviewed people and wrote field notes. The view from the bus afforded glances at the organized chaos around us and opportunities to capture it in passing with our cameras. But even on the bus we were not "disembodied travelling eyes" (Urry & Larsen, 2011, p. 199), but travelers eager in the morning, comfortable, car sick or too cold during the day and physically and emotionally exhausted by night, experiencing our own kind of compassion fatigue. Sometimes, when we were seemingly driving around for hours without any sense of where we were or where we were going, the feeling of disconnection from the outside world grew into a sense of disorientation and frustration. I seemed to be the only one interested in tracing our journeys on a map of Chennai, while the others, and especially Ananya, were focused more on our proximity to our hotel, a shower and dinner. How close we were was a question even our driver often could not seem to answer; after the first day we learned that "30 more minutes" usually meant another hour or two. This had a direct effect on our meetings, which we started to cut short like the one in Pulicat, or skip altogether. Pushed on by Ananya, we "perform[ed] the intense rhythms of strict time schedules" to which any organized tourist group is subjected (Scarles, 2012, p. 937). Time became a marker of difference and structured travelers' affect.

Final disembarkation at our destination invariably resulted in renewed feelings of embodiment (Diekmann & Hannam, 2012). Even in the safety of our group and led by Niti staff, stepping into the heat, noise and smell of crowded roads or narrow alleyways took adjustment, which gave way to anticipation at the sight of yet another multitude of sari-clad women. They were usually waiting for us surrounded by colorful patterns they had chalked on the ground, which symbolized life and prosperity. The women were sometimes shy and sometimes forward, as they welcomed us with the invariable procession of bindis, water, rock candy and flower garlands. Some tour members took the latter off because they feared stained clothes or disliked their smell; by doing so they conveyed a certain distance through these bodily expressions (Crouch et al., 2001). At the end of a hot day, the wilted flowers hanging from our bus seats were like a barely living document of our encounters. The colorful, tasty and fragrant start to these encounters always set the stage for the subsequent performance of microfinance, into which we were drawn together with Niti staff and borrowers. While our very first borrower group meeting was "a sensory and physical bombardment which precluded anything other than a contingent performance" (Edensor, 2001, p. 77), by the end of the week these welcomes had become routine and familiar.

Their intense embodiments stood in tension with the precautions we were urged to take so as to stay safe and healthy. For meals we usually retreated to high-end restaurants and resorts, which we shared with other foreign tourists and upper-middle-class Indian families. On all other occasions, Ananya was always at hand to advise us on what was safe to consume and where the best place to use the toilet was. We were counseled to accept the drinks that the women offered us during borrower group meetings because not to do so would offend, but not to drink them unless they were boiled chai or soft drinks, and even then the cleanliness of the cups aroused such suspicion that most people hid them behind their backs. Similarly, we never put the rock candy offered to us into our mouths, and therefore never actually tasted the way in which its sweetness was supposed to turn everything that followed its ingestion into something pleasing and delightful. The giving and receiving of hospitality was thus circumscribed by fears of gastrointestinal upsets (cf. Hutnyk, 1996), and it was with a certain pride that Ananya noted at the end of the trip that nobody had gotten sick. When tour members did stray from her advice, such as Mike who left us for 3 days to visit a mission his home church was supporting in northern India, divine intervention was sought. According to him, "many were praying for me because I ate every kind of food in India that was put in front of me, praise God no sickness period!"

Such culinary prescriptions are part of the "the cultural competencies and acquired skills that make up touristic culture themselves [which] suggest a Goffmanesque world where all the world is indeed a stage" (Franklin & Crang, 2001, pp. 17–18). On this stage, we enacted our roles as microfinance tourists according to certain cultural codes based on our gender, class and religion, which to some extent preformed our own contingent performance. These enactments were also guided by the Traveler's Code of Ethics in our Trip Guide, which exhorted us to "travel in humility and with a genuine desire to learn more about the people of your host country." In contrast to the most popular travel guide on India, Lonely Planet's *India: A Travel Survival Kit*, which contains only minimal guidelines for appropriate female tourist behavior (Bhattacharyya, 1997), our Trip Guide made repeated and numerous suggestions for culturally sensitive conduct, such as "listening and observing, rather than merely hearing and seeing," "not interpreting different time concepts and thought patterns as inferior" and "avoid[ing] the Western practice of knowing all the answers." These dos and do nots reflected the particular nature of our journey as one of alternative tourism, combining education about Opportunity's microfinance work in Chennai with poverty tourism. The latter refers to travel to marginalized places with the explicit purpose to view how poor people live and work (Freire-Medeiros, 2012), and according to our Trip Guide, our Insight Trip was an opportunity to understand first-hand "what poverty is all about." Poverty tourism, and especially its extreme cousin slum tourism, has been critiqued for being voyeuristic, invasive, commodifying and ultimately exploitative of poor people's precarious circumstances. On the other hand, participants of such tours feel that they come away with a new, more realistic and positive perspective on poverty and those it affects (Diekmann & Hannam, 2012). Similarly, my fellow travelers wanted to encounter poverty and see how microfinance mitigated it. They also wanted to remind themselves of their obligation to help the poor, and the prescriptions in our Trip Guide were meant to ensure the forging of social and emotional bonds that would facilitate this help.

Linguistic Limits

Much of our encounter with microfinance, in the form of Niti staff and borrowers, was discursively mediated in several ways. Information was primarily conveyed through language, translated by Niti staff, since none of us, including Ananya, spoke Tamil. In this context, Niti staff as well as Raj and his daughter Nishtha, who accompanied us on several trips, emerged as critical local guides. Because they controlled the flow of information between Ananya, tour participants and borrowers, what they said/translated and left unsaid/untranslated was significant (Brin & Noy, 2010). During the borrower group visit in the leper colony, I became exasperated by the obvious difference between what the loan officer was telling the women and what the translator, another Niti staff member, relayed to us. I asked Nishtha, who was sitting beside me, about this, whereupon the translator asked Nishtha to come up front and translate for the whole group. The topic of the loan officer's instruction was loan recycling, a potentially contentious subject as I will show below. When nobody from our group engaged with it, the loan officer moved swiftly to the business training part of her talk, which was a lesson about the importance of selling things that would be "attractive to the customer," for example, umbrellas in the winter, cotton clothes in the summer and sweets during the festival season.

This led into a Q&A session with us, started off by Mike asking the women about their different businesses. This was a standard question that was invariably asked by someone during every single one of our borrower group meetings. It was also one of the questions suggested in the Trip Guide, which listed a number of them as recommended points of departure for our own enquiries. The women's answers were also always similar: making and selling flowers, running a grocery shop, tailoring, selling rice or biryani, making jewelry or plastic components. They showed the narrow choice of activities the women could pursue based on their skills, loan terms and circumstances, which sometimes can bring them in competition with each other (Brett, 2006). Subsequent questions were often about loan amounts and repayment schedules, but never about possible financial challenges. There was usually a point in the meetings when we all went silent and when Bill or Ananya took over asking questions. During this particular meeting, Ananya asked the women about their dreams for their children. After answering that they wanted a good education that would lead to a good job, the women listed the different subjects their children were studying, ranging from electrical engineering to nursing to policing. In promotional microfinance representations, such replies are interpreted as women the world over sharing the same aspirations for their children. Within the performative frame, this exchange speaks to the scripted nature of microfinance encounters instead. These scripts, framed by microfinance's obligatory success story, limit the range of both questions and answers to those that are safe and uncontroversial.

This became especially obvious when Ananya asked, as she always did, how the women felt about their loan officer. As always, the women said that they liked her, in this case because she did not show any prejudices against her clients in the leper colony. The Niti translator, hamming it up a little, asked them if they wanted another loan officer, whereupon the women laughingly shouted "no." While it seems absurd to ask poor women borrowers, in the presence of their loan officer, MFI CEO and foreign visitors, if they liked their loan officer – as if they were in a position to say no – this exchange highlights that the women were also subject to the "collective disciplinary gaze of co-participants and onlookers" that directed, normalized and ultimately constrained their behavior (Edensor, 2000, p. 327). This gaze did not just come from us and Niti staff, but also from fellow borrower group members, who need to keep an eye on each other because they cross-guarantee each other's loans. In other words, the limited and scripted nature of our encounters was partly an issue of lost in translation, and partly the result of the tightly circumscribed and controlled representation of microfinance, leading to the constant reinforcement of its obligatory success story.

Embodied rituals can further support this story. The Niti borrower group routines are crafted on the archetypal Grameen solidarity group script, beginning with verbal attendance taking that signals to everybody that a particular woman is (not) present. In the Bangladeshi context in which this technology was developed, a usually male loan officer saying a woman's name is seen as a sign of empowerment because women are publicly referred to by their husband's name only. A woman being absent usually means that she is not able to make repayment and that all other group members have to wait until she shows up or until they have paid for her (Karim, 2011). In Chennai, roll call was followed by the group pledge, during which Niti borrowers promised, with their right arms stretched out in an embodied and visible sign of commitment, to "follow discipline, unity, courage and hard work," to boil water, provide education, but also to "tell others about the usefulness of financial services provided by Opportunity International India to help them also benefit from these services." As an instance of social engineering, this pledge has been modeled on the 16 commitments that Grameen borrowers have had to repeat at the beginning of each solidarity group meeting (Rankin, 2001). In one meeting, I observed an older woman holding up the arm of her toddler granddaughter while saying the pledge, thereby transferring bodily knowledge from one generation to the next. A unique part of the Niti pledge is the women's assertion that "I believe there is a God," which in turn was reinforced by the non-denominational prayer that followed. Lastly, the business lesson or health education that closed the formal meeting part marked Niti's work as social, or in its own words transformational microfinance, in contrast to the finance-only approach that more commercially oriented MFIs pursue. It is through these rituals, which are standardized across Opportunity borrower group meetings the world over, that the practice of microfinance becomes recognizable, and often celebrated, as a global development intervention. In addition, rituals mark particular modes of microfinance and thereby situate an MFI in the politically charged landscape of financial inclusion in India.

What we did not see during our tour was a loan repayment session, which is often the quintessential part of a microfinance performance and its most character-istic ritual, as I had come to know during my research with INM. According to Raj, it was too difficult to coordinate the various temporalities of our route, repay-ment schedules and visitation programs. Instead, the general objective of our bor-rower group visits was "to give a snapshot of Niti, where we operate, the kind of people we serve, their background and culture." We therefore never saw money exchange hands, but instead were proudly treated to representations of it in the form of repayment and savings books (see Figure 5.1). These were shown to us as evidence that Niti's transformational microfinance is working. It also meant that there was no material evidence of debt, which further reinforced the positive message of transformation that Opportunity wanted to convey to its Insight Tour participants.

Besides borrower groups, we also visited a number of branch offices. One par-ticularly memorable visit was to the Chengelpet branch office, whose establishment Paul and his wife had directly supported. The previous day, Bill had impressed on the regional manager how important it was that Paul's contribution was directly acknowledged during the visit. Because the regional manager did not deem the branch manager articulate enough, he ended up thanking Paul himself during a short speech. As Tamils usually express their gratitude in less direct ways (Appadurai,

FIGURE 5.1 Group Photo with Niti Borrowers Showing Their Repayment Books (source: author).

1985), the manager's performance was a direct response to Bill's demands. Then the hunt was on for the best backdrop for a photo of Paul surrounded by the loan officers of "his" branch (see Figure 5.2).

The Q&A session that followed was dominated by numbers impressing on Paul and the rest of us the impact of his donation: how many years had the loan officers worked for Niti, how many clients did they serve, how many hours did they travel to reach them, and how long was the waiting list for new borrowers. These numbers also bestowed legitimacy on Niti's work, by showing its female loan officers as hard-working, caring employees who went the extra mile for their borrowers.

Throughout the trip, Bill especially kept commenting how impressed he was with the dedication of the women; coming as it did from a high-level executive of Niti's international donor, this praise must have been music to Raj's ears. Because it is through the loan officers that Niti's Christian-inspired work is carried out, and continued support for Opportunity would trickle down to Niti, in hindsight our encounters with the loan officers emerged as even more important than our meetings with the borrower groups. Mike told me how moved he was

> by how the borrower groups connected so well with the loan officers and staff. You can tell that the groups work well together like a family with love and friendship. Hearing about the successes of their businesses and the hope

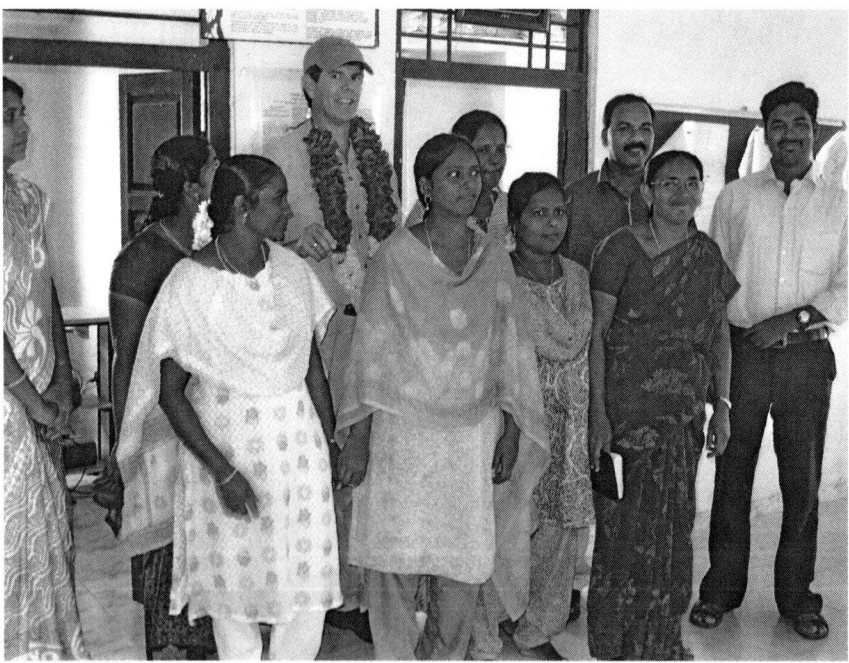

FIGURE 5.2 Paul Surrounded by Loan Officers at Niti's Chengelpet Branch (source: author).

that they have for their children's future was amazing. I felt and saw Christ walking along with them, I could see it in their faces with those beautiful smiles!

Even Paul, who was more skeptical about the Christian nature of Niti's work than the rest of the group, told me that he was happy with the way the organization worked and with how faith seemed to motivate Niti staff in a positive way, manifesting in working for low wages and riding 3 hours on a motorbike to reach distant clients. His inspection of the Chengelpet branch, then, had been a success; his affective investments had borne direct, visible, touchable fruit and therefore would continue. As we left, a last benefit was in store for us: we all lined up to use the office's Western-style toilet, and on the way out Susan jokingly thanked Paul for donating such a good toilet. Once again, embodied materiality articulated with the charitable impulse. I left the branch feeling touched by the direct encounter of Paul and his branch and imagined that he must have similar feelings. He probably did, although he did not show his emotions as much as other tour members did.

These affective performances happened especially when tour members were left speechless, unable to express their feelings during moments that were beyond words. Paralleling tourists' linguistic limitation to describe awe-inspiring encounters with overwhelming natural wonders (Picard, 2012), during our trip these instances usually took place around children. When we visited a private school to hand out Niti scholarships to deserving students from poor families, several parents started crying while telling us about the differences these scholarships made in their lives. Most of us choked up as well, and a few people let their tears flow freely. These were intensely sentimental moments, filled with empathy and gratitude. As I have shown, children are a tried and true vehicle for such emotions as they often evoke feelings of compassion and caring that are well-suited to the forging of affective investments. In contrast to the lone child represented in child sponsorship materials, however, here were children surrounded by their grateful parents, and what was celebrated was the promise of a better future for the whole family, via the scholarship and the education it enabled. The Christian charitable sentiment that "if I change one person's life, I will have done a good deed," which was frequently evoked by tour participants, holds especially true when that person has her whole life ahead of her.

During these emotion-filled moments, especially Susan often commented how "full" she was, as she carefully wiped tears from her eyes. In a similar fashion, frequent comments that the women we met were always smiling, which was taken as a sign of their surprising happiness amid the hardship of their lives, manifested non-linguistic affects. Smiles are prime expressions of affective interactions, often standing in for words. Such projections of joy unto the other can lead to tensions between the "cultural stereotype of contended Third World societies and tourists' own distress in the face of poverty" (Crossley, 2012, p. 249). While one way to resolve this tension is for the latter to feel grateful for the good fortunes of their own lives, some tour participants like Frank commented that it served to clear "the fog of materialistic complacency" to see what really mattered and to rally behind it. According to him:

> prosperity brings with it complacency and lethargy. We complain so much about so many grossly unimportant things. During a trip like this, it's embarrassing to think about it. We continue to "up the ante" for more excitement with imagery, technology, relationally while our impoverished brothers and sisters find joy and excitement in the simplest of things that require absolutely no money or technology.

For Frank, encountering the poor shone a light on the importance of the simple yet essential things in (his) life, which back home got buried under mountains of unnecessary stuff.

Frank's thoughts are similar to those of evangelical Christians in North Carolina who claim that they need the poor children they are sponsoring in Guatemala to liberate themselves from materialism, consumerism and the general distraction of their lives of affluence (O'Neill, 2013). It is especially during short-term mission trips to Guatemala, which are not unlike microfinance tours, that such emotions are cemented, when visceral encounters with filth, poverty and violence sometimes make it impossible for sponsors to return to their previous material trappings. The emphasis of this rising "Christian humanitarianism" is on relationships between the faithful, their close and distant neighbors and God (O'Neill, 2013, p. 206). Likewise, coming face to face with the recipients of his charity reinforced Frank's Christian virtues at the same time as it challenged his middle-class comforts. It is here where personal encounters differ from mediated ones like those produced by Kiva. Having exchanged one's chair in front of the computer for the journey of poverty tourism, it is easier to question one's complicity in the making of distant poverty. Although truth claims based on affective encounters need to be interrogated like all other assertions to authority (Pedwell, 2012), personal encounters with poverty often force a visceral reaction that can be harnessed by appropriate humanitarian technologies.

In the face of my fellow travelers' emotionality, I often felt inadequately moved, overtly analytical and unnecessarily critical. My personal discomfort showed that tour participants inhabit their roles differently and that "total immersion in a performance, or role distantiation (an awareness which inculcates critical reflection upon a performance), is defined by the conditions under which it is performed" (Edensor, 2000, p. 327). In addition to audience expectations, stage regulation and conformity pressure, our widely differing knowledge of microfinance also shaped our personal encounters. While all tour participants had a rudimentary understanding of what microfinance entailed, and those who had been involved with Opportunity for a while were familiar with Opportunity-style microfinance to varying degrees, nobody was aware of any of the critiques that have been advanced in the academic literature. By asking tour participants about these in my interviews, I drew their attention to the fact that such critiques existed, and invariably was asked

for more information and thanked for providing it. However, such a critical awareness very rarely made its way into our meetings.

(Im)possible Engagements

During our visit to the leper colony, we observed an animated lecture by the loan
officer to her borrowers. According to the Niti translator, she asked the women
"what will happen if you get five or six loans?" and the women answered "it will
be a burden to us and bring down our families." It was at this point that I had
turned to Nishtha to ask about the obvious gaps in the translation. It turned out that
what was missing was the loan officer's warning that

> all family happiness will be gone if too much is borrowed. The husband will
> start abusing the wife, because the husband is ultimately responsible for repay-
> ing the loan, and this can create tensions in the family. So you should only
> borrow as much as you can recuperate in income and therefore pay back.
> You should also understand the terms of the loan.

As described above, when none of us engaged this interchange, the loan officer
moved on to a less controversial business lesson.

Loan recycling happens when borrowers use a new loan to pay off an older one,
often held with another MFI. The practice is usually taken as a first sign of over-
indebtedness (Guérin et al., 2013). It has also been linked to the high-profile microfinance crisis that gripped the Indian state of Andhra Pradesh in 2010, leading to
politically incited mass repayment refusals, tighter MFI regulations and borrower
suicides (Roy, 2012; Young, 2010). Any discussion of loan recycling therefore has
the potential to disrupt microfinance's obligatory success story, and this might have
been why the translator had been trying to truncate the exchange in our presence.
In Raj's initial presentation, after Robert had asked him about regulatory challenges
in Indian microfinance that were briefly mentioned in our Trip Guide, Raj had
explained the crisis in Andhra Pradesh with the good intentions of MFIs going
awry when microfinance becomes an easy way to make money. As often happens,
he laid blame on the doorstep of wayward MFIs but left the principle of microfinance intact. Raj furthermore opposed the transactional microfinance model of
commercial MFIs to Niti's transformational model, under which borrowers who
already have loans with two or more MFIs will not be able to borrow from Niti.
During the same discussion, Bill had admitted that Opportunity had received calls
from anxious donors who had read about the crisis in the *Wall Street Journal*. "It did
hurt Opportunity, and we had to remind donors that we are mission-minded, that
we are not SKS [in reference to a large Indian MFI that had gone public in 2010]."
Changing microfinance regulations were also briefly discussed during our meeting
with the US consulate staff.

While some of the downsides of microfinance had therefore been mentioned in
passing during our meetings, where they were usually attached to discussions of

how changing microfinance regulations affected Niti's operations, here in the leper colony was a chance to ask borrowers themselves if they ever had difficulties repaying. What would happen in such cases? And how did the women feel in general about being in debt, even to an organization as caring as Niti? Such questions had not figured in our Trip Guide, and they were not asked that afternoon. In their absence, it would have been up to Ananya, Raj or the Niti translator to point out to us the importance of the interchange we were witnessing, but they did not challenge the story of transformative lending we were all co-creating that afternoon. In other words,

> the performance [of a tour] builds on what a particular guide chooses to relate to his or her audience(s), and what to omit, highlight and downplay, and reciprocally, on what issues the audiences of guided tours ask about, or accept as fait accompli. The spoken and unspoken elements of the performance are not randomly distributed [and] guides and their audiences do not act in a void.
>
> *(Brin & Noy, 2010, p. 30)*

In our case, the obligatory success story of microfinance and the resulting scripted nature of our encounters set clear boundaries for everybody's performative engagement.

Initially, I saw it as my role to ask some of the questions that would turn these encounters into more balanced learning experiences, but I soon found that there were real constraints to more searching exchanges. All of my questions, about existing competition, for example, were curtly dealt with through answers that reaffirmed that whatever business I was asking about was doing well. There simply was no space to ask tough questions, because of time constraints, the repetitive nature of the meetings and the discouragement of dissenting voices. After a while, I began to censor myself, submitting to the tour group's discipline and ultimately performing my proper, expected role. The "rigid script" that typecast us and resulted in our "dutiful disposition to perform efficiently in appropriate fashion" was proving to be effective (Edensor, 2000, p. 334). In the end, we all enacted our roles as microfinance tourists well, by asking the right questions and avoiding the wrong ones, by accepting the flowers and rock candy even if we did not embrace them, and by not outright rejecting the drinks offered to us but making them disappear behind our backs.

Literature on "the performance of development" (Roy, 2010, p. 167) can shed further light on our impossible engagement with microfinance critiques. Roy shows that microfinance in Egypt is intimately tied up with various performative aspects, which does not make it any less authentic. Rather, its performance is a reality because "it comes to be accepted and legitimized as common sense," because it is financially productive and because it showcases the continued role of the sovereign Egyptian state in its nation's developmental landscape (Roy, 2010, p. 163). This is especially important in light of frequent tours by World Bank representatives to development sites in Cairo's poor neighborhoods (Elyachar, 2002). These tours enacted a more classical version of development tourism (Chambers, 1983): from the visitors' encapsulation in their cars and entourages of officials to the best faces put forward by the toured subjects to the Coca-Cola and photographs, such brief visits are more than anything curtailed by a lack of time that inhibits any kind of meaningful learning. Microfinance borrowers groups are also not unlike Chambers'

> self-conscious groups, dressed in their best clothes, [who] are seen and spoken to. They nervously respond in what they hope will bring benefits and avoid penalties … [because] they have to live with the officials and with each other after the visitor has left.
>
> *(Chambers, 1983, p. 12)*

Performing out of line would be foolish for anybody involved in such encounters.

Microfinance also becomes "a performance of labor" by poor entrepreneurs themselves, who display their microloan-enabled productions for the visitors (Elyachar, 2002, p. 503). In Chennai, borrowers proudly showed us their saris, jewelry and candles. Their groups had been picked by Niti's regional manager, and according to Raj, one important selection criteria was that they were "not too shy" to talk to us. They had been told to prepare for US visitors, labeled as partners rather than donors so as to lessen any possibility of asking us for money directly. Ananya often pointed out to us how excited the women were to receive us, visible in their best clothes and gold jewelry worn for the occasion. Raj confirmed that because they normally do not have contact with foreigners, our visits were much cherished highlights in their lives.

During one of my interviews with her, Ananya explained to me that Opportunity's aim is to create an "authentic" borrower group meeting experience for Insight Trip participants. She thereby invoked a critical concept in the tourism literature, where authenticity used to be regarded as a quality that distinguished originals from their recreations for tourists, and has more recently come to be understood as a projection by tourists onto visited sites and objects, depending on their expectations and beliefs (Wang, 1999). In the context of poverty tourism in India, authenticity has been analyzed as slum tour participants' desire to see the true India found in its slums, as opposed to a staged tourist world (Meschkank, 2011). Furthermore, slum tour participants want to experience the real India in direct, non-media-mediated encounters. For many of these tourists, that means visiting poor India, and the places where poor people could be seen living and working become marked, and marketed, as authentic. What stands out in these constructions of authenticity is tourists' surprise at the intense commercial activity found in slums, which in turn is highlighted by tour operators to counter the negative stereotypes held by most tourists before their tours (Diekmann & Hannam, 2012; Meschkank, 2011). Micro-scale commercial activity is also what microfinance aims to foster, and Ananya's demand for authenticity implied a direct and personal, as opposed to a distant and mediated, encounter with women microfinance clients.

But Ananya also had in mind a real encounter as opposed to a staged one, with the women being true to themselves and the challenges in their difficult lives. In other words, Ananya did not want the women to be, or be seen as, Goffmanesque actors. While Goffman's "insistence on the instrumentality of role-playing ... conjures up a continually self-reflexive individual, intentionally communicating values to an audience," the women's performance is better captured as "unreflexive, habitual and unintentional enactions" (Edensor, 2001, p. 60). Rather than as strategic subjects, borrower identities were normatively constituted by their subject position vis-à-vis Western visitors and guests of the MFI that disbursed their loans. They understood the importance of presenting themselves to us as deserving recipients of these loans, a performativity rehearsed in weekly meetings with their Niti loan officer. Through their clothes and comportment, pledging and praying, as well as the shape of their answers to our questions, the women borrowers showed themselves as worthy of our care. Anthropologists have identified such performances for refugees, who have to look and conduct themselves according to expectations of refugee-ness (Malkki, 1996), underscored by the "performance of a credible narrative of victimhood" that depends on possessing "authentic fear or suffering" (Sandvik, 2009, p. 228). Such performances often happen under extremely unequal power relations, where the group under scrutiny stands to lose much by not being judged authentic enough by the evaluators of their performance. While the stakes were not as high for Niti's borrowers as they are for refugees, they too had to present themselves as subjects suitable for a continuing affective relationship that was hopefully ensured by our mutual encounter (Sin, 2010). One way in which this relationship was cemented was through another quintessential tourist activity – photography.

Pictures of Microfinance

In the 3.0 remake of Urry's classic text *The Tourist Gaze*, Urry and Larsen argue that "photography was born, from Talbot's [Fox Talbot, the inventor of photography] sense of inadequacy as an artist when faced with an attractive, foreign scene" (Urry & Larsen, 2011, p. 164). In fact, many a traveler in the middle of the 19th century postponed his trip to await the invention of the Daguerreotype in 1840, in order to capture his travels more realistically. If taking pictures is "perhaps *the* emblematic tourism activity" (Haldrup & Larsen, 2003, p. 23), then our group was full of tourists. We not only took pictures of the typical tourist attractions – the Taj Mahal, the Red Fort in Delhi, the temples outside Chennai, the tomb of St. Thomas in the city's cathedral – visits to which constituted the tourism aspect of our Insight Trip, but in addition the performance of photography, enacted by "an engaged and multi-sensuous body" (Urry & Larsen, 2011, p. 209), was an integral part of mobilizing tour participants' affective investments in Niti staff and borrowers. This performance is central to how tourists "grasp their worlds," encounter others within them and build relationships through these encounters (Haldrup & Larsen, 2003, p. 26). On the one hand, our constant picture taking reinscribed a voyeuristic distance between us and the women borrowers, but on the other it also allowed for moments of "fleeting togetherness" through a co-performance of repeated photographic encounters (Scarles, 2012, p. 931). It is through the latter that social and emotional connections were built most strongly during our tour. The ultimate objective of the "future-perfect" (Crang, 1997, p. 366) created from these photographic encounters were continued financial contributions to Opportunity.

The Gift of Photography

Photography was marked as important even before we embarked on our journey. Ananya had informed us in an email that rather than giving money or candies to the children we would meet, the best presents we could give them and their mothers were to take pictures with them and show them the photo afterwards. In other words, photos, and the act of taking them, would be our gifts, however temporary and fleeting. This was especially so for children, many of whom, we were told, had never seen a photo of themselves. We also took a Polaroid camera to all our borrower meetings for more permanent pleasure, which indeed proved a hit until we ran out of paper. From then on, glances at the screens of our digital cameras had to do, which often elicited laughter (see Figure 5.3). This interaction was afforded by innovation in photographic technologies: while Kodak's launch of the user-friendly, lightweight and cheap Brownie camera in the late 1880s "in effect invented tourist

FIGURE 5.3 Frank and Niti Borrowers Looking at Their Picture on Frank's Camera (source: author).

photography through developing a new system, assembling together a novel set of material and social relations" (Urry & Larsen, 2011, p. 170), our sharing pictures with women and children in Chennai would not have been possible without digital cameras and their instant replay screens.

Children clearly enjoyed posing for our cameras, maybe not unlike Ladhaki children, who, when photographed by tourists, "get an identity reward, or some form of recognition, by virtue of being photographed – it positions them as valuable" (Gillespie, 2006, p. 351). This potential for recognition is negated when tourists feel overwhelmed by the many requests for pictures and end up only pretending to take them. When I asked Raj what the picture taking might mean for the women, he described an "afterglow" that comes from looking at cherished moments and remembering rare foreign visitors. However, this was a temporary pleasure, as the cameras did not belong to the women and the picture files were not shared with them, but remained with Opportunity and us, from where they made their way onto websites, blogs and coffee table (and academic) books. For the women, fading Polaroid photographs would have to suffice. Thus, technology ownership negates some of the potential of tourist photography. The same holds true for ownership over picture files; while Scarles (2012) argues that digital technology has the potential to renegotiate positions of power by allowing locals to ask to delete those pictures they do not like, this never happened in our case. Instead, our picture taking was mostly voyeuristic.

Voyeuristic Distance

Susan Sontag once remarked that "tourists feel obliged to put the camera between themselves and whatever is remarkable in the encounter" (cited in Urry & Larsen, 2011, p. 155). In Chennai, this distancing started the moment we disembarked from our bus, when tour participants pulled out their cameras, pointed them in the direction of the waiting women and took pictures while walking toward them. Thus, even before any greetings were exchanged, cameras were drawn and firing away. Like Emilie Crossley, who during her research on volunteer tourism was "horrified" when the majority of tour members started photographing children in a classroom as the teacher was trying to introduce them (2012, p. 246), I felt that taking pictures of people before even meeting them was a clear manifestation of the objectifying nature of much tourist photography.

Zoom lenses amplified our voyeurism, enabling us to take close-up pictures of women praying with their eyes closed and of children sleeping in their mothers' arms.[16] At the same time as searching for the photogenic like any other tourist, I felt ashamed for intruding into the women's private, intimate moments, a feeling that is not uncommon in tourist encounters with distant others and is brought about by a heightened awareness of the self that sees itself through the eyes of the other (Tucker, 2009). The question as to whether "the very politics of authenticity … embodied in tourism encounters … might evoke feelings of shame in any reflexive tourist who has an interest in living ethically" (p. 455) extends the discomfort I was experiencing from the photo moments to the tour itself. It throws into doubt the very project of microfinance tourism, which ultimately only seemed to re-enact the problematic power relations for which tourism in general has been so roundly criticized.

My discomfort was also caused by the "reverse gaze," whereby the women's glances at me revealed myself as just another picture-hunting tourist (Gillespie, 2006). Instead, I wanted to be seen as the resident ethnographer, and most of my pictures were of my fellow travelers taking pictures of or with the women (see Figures 5.4 and 5.5). Since that was not evident to the women in front of me, at least I wanted to be perceived as a caring person interested in microfinance and genuinely wanting to see the difference it had made in the women's lives, in spite of my critical disposition toward it. This reverse gaze, which can also cause embarrassment, guilt and shame, creates situations where "romanticism, voyeurism, and superiority are delicately balanced" (Gillespie, 2006, p. 359). Finally, voyeuristic distance was made manifest in each group photo taken at the end of borrower group meetings. The performance of static poses, with us either towering behind the women or sitting on chairs behind the women on the floor, visually displayed the hierarchical distance between us and them (see Figure 5.1). However, these staged photos were preceded by a markedly different kind of performance that had almost opposite effects.

FIGURE 5.4 Sam and Niti Borrower Being Photographed in Front of Her Store by Insight Trip Participants (source: author).

FIGURE 5.5 Bill with Niti Borrowers, Being Photographed by His Son (source: author).

Photographic Communitas

Toward the end of each borrower group meeting, there was much jostling among the women who wanted to have their pictures taken together with us. This was the women's opportunity to get close to us, allowing literal connections through furtive touches. Touch, as a powerful sense that acts directly on the body, comingled with sight, sound and smell to create intense embodied and emotive moments that resulted in "performative objects generating affective sensations" (Urry & Larsen, 2011, p. 155). Here, tourist photography produced not distance, but intersubjective connections. Just like in family vacation pictures, where "to produce signs of affection, families need to be affective" (Larsen, 2005, p. 430), in Chennai the Niti family was on display. Born from the Christian devotion of its leaders, staff and funders to poor women borrowers, this family temporarily included us (see Figure 5.6).

These photographic moments were necessarily brief: "the immanence and unpredictability of photographic encounters coupled with the ability of tourists to instantly show locals photographs on digital cameras generates a fleeting togetherness: an immersion into experience through an investment of desire" (Scarles, 2012, p. 931). It was precisely their fleetingness that enabled their intensity. In classical anthropological terms, these moments were instances of Turnerian communitas. While the formal parts of our borrower group meetings, the greetings and microfinance performances, constituted the entry into the ritual

FIGURE 5.6 Susan Holding a Child's Hand to Her Face (source: author).

period, and the final group photo and goodbyes marked the exit, our shared picture taking was a period of liminality or anti-structure, where hierarchies were temporarily leveled and where the women felt comfortable to be in playful togetherness with us (Turner & Turner, 1978). Pushing and pulling was accompanied by laughing and giggling. Susan and I were in equal demand to the men in our group (see Figure 5.7).

We often put our arms around the women next to us, and I felt as if these hugs were reciprocated. It was only when I looked at the pictures that I realized that most of the women held their arms stiffly against their bodies. This was especially the case when being photographed with Bill, Frank, Paul or Mike (see Figure 5.8). The gendered limits of liminality reasserted themselves in the products of our fleeting encounters.

Microfinance tourist photography, then, defies easy categorization. On the one hand, microfinance itself became flattened to smiling faces, group rituals and photographic performances to be "consumed as lightweight pre-arranged photo-scenes" (Urry & Larsen, 2011, p. 187). Furthermore, "the cavalier use of photography is likely to produce a barrier to the engagement and intimacy with local people that … tourism endorses, as well as enacting damaging power relations" (Crossley, 2012, p. 247). Staged pictures and voyeuristic intrusions contributed minimally to the connections that Opportunity and Niti hoped to produce during our Insight Trip. On the other hand, taking pictures afforded the only opportunities for the

FIGURE 5.7 Author with Niti Borrowers (source: author).

women to approach us. Their temporary overstepping of physical boundaries and social rules produced momentary feelings of togetherness and affirmed a common humanity that had been negated with prior clicks. Did this photographic communitas, and the meetings during which they took place, help mobilize affective investments?

According to Ananya, the main aim of Opportunity's Insight Tours is to educate the general public about the organization's work. While initially these tours were reserved for donors who had given at least US$5,000 to Opportunity, under her management, the tours have been opened up to all interested current and potential future supporters. As an "indirect fundraiser," Insight Tours were part of an organizational shift from "high net worth donors" whose support had waned in the wake of the global financial crisis to generating "consistent income from everyday people." The latter are often not (yet) acquainted with Opportunity, and therefore Insight Tours also serve as a word-of-mouth awareness-raising strategy. Mike commented that as a result of his trip to Chennai,

> my life is changed, I hope to tell the story of [Niti] to as many who will listen including my church, co-workers, family and friends. I'm going to encourage others to give because even if one life can be changed through this ministry it's all worth it.

For him, Niti was more than a bank, but a "human, caring, loving ministry," and that was worth supporting, through further donations to Opportunity. During our

FIGURE 5.8   Mike with Niti Borrower (source: author).

conversations, both Ananya and Bill repeatedly referred to Opportunity as "the best kept secret" and in order to change that status, in 2012 Opportunity's newly hired CEO was tasked with rebranding the organization and making it more of a household name in the global and US Christian philanthropic landscape.

This means that financial commitments from Insight Trip participants, while not mandatory, are an expected outcome; they are to be mobilized through the social and emotional connections forged during the tours. These connections were built through meetings with local MFI partner staff and borrowers. I have shown how these borrower group and branch meetings were performances that conveyed information about Opportunity's and Niti's lending and brought us in direct contact with its beneficiaries. In my follow-up questionnaire for tour participants, all stated that their support for Opportunity's work would continue if not grow, on the basis of having witnessed in person the difference this work makes in the lives of poor women. Paul's answer was a good example: "I am just even more committed to supporting microfinance, as long as the social support mechanisms are also provided. It does give me more hope that poverty can be reduced around the world through microfinance." Tour participants became not only financially, but also socially and emotionally invested in the women and their families they had met. This shows that "affect as a relational resource can travel beyond its space of genesis" (Solomon, 2011, p. 112). And travel is a good way for this to happen. According to Frank:

> this trip has continued to change me. When I make new friends like you and the others, when I visit a place never traveled to before, when I learn about other cultures and people with strange customs from my own, when I eat their food, when I smell them, when I hear their strange language and accents, I am expanded. Expanded emotionally, psychologically, socially and intellectually. Not always hugely so, but expanded none the less.

In my own post-trip evaluation for Opportunity, I had recommended that more microfinance information be included in the Trip Guide, and had offered to write something myself. This offer was not taken up, also because Bill became quickly engulfed in his daily responsibilities at Opportunity. While this means that Insight Tour participants continue to gain only minimal critical insights into microfinance, for people with no prior awareness of some of its downsides, this was a much appreciated start. Frank noted:

> a new thing I became more aware of is the controversy over microfinance and the unscrupulousness of some of the for-profit organizations involved in microfinance. As for understanding the full extent of the controversy, I need to dig in and learn more about it. I must confess, I was a bit naive until this trip. Time to do my homework now.

Even though the scope of the Insight Tour's microfinance performance was restricted by various technologies of representation, surveillance and disciplining, some tour participants' understanding of microfinance was enriched.

Our encounters in Chennai were ultimately shaped by the "covertly ideological nature of tour guiding as well as the contested and negotiated nature of toured spaces" (Brin and Noy, 2010: 29). What the Insight Tour enabled only minimally was "the second gaze" that is aware that something is missing from every picture and becomes an invitation to look again and beyond (MacCannell, 2001). Microfinance tourism, while mobilizing affective investments among its participants, only provided limited opportunities for this to happen. Volunteer tourism has been suggested as an alternative to such limited engagement (McGehee, 2002). Microfinance volunteers who work for MFIs for longer amounts of time do obtain a deeper understanding of some of the challenges faced by their host organizations. Does this in turn allow for a more sustained and critical engagement with microfinance? Does it open up angles that turn touristic glimpses into seeing beyond stereotypes and obligatory stories? In the next chapter, I examine Kiva Fellows as particular kinds of volunteer tourists who learn to look again by becoming actively involved in microfinance work.

Notes

* Unless otherwise noted, quotes in this chapter come from face-to-face conversations during the author's tour in Chennai, India, in August 2012, or personal communications with the author immediately following this.
** Except for Opportunity, all names of organizations and individuals are pseudonyms.
1 India refused to accept aid from other national governments after the tsunami, and Indians themselves donated over US$90 billion in 2 weeks. While India used the disaster to present itself as a "benevolent donor [rather] than a needy recipient," the tsunami also served as "a portal into a larger moral critique of the government, of NGOs and of social welfare practices," mainly around the mismanagement of funds (Bornstein, 2012, p. 40).
2 Retrieved June 17, 2013, from www.ndtv.com/article/south/us-announces-ex-gratia-to-kin-of-tamil-nadu-fisherman-killed-in-dubai-251970.
3 Retrieved September 2012, from www.opportunity.org/news/blog.
4 INM had been an Opportunity partner organization for many years, and that is how Kiva learned about its existence.
5 Kristen was established in the 1930s when Christian converts were ostracized from their villages and forced to live in the forest. Here they survived against all odds and built a village around a small white timber church (Tyndale, 2004).
6 Maranatha can roughly be translated as "Come, oh Lord."
7 Retrieved June 11, 2013, from www.opportunity.org/about/#.UbZRSetzo10.
8 Retrieved June 11, 2013, from www.opportunity.org/about/our-story/#.UbZSZutzo10.
9 There is some debate over the naming of these organizations. While they have recently become known as faith-based organizations (FBOs), several scholars have pointed out the limitations of this categorization, which betrays its Western, Christian orientation (Jones & Petersen, 2011). I will use the more encompassing term religious organizations (ROs) to escape this somewhat narrow focus.
10 In line with the scholarship on the topic, I define spirituality as a personal relationship with the spiritual realm, religion as an institutionalized expression of this relationship and faith as belief in a transcendent reality (Lunn, 2009).
11 Oxfam was founded by a vicar at Oxford University to help Greek Cypriot civilians during World War II, Voluntary Service Overseas was started by two Anglicans with support from the Bishop of Portsmouth and Amnesty International was started by a Christian whose religious convictions inspired him to help prisoners of conscience under dictatorships (Deneulin & Bano, 2009).
12 An example of this is Shri Kshetra Dhamasthala Rural Development (SKDRDP), an MFI in southwest India based around a Jain-led temple, which serves primarily Hindu but also Muslim and Christian faith groups. Borrowers believe that the loans they receive are God's money, given to them as a divine gift, and all transactions are carried out in front of religious items. This ensures that defaults are kept to a minimum because defaulters feel that they are cheating not only SKDRDP, but also God (Harper et al., 2008).
13 Retrieved June 14, 2013, from www.opportunity.org/about/our-beliefs-about-christian-microfinance/#.UbpDretzo10.
14 Governors are central to the work of Opportunity in the United States. In 2011, the over 600 Governors donated US$14.2 million, or 49 percent of Opportunity's private fundraising budget. (Retrieved June 11, 2013, from www.opportunity.org/board-of-governors/#.Ubefz-tzo10.)
15 Niti was established in 2006 by the founders of Inter-Mission Industrial Development Association (IIDA), a skills training program for poor women, especially widows, that had been in existence since the 1970s. Combining this training with financial support brought Niti into the Opportunity network and as of 2011, the organization has served over 50,000 mainly female clients through business, housing and school fee loans as well as microinsurance products.
16 We uploaded all of our pictures on a shared photo website, which allowed me to see the photos of other tour participants.

Bibliography

Appadurai, A. (1985). Gratitude as a social mode in South India. *Ethos, 13*(3), 236–245.

Bandyopadhyay, R. (2009). The perennial tourism representations of India that refuse to die. *Tourism Studies, 57*(1), 23–35.

Barbieri, C., Santos, C. A. & Katsube, Y. (2012). Volunteer tourism: On-the-ground observations from Rwanda. *Tourism Management, 33*, 509–516.

Bhattacharyya, D. (1997). Mediating India: An analysis of a guidebook. *Annals of Tourism Research, 24*(2), 371–389.

Bornstein, E. (2012). *Disquieting gifts: Humanitarianism in New Delhi*. Palo Alto, CA: Stanford University Press.

Brett, J. (2006). "We sacrifice and eat less": The structural complexities of microfinance participation. *Human Organization, 65*(1), 8–19.

Brin, E. & Noy, C. (2010). The said and the unsaid: Performing guiding in a Jerusalem neighbourhood. *Tourist Studies, 10*(1), 19–33.

Brown, K. (2009). Economics and morality: An introduction. In K. Brown & L. Milgram (Eds.), *Economics and morality: Anthropological approaches* (pp. 1–42). Lanham, MD: Altmira Press.

Bussau, D. & Mask, R. (2003). *Christian microenterprise development: An introduction*. Oxford: Regnum Books International.

Calhoun, C. (2010). *The idea of emergency: Humanitarian action and global (dis)order*. New York: Zone Books.

Chambers, R. (1983). *Rural development: Putting the last first*. Harlow: Pearson.

Chant, S. (2008). The "feminisation of poverty" and the "feminisation" of anti-poverty programmes: Room for revision? *Journal of Development Studies, 44*(2), 165–197.

Chouliaraki, L. (2012). The theatricality of humanitarianism: A critique of celebrity advocacy. *Communication and Critical/Cultural Studies, 9*(1), 1–21.

Crang, M. (1997). Picturing practices: Research through the tourist gaze. *Progress in Human Geography, 21*(3), 359–373.

Crossley, E. (2012). Poor but happy: Volunteer tourists' encounters with poverty. *Tourism Geographies: An International Journal of Tourism Space, Place and Environment, 14*(2), 235–253.

Crouch, D., Arronsson, L. & Wahlstroem, L. (2001). Tourist encounters. *Tourist Studies, 1*(3), 253–268.

Deneulin, S. & Bano, M. (2009). *Religion in development: Rewriting the secular script*. New York: Zed Books.

Deneulin, S. & Rakodi, C. (2011). Revisiting religion: Development studies 30 years on. *World Development, 39*(1), 45–54.

Diekmann, A. & Hannam, K. (2012). Touristic mobilities in India's slum spaces. *Annals of Tourism Research, 39*(3), 1315–1336.

Edensor, T. (2000). Staging tourism: Tourists as performers. *Annals of Tourism Research, 27*(2), 322–344.

Edensor, T. (2001). Performing tourism, staging tourism: (Re)producing tourist space and practice. *Tourist Studies, 1*(1), 59–81.

Elyachar, J. (2002). Empowerment money: The World Bank, non-governmental organizations and the value of culture in Egypt. *Public Culture, 14*(3), 493–513.

Franklin, A. & Crang, M. (2001). The trouble with tourism and travel theory. *Tourist Studies, 1*(1), 5–22.

Freire-Medeiros, B. (2012). *Touring poverty*. New York and London: Routledge.

Gillespie, A. (2006). Tourist photography and the reverse gaze. *Ethos, 34*(3), 343–366.

Graburn, N. (1977). Tourism: The sacred journey. In V. Smith (Ed.), *Hosts and guests* (pp. 17–31). Philadelphia: University of Pennsylvania Press.

Graburn, N. (2001). Secular ritual: A general theory of tourism. In V. Smith & M. Brent (Eds.), *Hosts and guests revisited: Tourism issues of the 21st century* (pp. 42–52). Elmsford, NY: Cognizant Communications.

Guérin, I., Morvant-Roux, S. & Villareal, M. (2013). *Microfinance, debt and over-indebtedness: Juggling with money.* Abingdon: Routledge.

Haldrup, M. & Larsen, J. (2003). The family gaze. *Tourism Studies, 3*(1), 23–46.

Harper, M., Rao, D. & Sahu, A. (2008). *Development, divinity and dharma: The role of religion in development and microfinance institutions.* Rugby, UK: Practical Action Publishing.

Hutnyk, J. (1996). *The rumour of Calcutta: Tourism, charity and the poverty of representation.* London and New Jersey: Zed Books.

Jones, B. & Petersen, M. (2011). Instrumental, narrow, normative? Reviewing recent work on religion and development. *Third World Quarterly, 32*(7), 1291–1306.

Karim, L. (2011). *Microfinance and its discontents: Women in debt in Bangladesh.* Minneapolis: University of Minnesota Press.

Larsen, J. (2005). Families seen sightseeing: Performativity of tourist photography. *Space and Culture, 8*(4), 416–434.

Lunn, J. (2009). The role of religion, spirituality and faith in development: A critical theory approach. *Third World Quarterly, 30*(5), 937–951.

Lutz, M. (2010). *Unpoverty: Rich lessons from the working poor.* Glen Ellyn, IL: Unpoverty Communications.

MacCannell, D. (1976). *The tourist: A new theory of the leisure class.* Berkeley: University of California Press.

MacCannell, D. (2001). Tourist agency. *Tourist Studies, 1*(1), 23–37.

Malkki, L. (1996). Speechless emissaries: Refugees, humanitarianism and dehistoricization. *Cultural Anthropology, 11*(3), 377–404.

Malkki, L. (2010). Children, humanity and the infantilization of peace. In I. Feldman & M. Ticktin (Eds.), *In the name of humanity: The government of threat and care* (pp. 58–90). Durham, NC: Duke University Press.

Mathers, K. (2010). *Travel, humanitarianism, and becoming American in Africa.* New York: Palgrave Macmillan.

McGehee, N. (2002). Alternative tourism and social movements. *Annals of Tourism Research, 29*(1), 124–143.

McGehee, N. & Andereck, K. (2008). "Pettin' the critters": Exploring the complex relationship between volunteers and the voluntoured in McDowell County, West Virginia, USA and Tijuana, Mexico. In K. Lyons & S. Wearing (Eds.), *Journeys of discovery in volunteer tourism: International case study perspectives* (pp. 12–24). Wallingford: CABI.

Mersland, R., D'Espallier, B. & Supphellen, M. (2012). The effects of religion on development efforts: Evidence from the microfinance industry and a research agenda. *World Development, 41*, 145–156.

Meschkank, J. (2011). Investigations into slum tourism in Mumbai: Poverty tourism and the tensions between different constructions of reality. *GeoJournal, 76*(1), 47–62.

Mühlebach, A. (2013). The catholicization of neoliberalism: On love and welfare in Lombardy, Italy. *American Anthropologist, 115*(3), 452–465.

Navaro-Yashin, Y. (2009). Affective spaces, melancholic objects: Ruination and the production of anthropological knowledge. *Journal of the Royal Anthropological Institute* (N.S.), 15, 1–18.

O'Neill, K. L. (2013). Left behind: Security, salvation, and the subject of prevention. *Cultural Anthropology, 28*(2), 204–226.

Pedwell, C. (2012). Affective (self-) transformations: Empathy, neoliberalism and international development. *Feminist Theory, 13*(2), 163–179.

Picard, D. (2012). Tourism, awe and inner journeys. In D. Picard & M. Robinson (Eds.), *Emotions in motion: Tourism, affect and transformation* (pp. 1–19). Farnham: Ashgate.

Rankin, K. (2001). Governing development: Neoliberalism, microcredit and rational economic woman. *Economy and Society, 30*(1), 18–37.

Redfield, P. & Bornstein, E. (2010). An introduction to the anthropology of humanitarianism. In E. Bornstein & P. Redfield (Eds.), *Forces of compassion: Humanitarianism between ethics and politics* (pp. 3–30). Santa Fe, NM: SAR Press.

Richard, A. & Rudnyckyj, D. (2009). Economies of affect. *Journal of the Royal Anthropological Institute* (N.S.), 15, 57–77.

Roy, A. (2010). *Poverty capital: Microfinance and the making of development.* New York and London: Routledge.

Roy, A. (2012). Subjects of risk: Technologies of gender in the making of millennial modernity. *Public Culture, 24*(1), 131–155.

Rudnyckyj, D. (2010). *Spiritual economies: Islam, globalization and the afterlife of development.* Ithaca, NY: Cornell University Press.

Sandvik, K. B. (2009). The physicality of legal consciousness: Suffering and the production of credibility in refugee settlement. In R. A. Wilson & R. D. Brown (Eds.), *Humanitarianism and suffering: The mobilization of empathy* (pp. 223–244). Cambridge: Cambridge University Press.

Scarles, C. (2012). The photographed other: Interplays of agency in tourist photography in Cusco, Peru. *Annals of Tourism Research, 39*(2), 928–950.

Sen, A. (1999). *Development as freedom.* New York: Doubleday.

Sharpley, R. & Sundaram, P. (2005). Tourism: A sacred journey? The case of ashram tourism, India. *International Journal of Tourism Research, 7*, 161–171.

Sin, H. L. (2010). Who are we responsible to? Locals' tales of volunteer tourism. *Geoforum, 41*, 983–992.

Solomon, H. (2011). Affective journeys: The emotional structuring of medical tourism in India. *Anthropology and Medicine, 18*(1), 105–118.

Tomalin, E. (2012). Thinking about faith-based organizations in development: Where have we got to and what next? *Development in Practice, 22*(5–6), 689–703.

Tucker, H. (2009). Recognizing emotion and its postcolonial potentialities: Discomfort and shame in a tourism encounter in Turkey. *Tourism Geographies: An International Journal of Tourism Space, Place and Environment, 11*(4), 444–461.

Turner, V. & Turner, E. (1978). *Image and pilgrimage in Christian culture.* New York: Columbia University Press.

Tyndale, P. (2004). *Don't look back: The David Bussau story.* Sydney: Allen & Unwin.

Urry, J. & Larsen, J. (2011). *The tourist gaze 3.0.* London: Sage Publications.

Ver Beek, K. (2000). Spirituality: A development taboo. *Development in Practice, 10*(1), 31–43.

Wang, N. (1999). Rethinking authenticity in tourism experience. *Annals of Tourism Research, 26*(2), 349–370.

Wilson, K. (2007). The moneylender's dilemma. In T. Dichter & M. Harper (Eds.), *What's wrong with microfinance?* (pp. 97–108). Rugby, UK: Practical Action Publishing.

Young, S. (2010). The "moral hazards" of microfinance: Restructuring rural credit in India. *Antipode, 42*(1), 201–230.

6

AFFECTIVE LABOR

My experiences here in Tajikistan over the past several weeks have run the full spectrum of human emotion. I have laughed with astonishment at the absurd amounts of food that have been forced down my throat, stuffed like a pig all in the name of "hospitality"; I have been saddened and amazed by the industry of young porters who abandon school at the age of ten, forgoing their childhoods in order to earn a couple of dollars a day carrying fruit, bread and meat through the vast, chaotic scene of the Panjshanbe bazaar; I have been humbled by the sheer generosity and kindness of people, who despite receiving a salary of less than $200 a month give this privileged American almost everything they have, asking for nothing in return; I have smiled with joy when the kids at my apartment block treat me like a minor celebrity, and I have gawked in astonishment at the sheer indifference of the government to the blight of its people.

(Kiva Fellow posted to MFI in Tajikistan)

Kiva would not be able to function without the work of its thousands of volunteers, who by the end of 2012 had contributed 200,000 hours of free labor to the organization.[1] For every one staff person, there are six volunteers who do everything from administrative work at the Kiva headquarters to translating and editing borrower profiles from their homes to serving as Kiva Fellows in all corners of the world. Being a Fellow is arguably the most intense and celebrated Kiva volunteer experience. Fellows are posted for a minimum of 4 months with a partner MFI, where they serve as a "liaison, language translator, cultural interpreter, tech support representative, writer, photographer and videographer," in the words of a former employee working as the Kiva Fellow Coordinator at the organization (quoted in Harris, 2013, p. 81). Their most important job is to make local MFIs into better-integrated Kiva partners, which often involves setting up technological information management systems and training MFI staff on how to fulfill Kiva's borrower recruiting and profiling requirements. Fellows often talk about "following their hearts" in pursuing their volunteer work for Kiva, in the process sometimes giving up well-paying and high-status jobs, much to the initial bewilderment of friends and family.

In this chapter, I draw on the anthropological literature on volunteering (Adams, 2012; Bornstein, 2012; Mühlebach, 2011; Parreñas, 2012) and the literature on volunteer tourism (Conran, 2011; Crossley, 2012; Mostafanezhad, 2013a, 2013b), both of which have recently begun to explore volunteering as a form of affective labor. This term draws attention to the sentiments that inform volunteering and that can also result from it. While some Kiva Fellows would surely bristle at being called tourists, the definition of volunteer tourists as "people who invest their time, budget and manpower at a destination far from home to gain cultural, environmental and spiritual experiences" (Wearing, 2001, p. 5) is applicable to the activities of the great majority of Fellows. In particular, they fit the description of "deep" volunteer tourists who stay for longer periods of time, have skills that make a direct contribution to their host organization and are motivated by altruism over self-interest (Callanan & Thomas, 2005, p. 196). Depth here refers to a temporal and personal commitment to a host organization, which leads to intense experiences that go below the surfaces that microfinance tourists can only scratch. For Kiva Fellows, it is their work at MFIs and the immersion into local places, institutions and practices that this work allows that is the defining aspect of a Kiva Fellowship.

Similar to the volunteer tourists in Thailand studied by Mary Conran (2011), Fellows tend to be middle and upper class, well educated, globally conscious and sympathetic to ideas of global justice. However, there are also important distinctions that mark Kiva Fellows as a particular kind of volunteer. While 95 percent of Fellows are born in or reside in the United States, a similar number have substantial international living experiences, either through moving around with their parents, long-term travels, volunteering or living and studying abroad. They are between 25 and 35 years of age, are equally split along gender lines and the great majority are young professionals in technology, finance or business areas, as well as some self-proclaimed entrepreneurs. Quite a few are also between undergraduate and graduate studies, looking to gain work experience. About a third of the Fellows have some form of international relations or development study experiences, often focusing on business, economics or policy aspects, and almost all speak another language besides English. Most importantly for their Kiva assignment, Fellows believe, to varying degrees, in the power of microfinance to alleviate poverty through fostering microentrepreneurship.

The above information was collated from the personal webpages of 323 Fellows, who participated in the program between June 2007, when it began, and the end of 2010. As an important part of their placement, Fellows have to write bi-weekly blog posts for the official Kiva Fellows blog, which was started in 2008 by Kiva's first Fellows Coordinator who had a BA in Modern Literature and understood the power of language. For this chapter I analyzed, manually and with the help of research students, over 1,000 posts written by the 323 Fellows, first ordering their content into four broad categories of microfinance and Kiva; poverty and development; cross-cultural understanding; subjectivity; and identity. Keywords were established and searched for each category, and emic themes were also noted. While the blog contains many photos and a number of videos, I have focused here on the text rather than these images because words are the primary medium in which the blog communicates. To contextualize this narrative analysis, I conducted in-person and Skype interviews with the five Fellows posted at INM, the Indonesian Kiva partner microfinance institute (MFI) where I conducted field research between 2009 and 2011, and observed one Fellow's work at that organization.

This chapter uses a very different methodology from the previous chapter, where I carried out participant-observation at a microfinance tour. Reading and analyzing the blog posts of over 300 individuals gave me insights into a wide variety of experiences and allowed me to see which ones were representative of a Kiva Fellowship. These were mediated insights, but their reading was greatly helped by my in-depth knowledge of Kiva itself, by my interviews with the INM Fellows and by my observations of Heike, the resident Fellow at the time of my own research at INM. Especially the latter made me aware that what the blog posts could not provide were the unexpected encounters of fieldwork, the unprompted understandings that provide rich research details. On the other hand, blog posts afforded me the opportunity to represent Fellows' sentiments in their own words, as already written for public consumption. Consequently, all of the quotations in this chapter are from blog posts on the Kiva website (www.kiva.org/updates/kiva), accessed between January 2009 and December 2013, unless otherwise noted. Just like the photographers who produced the CGAP photos, Fellows are the creators of their representations of (Kiva-style) microfinance.

In my analysis, then, I regard Fellows as "volunteer tourists [who are] active narrators of their experiences" (Sin, 2009, p. 491). These experiences are expressed in their blog posts, which constitute a particular genre of writing that shapes what Fellows say and how they say it. Research on blogging in international development has identified two main purposes: allowing practitioners to reflect on their work practices and experiences, and engaging with an audience on the basis of shared interests (Ferguson et al., 2013). In addition, the Fellows Blog acts as a kind of corporate blog, as it is "part of the communication practices imposed by [Kiva's] top management" (Panteli et al., 2011, p. 366). Even though Fellows have great leeway in what they write about, as long as their posts relate in some way to microfinance, their blogging is prompted by Kiva managers, who see it as an important way of informing website visitors about Kiva's work in the field, cementing the support of current lenders and attracting new ones.

Blogs have been called "internet-based personal journals" (Panteli et al., 2011, p. 365) and "public diaries" (Lovink, 2008, p. 15). They are thus a personal affair, allowing bloggers to chronicle their experiences, ideas and other things in chronological order. This often results in reflexivity, which see bloggers engaging in a process of "incremental and public sense making" (Ferguson et al., 2013, p. 315). For Kiva Fellows, this sense-making becomes visible in their writings about the complexities of local poverty and the thorny questions of microfinance. However, blogging is also a public, socially mediated activity, and there is a tension in blogging as an "inherently personal medium in content while its reach extents to a potentially broad, public and largely anonymous audience" (Ferguson et al., 2013, p. 320). This is exacerbated by the fact that blogging is not a voluntary act for Fellows but a required part of their job. Audience is central to the process of blogging, as bloggers engage in virtual self-presentation and identity management (Panteli et al., 2011). The Kiva Fellows Blog has multiple audiences, encompassing family and friends, other Kiva Fellows, staff and lenders, and people interested in microfinance, all of whom are overwhelmingly sympathetic.[2]

While all of the Fellows' blog posts are written for public consumption, their tones range widely, from intensely personal accounts, especially of the experience of foreign places and encounters with borrowers, to very analytical descriptions of microfinance topics and MFI activities. Blogs also have an element of interactivity by allowing readers to post comments, which happens frequently. I am less concerned with this interaction in this chapter, but rather focus on the way in which these blog posts shine a light on the affective dimension of volunteering for microfinance organizations. In this context, affect bestows "an emotional sense of urgency ... and an injunction to action" (Adams, 2012, p. 201). While the Fellows' stories from the field can contribute to turning their readers into microfinance supporters, I am more interested here in the constitution of Kiva Fellows as such supporters. I show how being a Kiva Fellow mobilizes affective investments by first examining Fellows' accounts of their MFI placements and changing understandings of microfinance, poverty and development. I will then analyze their personal transformations and lastly their encounters with MFI staff and borrowers.

Kiva's Eyes and Ears

One afternoon I went with Heike, INM's Kiva Fellow at the time of my research, and other INM staffers to a village where she was delivering a health lesson to INM borrowers. In the car, I overheard a conversation between Heike and one of the loan officers, who in the course of it referred to Heike as a "volunteer." She sharply reminded him that she was not a volunteer but a Fellow, which meant a "higher standing" than a mere volunteer would have. When the loan officer (half jokingly) apologized, Heike explained that during their training in San Francisco, future Fellows had been told to insist on being called Fellows to reinforce their status as "official Kiva representatives" at the partner MFIs. However, when I interviewed Heike later, she prefaced her words by saying that she was not speaking in an official Kiva capacity but as a Fellow, which had to be made clear in my writing. Every single Fellow I spoke to repeated these same words, as asked to do by Kiva.

Kiva Fellows thus occupy an ambiguous middle ground between Kiva's headquarters in San Francisco and the partner MFIs in over 70 countries around the world. According to the Kiva website, the Kiva Fellow is an integral part of the Kiva Team, acting as Kiva's eyes and ears in the field and helping to extend limited resources to maximum effect. Kiva Fellows fulfill tasks set out in a Work Plan, defined by Kiva along with the host MFI. These include 1) Facilitate connections between Kiva's borrowers and lenders, 2) Assist communications and maximize the host MFI's partnership with Kiva, 3) Support Kiva's Mission, Product and Procedures.[3]

Fellows are volunteers in the sense that they are not paid by Kiva, but they clearly occupy a position of authority within the partner MFI, acting as agents of an organization that provides up to a third of the MFIs' microlending capital. This authority is reinforced by the Fellows' main task, which is to verify that the MFIs' Kiva borrowers are indeed who the MFIs claim them to be and that Kiva procedures are followed properly. As Heike put it, "Kiva Fellows are very demanding on the organization, but they can also help it be a better Kiva partner."

The Kiva Fellows website states that successful Fellows share, among others, an "enthusiasm for Kiva!, dedication to working in the field with a microfinance institution and a sincere interest in microfinance." When Fellows write about their motivations for becoming Fellows, they often talk about "wanting to give Kiva love" and "wanting to work for love, not the money." I have already analyzed Kiva's potential contribution to a political concept of love in Chapter 4, and here examine how this can be expanded through personal encounters with microfinance borrowers. One Fellow, a self-proclaimed Kiva Diva, wrote that she wanted to be a Fellow

> so that I could become a channel though which disadvantaged people could connect to a network of financial support thereby presenting them with a chance to improve their lives. It is a perfect opportunity that will enable me to pursue my true passions: traveling, experiencing new cultures, and being part of a noble cause which helps empower underprivileged individuals.

While Kiva's mission animates these statements, they also show Fellows' location within a current moral economy where working for poverty alleviation is a popular cause. Often, it is volunteer tourism that allows Northern publics to become everyday humanitarians and fulfill their ideals of making the world a better place (Mostafanezhad, 2013a).

Training Days

To make sure that Fellows are up to their tasks, they undergo a lengthy and rigorous selection process, which includes a substantial written application and Skype interviews with former Fellows and the Kiva Fellows Coordinator. About 25 percent of applicants are chosen, and subsequently have to take a United Nations Capital Development Fund online course about microfinance. Then they participate in weeklong intensive training at Kiva's headquarters, to be transformed, as one Fellow wrote, "from civilians into capable Kiva Fellows." The training not only teaches them the ins and outs of the Kiva process, but is also meant to prepare the Fellows for the physical, emotional and work challenges ahead of them. Sometimes they get to meet Flannery and Shah, and one Fellow recounted that "I felt like I was in the presence of celebrities, although their demeanor suggested that I was in every part their equal." Bob Harris, author of *The First International Bank of Bob*, who went through the training in 2009, recounted that JD, the Kiva Fellows Coordinator at the time, told them "every Fellow says that this training was their favorite part of the process. It's all downhill from there. You honestly have no idea what you're getting into" (quoted in Harris, 2013, p. 82). JD then ran through a list of possible dangers: traffic accidents, health issues, communication difficulties, police discrimination and sexual harassment, all summarized in the fact that many of the locations where Fellows will be placed feature on the US State Department's Travel Warning website as places where US citizens are discouraged from going. Then,

> JD's smile softened, turning compassionate and encouraging despite the difficult words. He continued that "we wouldn't send you there if we thought you couldn't handle it and come home okay. But the dangers are real and we will need you to keep your eyes open to stay safe."
>
> *(quoted in Harris, 2013, p. 82)*

Finally, JD assured them that they would all go from thinking that they had made the single worst decision of their lives to being convinced that the Fellowship was one of the best and most important experiences they will have had. The Fellows' blog posts bear witness to that transformation.

In their initial posts from the field, Fellows remember their training fondly. One of them, a public accounting consultant who was posted to Armenia in 2009, wrote that

> Last week's training was overwhelming to say the least – the community and caliber of relationships I established was completely unexpected. I thought I would go in and learn about my host MFI and the nuts and bolts of micro-finance, which I did. But what I really came away with was a family of Fellows, a group that will be my first level of support out in the field, and the few to truly understand my fellowship experience ... it is a group of extremely talented, motivated and compassionate people ... As training fades into the past and we are now officially "Kiva Fellows," I hope to keep that Kiva Love fresh in my mind. [When times get tough] I will also remember why I'm here, and why 49 others have willingly dispersed themselves across the globe at great sacrifice to help empower poor entrepreneurs as well as find out something about themselves.

Kiva Fellows, especially those of each cohort who undergo their training together, become another of Kiva's "affective collectivities" (Richard & Rudnyckyj, 2009,

p. 66), joined together not only by the shared experiences of long hours at Kiva HQ and long nights partying in San Francisco, but also by a shared passion for Kiva and its mission. They form a tight-knit group that becomes their first port of call for logistical and emotional support in the field, in part through commenting on each other's blog posts with advice and encouragement. When questions or problems arise, Fellows first discuss them with their cohort members, then with the wider Fellow community and lastly with Kiva staff. This line of command also means that the work of troubleshooting is outsourced to the volunteers, once again reinforcing the crucial work they do.

Before joining Kiva as its Fellow Coordinator, JD had been a Peace Corps volunteer, as have a number of Fellows. This important rite of passage for many young, civic-minded Americans shows "voluntarism as a classic component of a coming-of-age ritual that has become popular in American higher education" (Bornstein, 2012, p. 17; Fischer, 1998). The US culture of volunteering provides the meanings and practices that frame Kiva Fellows' work, which does not exist in a cultural vacuum (Mühlebach, 2011). There are other parallels. A 1999 brochure aiming to recruit Peace Corps volunteers to Africa contained the following poem: "You will learn lessons/Upon the dirt floor/Of a poor South African school/That you will never learn/Inside the ivy covered walls of/The finest American university" (cited in Mathers, 2010, p. 174). Kathryn Mathers shows that the "ethos of caring" that is promoted here presents international volunteering as an inner journey, whereby young Americans "can save themselves so much better under a tree in Africa than in an American classroom" (Mathers, 2010, p. 174). Similarly, a Kiva Fellowship is as much about an authentic experience of microfinance, in the process helping to spread its benefits, as it is about Fellows discovering something about themselves. This they can only do through their close interactions with distant others.

Kiva Works

Once Fellows arrive at their MFIs, it is their job to make them into better Kiva partners; or, as one Fellow described it, to "make myself irrelevant." While their primary, and favorite, task is to conduct Borrower Verification, whereby they visit randomly selected Kiva borrowers, check their details, tell them about Kiva and collect their stories, they also spend much time in the office, training field officers or HR personnel about Kiva procedures and helping to integrate financial information management and reporting systems. This can be tedious and somewhat disappointing. One Fellow remarked that "most of the time I look at the back of a computer. It wasn't exactly the vision I had when I dreamed of joining the ranks of Kiva Fellows." However, it is here that their backgrounds in business, finance, technology or management consulting come in handy. This does not necessarily make the job any easier. One management consultant described his training of field officers in Vietnam as an "emotional rollercoaster," which took him from enthusiasm to anxiety, chaos and frustration and finally relief when at the end of the day everybody had learned how to post borrower profiles.

The question of volunteer expertise is a thorny one in discussions of volunteer tourism, which mostly sees untrained young gap-year-style Northerners carrying out tasks, such as construction work, that sometimes take jobs away from locals. Their activities rest on and reinforce simplistic boundaries between a Third World, a bleak, helpless place of poverty and despair that is defined by its neediness, and a First World, whose enthusiastic young global citizens are seen to have the abilities and the right to meet this need. The results are equally simplistic ideas of development, which "legitimize the validity of young unskilled international labor as a development solution" (Simpson, 2004, p. 682). In other words, volunteer tourists "inappropriately take on roles of 'expert' or 'teacher' regardless of their qualifications, [which] can be seen to represent the neo-colonial construction of the westerner as racially and culturally superior" (Raymond & Hall, 2008, p. 531).

Kiva Fellows definitely do not fill this slot of untrained Northerners, as most of them have financial or technological expertise that is valued by their host MFIs. Still, the unequal power relations between Northern dispensers of aid and advice, no matter how appreciated, and Southern recipients of the same, persist. As temporary outsiders coming from a US organization that is a significant funder for especially smaller MFIs, Fellows often act as powerful change agents. Even at well-established MFIs this shift can be a struggle. One Fellow, who was placed at a large MFI in Honduras, described her job as bringing about "significant cultural change for the loan officers and MFI Kiva coordinators, who are suddenly asked to complete entirely new tasks that have never been part of their daily routine." She had to balance "being aggressive about getting Kiva onto the docket" with the need to be "delicate," also because the MFI's management asked her to motivate loan officers to find more borrowers that fit the Kiva requirements and to devote extra time to writing and uploading their profiles. What this Fellow, who prior to her Fellowship had undertaken research, travel and community health work in Latin America, took away was an understanding of the nuanced role of her position in the partner organization, something that she felt was not conveyed sufficiently during the training.

Another Fellow had to convince the leadership at her MFI that a dedicated Kiva coordinator should be hired, which she did, in true consultant style, by putting together a cost–benefit PowerPoint presentation showing that the MFI could save around US$18,400/year by getting 0 percent interest loans from Kiva. One INM Fellow I interviewed confirmed that some Fellows (albeit not her) are met with "a lot of resistance," especially when they are placed with MFIs that do not necessarily want a Fellow. In these cases, the oversight and verification part of the job is paramount, which can cause "political difficulties of the 'who are you to tell me to do that' kind" with MFI leadership. As a management consultant, she likened it to the high-pressure situations that are a daily part of her job. Not surprisingly, the Kiva Fellows website states that "a background in economics/finance/consulting will greatly enhance your ability to provide support to the host MFI." Fellows' surveillance has material implications for partner organizations. It was one of the first ever Kiva Fellows who discovered that Moses Onyango, the Ugandan pastor who had recruited Kiva's first seven borrowers, was committing fraud, which led to the withdrawal of all Kiva funds from the organization he had set up and the termination of the Kiva partnership (Flannery, 2009).

Sometimes mistakes complicate the already uncomfortable change process. When in 2010 several of INM's loans were posted as being delinquent on the Kiva website, the Fellow at the time had to admit that, even with her help, errors were made when INM started reporting repayment data on Kiva's internal site for the first time. Her blog post to all INM lenders gave a glimpse of the complexities of integrating MFIs into Kiva's technological infrastructure, also speaking to the digital gap between a Silicon Valley organization and small institutions in the global South, some of which did not even have broadband before they became Kiva partners. Unreliable electricity supply and intermittent connectivity further compound these challenges. Reporting errors can have consequences in the reputation-based and highly competitive environment of the Kiva website since they affect MFIs' risk rating. The Fellow's blog post also admitted, however, that some of these loans might actually have been delinquent, and a few days later she blogged about a microfinance-not-so-success story of a borrower who had taken a risk with a new, potentially more profitable line of business. The risk had not paid off and the borrower had to default on her loan, a rare occurrence on the Kiva site. It is precisely this opportunity to witness microfinance and its impacts first-hand that is cited by all Fellows as the main motivator for taking up a Fellowship.

Microfinance on the Ground

Learning how microfinance works on the ground is a central feature of the Fellowship. During their training, Fellows are warned that "four weeks in, microfinance sucks," which Kiva hopes will turn into a "well-rounded knowledge" of financial inclusion (quoted in Harris, 2013, p. 82). More than anything, however, a Kiva Fellowship provides a "visceral experience" of microfinance, according to the Fellow who had found a family during his training. In direct contrast to the virtual experience most Kiva users have, he described for his readers how his visits to borrowers in Armenian villages entailed trudging through muddy pigsties and their awful smell, which was very different from his prior work experience in financial services in New York. At the end of his fellowship he reflected that

> as a Kiva Fellow who has been lucky enough to see these borrowers and loans firsthand, it really has put "microfinance in Armenia" in perspective. Statistics turn into stories and you forget questions like "does microfinance really work?" and "why are interest rates so high?" as well as all of the other academic jargon that comes along with development. Instead, the human side continually reemerges as the defining thread of each borrower visit.

His Fellowship thus also provided a material critique to academic virtuality.

This shows that from the standpoint of their personal experiences, Fellows also address many of the thorny questions of microfinance, such as high interest rates, repeat and consumption loans, and MFI oversaturation and commercialization. In the process they explain to their readers how microfinance works on the ground in particular locations. What emerges is a picture of microfinance as a very site-specific practice, which is supported by posts of roving Fellows who have been placed at more than one MFI and often draw comparisons between them. In these posts, microfinance becomes nuanced, but is never questioned. Instead, initial idealistic hopes often turn into an appreciation of microfinance's "no-frills simplicity." Faced with incremental, "watching grass grow" kind of changes, Fellows become pragmatists who recall being told during their training that microfinance is but one tool for poverty alleviation. Often, this tool is described as a safety net, helping people to stay afloat and cope with what life throws at them rather than bringing about radical improvements. This can be frustrating to some Fellows who expect to see the almost miraculous changes presented by microfinance advocates like Yunus. One Fellow, posted in Honduras, wrote "I so badly want to see the extreme transformations that I have to make sure I am not fabricating it. Progress is so incremental, often non-existent." Another Fellow described his reaction to meeting his first Kiva borrower in Vietnam, who emphatically told him that her loan had not brought about any positive changes in her life, as getting a

> gut punch … I felt confused and frustrated. I knew that as a Kiva Fellow I wouldn't be hearing dramatic stories every time I met a client, but I didn't believe that I would have a client tell me that their loan hasn't helped much.

Here, affect's embodied quality nuances Kiva's electronic success stories.

For many readers of the Fellows Blog, who believe in Kiva's work, these posts become authoritative accounts of microfinance. If the ability to make representative statements comes from first-hand experience, acquired through immersion over longer periods of time, then Kiva Fellows' blog posts do offer legitimate glimpses at the complexities of microfinance. While such claims to immersive authority cannot be taken at face value (Pedwell, 2012), on a website that capitalizes on micro-profiles, *Fellows Stories from the Field*, as the Fellows Blog is officially called, go beyond one-paragraph descriptions. They show smart, dedicated and articulate young people grappling with complicated questions, not only about finance, but also about ethics, responsibility and their role in the world as temporary "Kiva ambassadors." Their accounts draw the reader in, as is manifested in the many comments most blog posts get. Nevertheless, MFIs and their staff and borrowers continue to be spoken for by Northern everyday humanitarians, who assume authorship over the former's stories. Just like borrowers have no part in creating their profiles, so Kiva "partner" MFIs cannot speak for themselves. Except for occasional short videos allowing the voices of MFI staff or borrowers to be heard, representation remains mediated and controlled by foreign Kiva experts.

Most of the Fellows' posts are framed as stories of entrepreneurial empowerment enabled by microfinance. They are introducing their readers to the variety of businesses people run in the global South and thereby contribute to a condensed understanding of local economies. Just like on the website, overwhelmingly these are stories of success, mostly modest, but sometimes spectacular. There are also more probing posts, focusing on market scenes where rows of stalls sell the same imported or handcrafted items, so that competition is a real issue. One INM Fellow framed it as a question of ticky tacky boxes looking all the same, in a tribute to San Francisco, Kiva's location.[4] He mused, "how any store owner can make a living when there are so few customers and so much competition is an absolute mystery to me." Another Fellow was "disconcerted" by the fact that a borrower in Cambodia had taken her children out of school so that they could help with her clothing business.[5]

One particularly reflexive post by the Fellow who had complained about too much computer time questioned the very heart of her own stories. Her post recounted an exchange she had with her mum, who edited her posts before they went public. The mother had a number of probing questions about two run-of-the-Kiva-mill borrower stories, wanting to know about profits, business tactics, scaling and green alternatives. The Fellow finished her reply to her mum by writing: "the complexity of beginning to answer to [sic] your questions feels like it is enough to break the hope that these stories begin to tell." She was worried

> that my responses are discouraging as I write them to my mum, I am even more concerned that they are discouraging as I write them for a wider audience. I don't worry that microfinance "isn't working." I worry that people will forget to ask what happens without it, I worry that people will give up on it.

The Fellow's concern touches on the need to ask the right questions, but ultimately reaffirms the pressure to tell microfinance's obligatory, albeit scaled back, success story.

It is therefore no surprise that there are very few tales of unsuccessful borrowers in the Fellows blog. It is in the small number of posts that describe how loan officers deal with late or missed payments that microfinance as microdebt, and the power relations within which it operates, comes most strongly to the fore. During her time at INM, Heike, who is a medical doctor by training, wrote a post dramatically titled "License to kill – similarities of being a doctor and a field officer." It tells the story of an INM client, who, after a number of successful loans, tried out a new business idea, which failed. The client's bankruptcy coincided with a severe illness of his wife, and Heike reflected on the hard job of the field officer having to collect every possible repayment, which she compared to a doctor having to break the bad news of a terminal illness. Her post ended on a hopeful note; upon the field officer's suggestion, the loan was completely written off by INM's management. What Fellows never seem to witness, however, or never choose to write about, are incidences of house-breaking, taking of personal possessions or other harassments of delinquent borrowers that have been described by academic researchers (Karim, 2011; Roy, 2010). Instead, for most Fellows microfinance gives borrowers choices and opportunities, but their success is not guaranteed.

No matter what the content of the story, it is always an invitation to make loans to the borrowers of the Fellow's MFIs. Often these are represented as a good investment into risk-rated investment products, a phrase that pierces the veil of Kiva's human stories and person-to-person illusion and brings its financial and competitive aspect to the fore. In parallel, Fellows' accounts of poverty, which often include the usual World Bank/UN statistics, are always framed by the relief brought by microfinance. One Fellow, a young woman from the United States who grew up in Colombia where her parents worked for a development organization, described the poverty she saw in Mexico as a "vulnerability to random acts of life or just plain dumb luck, rather than the economy." While this can lead to delinquent repayments, loans are nevertheless represented as "a little voice of hope and encouragement" in the face of the emotional strain that comes with poverty, a reminder not to give up. The Fellow did not explore why poor people might live in such vulnerable situations or the role economic systems play in perpetuating inequality. Another Fellow learned in Vietnam that, while it might not make sense to her that a family living in a house with holes in the roof would use a loan to buy a TV, the TV relieved them from constantly being reminded of their poverty. It also meant that the borrower's children would not be shamed because of their dirty and torn clothes when they went to the neighbor's house to watch TV.

More provocatively, one Fellow titled one of her posts "Slavery – abolished or reinvented?" She wrote about a woman in the Philippines who, in spite of taking out loans, is forced to sell her products to the same person who sells her the materials to make it. This means that she gets only a fourth of what she would get in the local market and makes $1/day in a country where the legal minimum wage is $5. For this Fellow, the borrower is "an exploited slave to this system," which includes her products being sold overseas with astronomical markups.[6] For her, microfinance is the "Robin Hood" of a world in which the rich get richer and the poor get poorer. "The best thing is, Robin (aka Kiva) doesn't need to steal, he simply asks anyone with a heart to lend $25. It's too easy." In Kiva land, it takes people with big hearts, who care about the fate of distant others, to bring justice to a world gone wrong.

Within this geography of poverty, Africa – Kiva's birthplace – occupies a special location, as a continent that is originally defined by its poverty but often ends up becoming a story about the resilience of the human spirit (Mathers, 2010). A Fellow in Uganda described that upon his arrival in Kampala, he realized that "Africa is poverty. Breathing, smelling, feeling; indeed, being among poverty is an assault on my sense of humanity and morality." Another Fellow in the Democratic Republic of the Congo wrote: "I had clearly fallen into the all-too-common trap of focusing on African tragedy and misery, rather than hope and ingenuity." His words seemed to come straight out of Bono's playbook, who declared "our habit – and we have to kick it – is to reduce this mesmerizing, entrepreneurial, dynamic continent of 53 diverse countries to a hopeless death-bed of war, disease, and corruption" (Bono, 2007). For Kiva Fellows, poverty might cease to be an undifferentiated global condition, but it remains defined as a lack of things that can be addressed through supporting businesses generating the capital to acquire what is missing (Mathers, 2010).

Often, the lives of the poor become part of Fellows' colorful travel accounts, which reveals that they are volunteer tourists after all. An Indian-American woman with extensive study and travel experiences in Latin America who was posted in Bolivia blogged about a trip to visit borrowers on the outskirts of Cochabamba. As she rode on the back of the loan officer's bike through green pastures dotted with cows and women in colorful skirts, she proclaimed "I love this part of the town." The loan officer replied in shock "I thought you would be horrified; this is the poorest section of town." She recounted:

> I suddenly felt ashamed, as if I were viewing this community like a sheltered tourist who did not fully realize or empathize with the economic realities of its inhabitants. But on the other hand, isn't it necessary to see the beauty in poor communities and its people? Isn't that what inspires me to help them? I realized that the conflict I was going through has something to do with the specific idea of poverty that the developed world has … These images [which are] those that are propagated by the media, are of dire poverty, filth and crime. This is most likely not a malicious attempt to malign other nations, but a reflection of the stories that sell. People are fascinated by extremes and probably like the reassurance that their own country is the best place to live. Then I realized why I was feeling conflicted – I did not want to be fascinated by my first exposure in Bolivia to what American ideology has taught me is Poverty: women in plaid skirts, men in farmer hats, donkeys, and dirt roads. I did not want to be a tourist of poverty. I realize now that that is not the reason I like the poor section of Cochabamba. On the contrary, I saw the care that went into the mini-farms and dairy businesses that the residents owned. I saw laughter, camaraderie and hard work. If this community of people did not find anything either wrong or shameful about how they lived, why should I? I had no reason to pity them or to be horrified at their "condition."

While the Fellow realizes the power of Western mainstream media to shape Northern publics' perception of poverty and the hierarchies this creates, this does not come with an awareness of the larger agendas of these representations or their role in perpetuating the current world order. Instead, affection for a beautiful but poor landscape of poverty assumes a redeeming quality that also implies people's contentment with their situation. What this Fellow saw were not so much impoverished lives but authentic ones, and therefore good ones (Mathers, 2010).

My definition of affective investments does not encompass the psychosocial notion of investment as "the conscious and unconscious reason behind a subject's adoption of particular subject positions and use of certain discourses" (Crossley, 2012, p. 239). Nevertheless, Crossley's analysis of volunteer tourists' engagement with poverty is helpful in understanding the Fellow's confusion. Crossley postulates three responses to poverty among the volunteer tourists she studied in rural Kenya. Most applicable to the sentiments expressed by the Fellow above, poverty becomes part of a "seductive landscape of Otherness, authenticity and the Exotic" (Crossley, 2012, p. 245). The landscape and its people are admired even though their poverty is recognized, leading to feelings of ambivalence. Here, poverty is put into an aesthetic and cultural framework and becomes part of consumable landscape. As one Fellow in Senegal proclaimed: "holy crap, I'm in the middle of a National Geographic spread." As a result, poverty's economic and social features are elided, which can also lead to its trivialization. Relatedly, poverty becomes a dismissible element in the lives of poor but happy people. Volunteer tourists are invested in this material poverty, which they contrast with social and spiritual richness and, most importantly, happiness. While this might help volunteers deal with their own anxiety, it romanticizes poverty and contributes to constructing the need for the volunteers' help (Crossley, 2012; Simpson, 2004).

Lastly, poverty acts as a force for the internal moral transformation of volunteers. Because poverty remains threatening and unsettling, they develop a sense of appreciation for the good fortunes of their own lives, which can also deal with any feelings of guilt the volunteers might have. This stance neutralizes poverty and turns it into something that can bring moral redemption by delivering volunteers from ignorance and ingratitude. In addition, an investment in poverty enables their status as helpers, or, in this case, as Kiva Fellows. As the Fellow who defined Kampala and Africa by its poverty continued:

> I lose myself in philosophical and conflicting thought: How does this happen? Is this a product of exploitation by wealthy nations and, if so, the result of the comfortable lifestyle I enjoy? I'm thankful, if not guilty, that I won the lottery of life at birth being born in America. Why did I elude such a miserable fate? Am I just lucky or do I hold an obligation? I question my reason for wanting to be here and wonder if I can endure three months. Surely I can last 12 weeks, these poor souls are serving a life sentence. Most have never left their village. At this moment, I realize my life was easier when I was unaware and unconcerned with such things as poverty. It's impossible to get that back.

For this Fellow, his encounter with poverty serves as a wake-up call, uneasily juxtaposing a belief in random luck with an awareness of banal complicity. For resolve, he turns to the story of Paul Farmer: if Farmer can live in Haiti year after year, then this Fellow can certainly survive a few months in Uganda. His blog post closes with a description of a young woman who is a shopkeeper of a clean, well-stocked store. Wondering whether she is a microfinance borrower and looking into her daughter's eyes restores "the hope and meaning of my [Kiva] Fellowship. I don't need to solve global poverty, but maybe – with luck – my presence here will help just one person triumph in her struggle over poverty." The microfinance version of the everyday humanitarian double bind holds out the promise of structural transformation, for one lender at a time. Of course, whether financial inclusion results in structural transformations remains hotly debated. The blog post also reveals that volunteering is not only an external journey but also an internal one, or more accurately, an external adventure that allows volunteers to go on an internal exploration as well.

Journeys of Self-Discovery

"Kiva is the ability to travel from your life into someone else's life." This statement neatly summarizes an important, albeit somewhat sidelined, aspect of the Kiva Fellowship. After a week of intense training and camaraderie in San Francisco, Fellows disperse to all corners of the world where they are roughing it for at least 4 months in often unknown, infrastructurally poor and linguistically challenging places. There, they are on their own and have to adjust to extreme climates, overwhelming traffic and pollution, challenging cuisine and work with complete strangers. The distant others and their lives are becoming real, sometimes uncomfortably so, and Fellows' performances of their identities includes intense negotiations with self and other.

Travelers' Tales

Often, volunteer tourists' choices of location are guided by a "geography of compassion," stepping up from the easy-to-handle Thailand to more challenging places like India and Africa (Mostafanezhad, 2013a, p. 326). By contrast, because most Kiva Fellows have extensive prior experiences of international travel, their locational preferences, which they can indicate on their Fellowship application form, are either guided by a desire to revisit places to which they have been or to explore new locations. This becomes especially interesting in the case of the rare Fellow who does not reside in the United States. A Mexican Fellow, for example, wanted to combine "a thorough learning about microfinance with a different and authentic travel experience" abroad, but was persuaded by Kiva leadership to work in Latin America, where her Spanish would be most helpful. Once she had warmed to this idea, she asked to be placed in Mexico and ended up in Chiapas.

This shows that Fellows are usually assigned a country and MFI based on linguistic abilities or previous travel experiences there.[7] In the end, the Mexican Fellow reflected that she discovered a completely new side of Mexico, which made her feel like a stranger in her own country. While for her the familiar became unfamiliar, most Fellows, very much like anthropologists, make the unfamiliar familiar for themselves and their readers. One of their main realizations is that while there is much that is different in the world, much is also the same, which is reinforced by occasional comparison to similar events or things in the United States.

Serving as a Kiva Fellow is about traveling and working off the beaten track, in the process "having the rare opportunity to get under the skin of a completely different culture," as one Fellow put it. Many Fellows comment in their blog posts that they have met people, seen places and done things that they would not have experienced "in a million years of traveling as a tourist." Even backpackers don't come that close to being deeply immersed in a particular geographic and social location. Nevertheless, backpackers' travel journaling provides a good guide for reading the many blog posts that talk about Fellows' adventures in foreign land. Not incidentally, backpackers increasingly use blogs as a low-cost, easy-to-use way to stay in touch with loved ones and other travelers (Panteli et al., 2011).

Just like the microfinance tourists to Chennai, Fellows experience their travels through their bodies. However, there is an important difference, because the Fellows' experience is embodiment on steroids. They cannot escape to the luxury of high-end hotels, air-conditioned buses and upscale restaurants as microfinance tourists do. Instead, from the moment they arrive, they are in the thick of overwhelming temperatures, noises and smells. The daily life of a Kiva Fellow is filled by the physical discomfort of being crammed into minibuses and makeshift taxis or bumping along on the backs of loan officers' bikes for hours; the disorientating searches for borrowers in urban mazes or rice paddies; the nights without fans, never mind air conditioning, and the nuisance of frequent black-outs. This can be extreme, as it was for an American Fellow, a recent college graduate with previous travel experiences to France and China, who was placed in Bénin:

> Africa. Bénin. It shattered my worldview, changed my perspective on life. It nearly undid me. I was at times stupefied by heat and pollution, tongue-tied by the language barrier, unable to process basic thoughts, uncomfortable from stomach ailments, so overwhelmed by poverty that I could not imagine how to improve the quality of life. But I was also fascinated by the many cultures, bonding with friends of every nationality, living each day full of adventure as it [sic] were my last, traveling, collapsing into bed bone-tired and loving it. Rediscovering my sense of wonder. My experience defies any easy summary, an attempt to put it in a box and file it away. It is living, breathing, still breaking out of my skin Africa.

Her blog post conveys the feeling of a young, white woman being thrown head first into urban Bénin, but it also shows that she was ultimately enriched by her experience. More concretely, what changes are Fellows' perceptions of the circumstances around them, so that in Togo the "huge chaotic spectacle becomes quotidian reality" and in Hanoi, traffic chaos becomes a "ballet of considerate motorists carefully navigating the streets with, not against, each other."

These descriptions also constitute proof of an authentic travel experience. Just as for backpackers, they show prowess and stamina and afford status within the close-knit community of Kiva Fellows. There is a distinct competitive tone to the blog posts: who has had the craziest taxi ride, eaten the grossest food, experienced the most extreme weather. And yet, this is a sanitized representation, with no mention of sex, drugs or excessive parties in the blog posts. Instead, "health risks, illnesses, eating habits and other bodily threats and practices are foundations often used to build identity narratives upon" (Elsrud, 2001, p. 609). Kiva Fellows show themselves to be tough, fearless and extremely adventurous. Sometimes, risks are real. Many Fellows write about becoming sick with malaria. When I interviewed Heike, she wore bandages on one of her arms, hands and legs; riding home on her motorbike one night she had been forced off the road by a bus, which did not leave her any option but to dive into the ditch. The bus driver never stopped, but helpful strangers assisted her. A few days after that interview, as we drove to her health training, Heike was in visible pain every time our car bumped over another hole in the unpaved road. Being in the final week of her Fellowship, for her the accident was a sign that it was time to go home. The MFI employees with whom Fellows work do not have that option. Various blogs talk about loan officers being in accidents or robbed at gunpoint, one of them right after she had safely deposited a Fellow on her bus home. What becomes visible in these accounts are the "post-colonial inequalities" that shape international volunteer work (Parreñas, 2012, p. 683).

In the end, Fellows' posts often become a declaration of love for their temporary homes. One young woman described it like this: "I fell in love today. It started out as an innocent crush, evolved into a dangerous infatuation and today turned into a full-blown, head-over-heels in love ... with Guatemala that is." While discovering the beauties and charms of foreign places, Fellows sometimes reflect on their own home countries. Gaining a "measure of perspective on it," as one Fellow put it, includes becoming grateful for life and especially material comforts back home. This is often paired with a sense of what one Fellow, quoting Warren Buffett, called "drawing the best tickets in the ovarian lottery." Volunteers come to feel lucky about the fortune of their own life circumstances. While this does not result in a "fatalistic faith in the 'luck of the draw'," it also does not usually lead to a discussion of the "structures and systems in which we all participate" (Simpson, 2004, p. 689). Rather, Fellows see themselves as using their luck "to help those who drew less fortunate tickets."

There are a few rare posts in which the Fellows' home country comes out last; one of them is Heike's post about "Seven Reasons to Fall in Love with Not-Perfect Indonesia." It starts by saying that "negativity, discontentment, racism, catastrophy-focusing, no interest in strangers. All this I know very well from home in Vienna but in Indonesia you can find right the opposite in the national spirit." The seven reasons that contributed to Heike's love at first sight with Indonesia are: personal friendliness and sincerity, a healing acceptance of cultural, linguistic and religious diversity, a contentment with and enjoyment of life, frankness and honesty, helpfulness, sympathies and natural beauty. What emerges is an image of Indonesians as people who truly, innately, care for other human beings. In the process, Indonesians become subtly othered, bearing their poverty with stoicism, dignity and happiness. As a German myself, I can understand Heike's sentiments and relate them to the particular Germanic character against which she is writing. Still, Heike's romanticization of her host country is not unique.

A young woman volunteer in Thailand stated that "When I reach America, I am going to hate it, everyone walks with their heads down, they don't look at each other. Lots of love, there is so much love here. I want to bring that back with me" (Conran, 2011, p. 1460). Once again, it is the loving character of poor but happy people that becomes a shining example to be followed by miserable and materialistic Northerners. The distant other becomes defined by love and care for those around them, which inverts the conventional aid relationship but ultimately does not undermine it. Furthermore, even when volunteers question the abundance and egoism of their home countries at first, they ultimately come to reaffirm it (Mathers, 2010). When they do return home, it is often as self-proclaimed "irreversibly changed" individuals.

Changing Selves

For many volunteer tourists, personal growth is part of their motivation for volunteering (Sin, 2009). This also holds true for Kiva Fellows. One Fellow "wanted to learn about microfinance, Ghanaian culture, common characteristics that make us human and myself." For Fellows, volunteering becomes a formative experience that "begins with shocks of pain or pleasure" (Turner, 1986, p. 35, quoted in Bornstein, 2012, p. 113). Travel is an intimate part of this experience, which gets ordered through travel blogs that also create a sense of continuity or "biographical whole" (Elsrud, 2001, p. 600). This is especially important given the disruptive and purposely challenging nature of volunteering abroad. One Fellow wrote:

> I have learned much about myself in the last few weeks. Traveling has a way of doing that to you. You are on an emotional roller coaster where one minute you have everything under control and the next you are completely lost.

To cope with this roller coaster, Fellows should be endowed with certain characteristics, which one Kiva Fellow enumerated as: enthusiasm (served with a smile), optimism (especially about microfinance's ability to change the world), fearlessness (in the face of roughing it in a foreign, unknown environment), compassion and empathy (allowing Fellows to connect with co-workers and borrowers). In their own eyes, Fellows, much like volunteers in Italy, exhibit "proper affect, a specific internal disposition that would translate into publicly useful action" (Mühlebach, 2011, p. 60). These personal attributes, and the ways in which they are strengthened or changed during a Fellowship, are socially structured through membership in the Fellows cohort and the larger Kiva organization (Bornstein, 2012). These provide guideposts for proper dispositions and conduct, producing a certain conformity to an ideal-type Fellow that is given expression in the blog posts.

Fellows' prior international experience, training and adventurous spirit do not prevent them from initially feeling like "bumbling cultural idiots," as more than one Fellow called himself. Being thrown in a new and often unfamiliar environment means that they have to "swallow pride and embrace awkwardness." Fellows "drink culture from a firehose" and "act like a sponge," in reference to the intensely immersive nature of their stay. As a result, "you are experiencing yourself amplified," with a heightened sense of self-awareness and place in the world. Some of the most difficult things for Fellows to leave behind are cherished Western values, foremost among them independence and timeliness. One Fellow, who was taking a break from his IT consultancy job in the United States, wrote:

> While grateful for (and in need of) all the help, if I'm honest I initially bristled a bit at the extent of my dependence. Generally, I had strived to be self-sufficient, to be independent – and now found myself in a position of vulnerability. My first week in Tajikistan required me to recognize that vulnerability and embrace the role of honored (and reliant) guest. It served as a reminder of how powerful a feeling it is to be helped – to be in a position of need and to have someone intercede on your behalf.

Overcoming (male) Western expectations of independence allowed this Fellow to recognize not only the positive side of receiving help, but also the unequal relationships it sets up between its giver and receiver. Becoming vulnerable is seen as a way to facilitate "unlearning," leading to "knowing that transforms the self who knows" (Bartky, 1996, p. 179). Acquiring cultural competency thus includes pushing one's comfort zones and engaging with others from positions of (temporary) weakness, which has the potential to provide an "affective route towards greater social justice" (Pedwell, 2012, p. 170). This process necessitates a critical awareness of how the experience of personal vulnerability and reverse caring relations might apply to the structures of international development relations in which Kiva is embedded. Only few Fellows showed this awareness.

A part of personal transformation is coming to terms with constantly being labeled a foreigner. While some Fellows write about enjoying the VIP status, others are more ambivalent. A Fellow in Ghana wrote about being called *obruni*, "a word that induces feelings of happiness, anger and indifference, all at the same time." Other Fellows assumed the status of "mini-ambassadors for the U.S.," especially in places where Americans are a rare sight. Fellows thus also negotiate their national identities, which more often than not evoke pride (Mathers, 2010). This was especially so in 2008, when many blog posts of Fellows working in Africa talked about reactions to the election of President Obama.[8]

Often the relations with distant others are compounded by the travails of travel, which can lead to intense transformations. One Fellow wrote that living in Cambodia is "frustrating and emotionally and physically draining. But at the same time, there is something incredibly … cathartic? … about not having every convenience handed to me." Although she was not sure whether cathartic was the exact word she was looking for, it is a helpful one in understanding the experience of a Kiva Fellowship. "Related to emotional release following the witness of tragic events that lead to a moral influence on the person that is later transferred into virtuous action," catharsis has been connected to volunteer tourism before (Zahra & McIntosh, 2007, p. 115, drawing on Aristotle). It can occur when volunteer tourists have profound interactions with distant others and confront their suffering, which provokes the emotive reactions that many Kiva Fellows, and other volunteer tourists, describe. Cathartic events have a long-lasting and life-changing impact and reinforce volunteer tourists' desire to do good in the world. The Fellow posted to Kampala described his desired outcome for his Fellowship as: "I hope I will return [home] a better man – wiser, more humbled and compassionate, and with greater clarify [sic] as to my purpose and priorities." Volunteering abroad becomes the road to self-knowledge, growth and transformation into a better everyday humanitarian.

Sometimes this growth can lead to a change in profession. Indeed, many Kiva Fellows either take time off from their current job to re-evaluate where it leads them or quit their jobs outright. The Fellow who wrote about finding a Kiva Fellows family and meeting pig farmers in Armenia reflected at the end of his Fellowship that

> Kiva was a catalyst for me to totally switch what I was doing and get involved in more microfinance as well as socially conscious work. My background [in public accounting] was relevant for becoming a Kiva Fellow, but at the same time, I don't know of a better way to have leapt so far away from what I was doing to enter a new industry.

Being a Kiva Fellow affords cultural capital; one Fellow reflected that "simply stating that I had been a Kiva Fellow, more often than not, gains instant recognition and respect from people all over the world."

A Fellowship can also act as an important CV booster. Some repeat Fellows have obtained jobs with Kiva itself, so that the Fellowship program becomes a recruiting tool for the organization. For students, it can provide much needed practical experience akin to internships. For others, it helps when looking for a job post-fellowship. A woman interviewing for a position with a top management consulting company found that her interviewers were much more interested in her Kiva experience than in her prior consulting expertise. Another former Fellow wrote that

> aside from personal bragging rights, excellent stories and epic fun and wild times, Kiva was very useful for me in my job search ... Employers were equally impressed with and interested in Kiva as they were in my internship. It shows initiative, independence, a taste for adventure and trying circumstances ... Huge Cool factor. People love it.

In a table produced by Kiva that looked at the top five industries in which Fellows work before and after their Fellowship, Finance and Accounting dropped from no. 1 before to not even being among the top five after any more, just as Government and Public Policy dropped out of the top five. Not surprisingly, Consulting was present in both columns and International Development and Microfinance went from no. 2 before to no. 1 after. In fact, the top three industries Kiva Fellows work in upon their return from the field are development-related, including social entrepreneurship and social change. This clearly shows that the Fellowship succeeds not only in mobilizing affective investments among Kiva Fellows, but also transforms many of them from everyday humanitarians into development professionals.

Neoliberal Fellowship

Volunteer tourism has been described as a "mini-mission … a journey to fulfill the soul, spirit and stewardship" (Brown & Morrison, 2003, p. 77), which is a reminder of its descent from missionary journeys (Mostafanezhad, 2013a). Much as modern humanitarianism is a secular extension of early Christian concerns with the welfare of distant others (Redfield & Bornstein, 2010), so volunteer tourism is a secularized version of caring at a distance for the bodies, minds and sometimes souls of today's poor people. When some Kiva Fellows describe their decision to join up as "taking a leap of faith," this does not (usually) refer to religious faith. It rather points to a suspension of rational, self-interested calculation – because why would one otherwise leave a well-paying job in the middle of the biggest recession in decades to go to a place that one has previously not even heard of and volunteer for 4 months?

Similarly, and not unlike their missionary predecessors, Kiva Fellows see themselves as being in the business of spreading love, albeit of a micro-financial rather than religious kind. As a former IT Director, who spent his childhood in Beirut until the war forced his family to emigrate to the United States, wrote about his Fellowship in Armenia:

> I have recently become a Kiva Fellow as my way of giving "Kiva Love" to Kiva partners, and borrowers by visiting them, getting to know them and understanding how I can help "define, measure, analyze, improve and control" the processes that can place needed resources in the hands of Kiva borrowers. Creating this connection between Kiva partners, lenders and borrowers is my way of starting a "love affair." Instead of waiting for love to miraculously come to us, we need to reach out and first and foremost make ourselves lovable. This is usually accomplished by doing unto others what we would have them do unto us. It's simpler than we sometimes think.

What is interesting about his post is not only its affective language, but that such affect, culminating in feelings of love – which English-speakers articulate quite liberally – is to be achieved through calculative management processes with the aim of facilitating financial flows. Neoliberal logics do not disappear, but Kiva has managed to infuse this rationale with affect, which in turn contributes to its success.

Caring for others is central to the idea of fellowship; one Fellow exhorted the readers of her post to "keep caring." What she liked most about Kiva had nothing to do with money, but with its realization of the fundamental human values of caring that are shared by people the world over. Caring about distant others, then, becomes central to Kiva's mission and to the Fellowship, in yet another affective sleight of hand that makes the organization's financial dealings invisible.

Like volunteer tourism in general, Fellows' practices of caring and sharing are animated by compassion, empathy and intimacy. However, there are important differences to the normative volunteer experience that brings young Western women, who make up 80 percent of all international volunteers, to the global South, mainly to work with infants and children in orphanages and schools (Mostafanezhad, 2013b). This gendered practice articulates women's supposed innate caring abilities with children as prime subjects of humanitarian compassion. Kiva Fellows do not look for connections of the cute and cuddly kind, but contribute technological, business and financial skills to their host organizations. Consequently, there are as many male as female Fellows. This does not mean, however, that affect is absent. It is created through intense encounters with MFIs' staff and especially borrowers, which are shaped by the larger politics of international development: "where and to whom volunteer tourists direct their compassion is reflective of and expands tendencies of modern humanitarianism" (Mostafanezhad, 2013a, p. 3). In their desire to have an authentic experience of microfinance, Fellows forge affective human connections that make them feel that "they were really there" (Parreñas, 2012, p. 679).

In the Company of Loan Officers

Fellows' performance of "relational labor" (Mühlebach, 2011, p. 65) takes on particular contours in comparison to the work of MFI loan officers. Similar to the Niti loan officers that impressed the microfinance tourists in Chennai, in the Fellows' unanimous assessment, loan officers are the "unsung heroes" of the Kiva story, the dedicated, tireless and inspiring workers who put in endless hours, never complain and always go the extra mile for their assigned borrowers. Often, this extra mile is the so-called last mile of microfinance, when loan money has to be brought to borrowers and repayments collected, often on a weekly basis. Loan officers themselves "use powerfully affective ties created through everyday interactions to pressure women into payment by calling on the obligations of the debt relationship" (Kar, 2013, p. 488).

Fellows often accompany field officers on these trips to carry out their own borrower verification and journal updates. Tales of such travel abound in the blog posts, recounting bumpy motorcycle rides, cramped taxis and long walks. These stories again show how exciting and authentic the Fellowship adventure is. More importantly, through juxtaposing the Fellow's painful exhaustion at the end of the day to the loan officer, who is still smiling and sometimes on his or her way to the office to complete paperwork, the latter emerges as a financial inclusion *übermensch*.

In addition, descriptions of long, arduous and sometimes dangerous travel convey how difficult it is to reach remote borrowers. Having to drive 3 hours to collect US$11 in repayment reinforces the common justification for high interest rates and legitimizes microfinance in the process, just as it shows that these borrowers would not have access to financial services were it not for the MFI and its dedicated staff. Implicit is the call for Kiva lenders to continue to support the MFIs' important work, and provide jobs for dedicated loan officers, through continued lending on Kiva.

MFI staff is often described in affective terms. One Fellow wrote: "I adore my [MFI] family, and am beyond finding the right words to convey my gratitude for what I have gained through this experience." The language of kinship is also invoked by MFI employees; one Fellow recounted how during the goodbye party his MFI in Cambodia gave for him, the head of the organization said "you came here a stranger, but just in a short time you became family." Anthropological studies have shown that kinship is a contested terrain, but in the quotations above it connotes relations of love and care. The young woman whose life was changed by her time in Bénin even invoked supernatural beings in her description of the MFI staff as "angels who showed me the true meaning of caring for others" through their intense devotion to their work and through keeping her, the *yovo* in their midst, safe.[9] The importance of the latter became apparent when 2 days after her departure from Bénin, a Peace Corps Volunteer was killed for no apparent reason. Once again, the caring relationship becomes reversed, and hosts become care-givers par excellence.

Sometimes as a token of gratitude, Fellows give their hosts Kiva gift certificates. After he and his colleagues had become Kiva lenders themselves, the director of an MFI in Cambodia emailed the Fellow who had given him the certificate:

> When we click lend, we feel proud to help people really need money for business. We chose to lend Amato [a woman with a child care business in Fremont, California] because she is a widowed mother of two, has always loved children and believes her mission in life is to help them. Women and children are the first priority in my mind, as well as clients that Maxima targets. We will continue to lend more as we have committed within our management and staff to have the art of contribution.

These Cambodian lenders made similar affective identification to Kiva lenders living in the global North. They were also excited about being able to lend to someone in the United States, as a way to give back, thereby seemingly fulfilling Flannery's dream that one day, people in the global South will be lending to people in the global North (Flannery, 2007). However, a group of Cambodians lending to a Mexican-American woman only creates a facade of equivalence. It does not level the economic playing field, as Kiva's leadership claims, but shows that there are inequalities within all countries and that individual stories only create the illusion of systematic change.

Encountering Borrowers

Working alongside MFI staff pales in comparison to Fellows' encounters with borrowers, however. As part of their job, Fellows have to meet, per week, at least 15 borrowers whom their MFI has posted on Kiva, to verify their details and write journal updates. These meetings are cited by all Fellows as by far the favorite part of their job, even if it is also the most physically and emotionally taxing one. Fellows are invariably deeply affected by meeting borrowers. One Fellow, an older American who became a Fellow with his wife after riding their bikes from the United States to Argentina, and who was working for an MFI serving indigenous women living in "incredible poverty" in the highlands of Guatemala, recounted that

> as I came home after the day of interviewing, the women's stories, tears, smiles and laughter stuck deep in my soul. I will never be the same, and I am so thankful for being able to have a day like this.

The women's stories of hardship and survival allowed this Fellow to be a more empathetic person, similar to the way in which microfinance tourists were changed by their encounters in Chennai and sponsored children enable Americans to be better Christians (O'Neill, 2013). Empathy can have a "radically unsettling" effect, which feminist scholars see as "potentially generative of both personal and social change" (Pedwell, 2012, p. 166). This happens through responding to the experience of others with greater understanding and through recognizing one's complicity in perpetuating the structures that maintain poverty. While all Kiva Fellows write about the first element of this process, the second is far more rare.

This is partly because finding appropriate feelings in the face of borrowers is not always straightforward. One Fellow argued that "empathy is fundamental, but emoting pity is condescending and counterproductive. It's almost always a delicate trade-off." Humanitarian sentiments are a mixed bag, and young middle-class Americans coming face to face with hardship and poverty often feel ill-equipped to respond properly. One Fellow returned from a visit to a slum for internally displaced Colombians in Cartagena, and especially from his encounter with a woman borrower who had arrived there with nothing after fleeing the violent interior of the country, "haunted and with an enraged sense of justice in the world." This former Goldman Sachs risk analyst "choked back tears" during the interview with the borrower and let them flow afterwards, also in the face of feeling "overwhelmingly thankful" that the MFI could provide the woman with a loan and a basic house. Thus, feelings are never clear-cut, and positive and negative emotions mingle as Fellows experience pleasure and pain as they encounter human beings who have often suffered deprivation and violence (Bornstein, 2012; Mühlebach, 2011).

Some sentiments dominate more than others, however. Only a few Fellows write about feeling anger, which is absent from the larger international development discourse as well. The closest Northern publics come is indignation, which blames the perpetrators of injustice (Boltanski, 1999). This feeling comes from a realization of historical or banal complicity: "in its most powerful manifestation, complicity transforms these emotions, often regarded as introverted modes of feeling towards suffering, into the more extrovert and assertive emotion of indignation" (Chouliaraki, 2010, p. 111). The great majority of Fellows do not express indignation in their blogs, and those who do never call for action against injustice. Kiva does not promote activism among its Fellows, lenders or borrowers. Rather, what are needed according to the organization are more loans. Similarly, Fellows' feelings are framed by their assignment to facilitate financial inclusion, and operating outside these limits seems impossible. Instead, microentrepreneurship enabled by Kiva-cum-MFI loans is presented as the only answer to alleviate the poverty of poor people, which has already been defined as a problem of lack of money. The poor themselves are always encountered and represented as tireless, hardworking microentrepreneurial borrowers.

Interpretations of what this means differ among Fellows. One Fellow wrote that any of the borrowers she met in the Philippines would qualify as contestants on Donald Trump's show "The Apprentice." This reference to the American icon of successful entrepreneurship echoes Yunus' notion of the poor as always already innate entrepreneurs. By contrast, another called poor people "necessity entrepreneurs" because they were often pushed into informal work by unemployment, the death of family members or the need to support families. Several Fellows talked about the difference between North American, and especially Californian, ideas of entrepreneurship as risk taking and innovation, and the poor people they met, who could not afford to take risks but more often than not used their loans to enlarge their inventory or to buy in bulk to hedge against inflation. These are important discussions in microfinance, framed as a debate between advocates of microentrepreneurship and living-waged formal labor (Karnani, 2007).

Most Fellows clearly fall into the first camp, and each Fellow has at least one post about an exceptional, unique and often very successful entrepreneur: a man who runs a small health-food business in the land of meat, rice and soup that is Colombia; a Cambodian woman who turned her loan not into one but three businesses and immediately understood and was interested in Kiva; a Palestinian woman who moved her clothing shop from her house to a nearby refugee camp to take advantage of the foot traffic through its market; or a young divorcee in Ghana who sold porridge in the morning, tailored clothes in the afternoon and sold fabrics to other vendors in between. As one Fellow put it, "these are the borrowers we all love to read about"; they are the lifeblood of the Kiva website and the living proof that microfinance works. They also leave Fellows inspired, humbled, "dizzy with humility" and celebrating the "amazing and inspiring ways" in which borrowers accept the hardships of their lives. In the process, Fellows romanticize the ability of poor individuals to survive, sometimes against all odds, and to be at peace with their fates. Instead of rage or anger, there is acceptance and admiration. On the Kiva Fellows Blog, the grand humanitarian emotions are alive and well. Fellows celebrate borrowers' ability to fend for themselves and their families, to make a living instead of succumbing to daily struggles. They very rarely ask why people should have to live like this in the first place, and they are not asking their readers to pose that question either.

This, then, is the limit of reflexivity on Kiva and the greatest shortcoming of the Fellows Blog. Similar to microfinance tourists, there are certain questions that cannot be asked. In the case of Kiva Fellows, this limitation is not an issue of overscheduled timetables or group conformity, however. Rather, it is the result of Kiva's relentless focus on microfinance, and of the larger financialization of poverty that makes Kiva's work possible. In order to promote microfinance as its solution to poverty alleviation, Kiva defines poverty as a financial problem manifest in the absence of money or of opportunities to make money (Schwittay, 2014). This problematization forecloses other discussions that might lead to other solutions.

Fellows' visits to borrowers are also the prime location for "the consumption of intimate experiences [that] is at the heart of volunteer tourism" (Conran, 2011, p. 1459). These are often embodied. One (male) Fellow wrote of spontaneously kissing an older African borrower on her cheek at the end of their conversation, which elicited shrieks from the gaggles of kids hanging around. Another talked of the Ghanaian custom of men holding hands for several seconds after a handshake and described his own discomfort when this happened to him while walking through a crowded market. There are many stories (and pictures) of hugs and other physical closeness. In such interactions between bodies, Fellows experience affect or "intra-action, in which the act of connecting produces subjects in relation to each other" (Parreñas, 2012, p. 682, drawing on Haraway). This becomes even more important when linguistic communication is restricted because Fellows don't speak borrowers' languages. However, there are exceptions to this lovefest.

Kiva Love, Interrupted

Some borrowers are not happy about being interrupted during their work to tell their stories to complete strangers. Often, they have been interviewed before and were promised things that never materialized. They are wary of having their stories taken from them. At other times, intimacy is not welcomed, but recognized as potentially intrusive and disturbing. One Fellow, on her visit to a borrower in Nicaragua, found

> an older woman in a nightgown opens the door to us, my exuberant colleague recognizes our intrusion and apologizes for the disturbance. We sit in the sala to explain what a journal update is, how Kiva is an odd funding entity that wants to know her dreams. She rocks back and forth, comfortable in her own home but not in light of our probing questions. She is tired. I cannot pick her out of a family picture resting on the coffee table. The cast on her left wrist rests on a pillow in her lap. She is thin and her movements are those of someone who is more than just tired. I am struck not by her sadness, but

by her honesty, her resolution. I sit in front of her embarrassed to be here as a business woman. She does not look to me for pity. As a business woman, she answers my questions. I am more grateful for Kiva's oddity, for its requirement that the practice of business recognizes this dignity. We ask a woman with cancer what are her dreams. She is 66 and says with equal pragmatism that she has no dreams and that her loan payments are never late.

The Fellow is clearly uncomfortable with her uninvited intrusion into the borrower's "ordinary affects" (Stewart, 2007) and her interrogation about the borrower's business. At the same time, it is the business that allows the Fellow to attribute dignity to a tired, worn-out cancer patient. Ultimately, the Fellow retreats behind the fact that the borrower is never late with her payments, so all is well in spite of appearances to the contrary. We do not know whether the Fellow asked how the woman was able to make her payments even though she is visibly unwell or what sacrifices she might be making to be able to report that she always pays on time.

The post also highlights that borrowers usually remain the object of empathy. The only feeling that is ascribed to them is gratitude, for strangers listening to them, lending them money, caring about them.

> The implication is that poor people's efforts to generate means of basic subsistence for their families mean that they do not have time or need for affective life, but also that it is inconsequential whether or not they experience emotional journeys. [Here], empathy functions as a capacity of those who are already privileged.
>
> *(Pedwell, 2012, pp. 172–173)*

A dialogic empathetic engagement is rare in situations where one party comes with queries aimed to fill questionnaires, verify identities and elicit stories of business success.

One question that has the possibility of opening up a dialogue is about borrowers' dreams, which all Fellows are required to ask. Sometimes the answers are what Kiva is looking for. One Vietnamese woman said without hesitation that her dream was to travel and visit lenders to say "thank you." A woman in the Ukraine talked about being an artist.

> In the life of a Kiva Fellow, an experience like this is golden. I was beyond excited that [she] was able to link her loan to her dream by explaining that when her business was more sustainable, she'll have more time to pursue her favorite pastime.

But more often than not, Fellows write about being taken aback when they realize that many borrowers only want to move ahead, grow their business, send their kids to school and maybe improve their homes. For these Fellows, these are modest aspirations, not higher dreams that would show borrowers being confident about a much better future. Ironically, it is at these moments, when hopeful responses should be elicited, that the realization of the trying circumstances in which many borrowers live really sinks in and the limits of microfinance and of Kiva become visible. The cancer patient cited above has no dreams whatsoever. One Fellow recounted how a loan officer told her about a conversation he had with a young boy, who wanted to grow up to be as strong as his father, so that he could carry heavy boxes like him. The loan officer commented that "the worse part of poverty here is that it takes away people's ability to dream." The Fellow answered that maybe the boy should not be judged by what he thinks would make him happy, but the loan officer corrected her: the boy dreamed about carrying boxes because that was all he knew; "he is so poor that he doesn't know what else to dream about." Not surprisingly, the Fellow concluded her blog post by saying that microfinance gives people the chance to live a better life and thereby the ability to dream. Fellows hang on to these ideas, not wanting to pierce the Kiva veil even when it starts to rip.

A Vietnamese-American Fellow wrote that her interview with a Vietnamese borrower went well until she asked about her dreams. She recounted that

> The borrower's eyes became soft with sadness. This completely caught me by surprise. Dreams usually generate smiles. [She] looked away and told me that her family has encountered much hardship since the passing of her mother . . . I could see through these words that it was the memory of her mother combined with the family's current financial struggles that brought tears to her eyes. I turned off the camera. I could not imagine grieving the loss of a parent and worrying about how the loss will impact family finances at the same time. It must feel like the weight of the world is on your shoulders. *Chia Buon* is a Vietnamese saying that means "to share sadness." The words are said in a low tone and the phrase itself sounds sad. In Vietnam, people will offer to share another person's grief and sadness. My imagination tells me it's like splitting up the cloud of sadness into puzzle pieces and distributing them across the universe, until the pain no longer exists. Of course, that is not reality. Despite anyone offering to *chia buon*, [her] sadness, just like yours and mine, cannot be easily delegated to others. I suppose then, it's more of a reminder to someone that they are not alone and that in the bigger picture, we are all one people. Then perhaps, stories that connect us to one another, no matter the distance, helps us *chia buon*.

Here, it is not anger but sadness that makes a rare occurrence and thereby interrupts the positive Kiva story. In response, Fellows come to bear witness to distant others' struggles. They thereby partake in the making of a common humanity, which is one of the leitmotifs of the Fellows Blog. The fundamental message of its posts is that we are all human, that we all strive for the same things and that some of us come out on top, because of lucking out in the ovarian lottery. This comes with an obligation to help those who are less lucky, through lending on Kiva. Even though Kiva Fellows are surrounded by the effects of global structural inequalities every day during their Fellowships, they do not seem to be aware of them. One of the reasons for this is the posts' focus on individual borrowers' stories, on the individuals in the MFIs that serve them and on Kiva as a collection of individuals that can assist them through continued lending. This up-close vantage point, especially when combined with the limits of Kiva's discursive frame and microfinance's obligatory success story, precludes recognizing larger structures for what they are.

This observation aligns with broader critiques of volunteer tourism, which have focused on its unequal power relations between carer and cared for (Sin, 2010), its hierarchical binaries between givers and receivers (Mostafanezhad, 2013b), its simplification of poverty and development (Simpson, 2004) and its neat fit with a neoliberal framework that cannot address poverty's structural conditions (Conran, 2011). The affective underpinnings of volunteer tourism are not sufficient to create systemic change, as the "politics of personal feeling cannot address the institutional reasons for injustice" (Woodward, 2004, p. 71). And yet, as "a border zone where intimacy scrapes up against development" (Conran, 2011, p. 1464), international volunteering, and especially a Kiva Fellowship, is a more complicated affair. On the one hand, Kiva Fellows do not conform to many of the shortcomings of gap-year-style voluntourists: they provide sought-after expertise, they often make sustained and useful contributions to the MFIs where they work and they do not perpetuate the usual relations of charity dependency (although they can create new, financial dependencies). On the other hand, and more broadly, while volunteering can enhance distinctions between groups, it can also contribute to overcoming them (Bornstein, 2012).

Often, local hosts become care-givers, keeping Fellows safe and sane. By inverting some of the conventional development relations, this gives volunteers insight into what it means to be dependent and cared for and shows them that the people whom they have come to help are equally capable of helping them and by extension themselves. A political concept of love can also work toward Kiva, which builds connections that invite care for its lenders and volunteers. This can foster Fellows' awareness of local abilities and initiatives and a simultaneous questioning of outside aid. In this way, volunteering can lead to an emerging critical consciousness that can inform more complex cultural understanding and participation in social change movements and public service (McGehee, 2002; McIntosh & Zahra, 2007). For this to happen, however, volunteer tourists need to extrapolate from their personal experiences to larger structures of power. This in turn necessitates a critical engagement with what they encounter, asking not only how poor people are able to make a living, but why they have to live in poverty in the first place.

While the Kiva Fellows provide moving accounts of their encounters with poverty and resilience, struggle and hope, they only very occasionally ask the hard questions that would deny them the possibility of always arriving at microfinance as the solution to the difficult circumstances they are witnessing. Instead, posts would provide historical accounts instead of local cultural snapshots and talk of global trade inequities rather than micro-economies, showing the critical awareness of their writers. But is that not asking too much of the Kiva Fellows Blog called *Stories from the Field*? Blogs kept by academics show that nuanced analysis is possible within the truncated space provided by this medium. But what about a blog kept by practitioners, not researchers, by individuals who want to inform, not educate? Kiva Fellows fall into the former group, and their blog posts aim to create and support a "community of like-minded people" that is manifest in the many, over-whelmingly positive comments to the Fellows posts (Lovink, 2008, p. 21). Kiva is in the business of providing online microloans, and the Fellows and their stories are a crucial part of it. What then can we ask of their posts? The stories they tell speak more than anything to the Fellows' dedication to their task of furthering Kiva's mission of connecting people through microfinance to alleviate poverty. Con-sequently, "the emotional ties built through [a Kiva Fellowship] have a potency that should not be underestimated. The fact that [Fellows' representations and prac-tices] produced through these are partial does not make the acts themselves so" (Mühlebach, 2011, p. 76).

Notes

1 Retrieved November 7, 2013, from www.kiva.org/annualreport.
2 All of the quotations in this chapter are from blog posts on the Kiva website (www.kiva.org/updates/kiva), accessed between November 2010 and December 2013, unless other-wise noted. All blog posts are in English. Occasionally Fellows with non-English mother tongues blog in French, German or Spanish, but these blogs are always translated into English as well.
3 Retrieved August 25, 2010, from www.kiva.org/fellows.
4 Drawing on a 1962 folk song about San Francisco.
5 Karim (2011) reports the same for a particularly successful Grameen borrower-cum-money lender she encountered in Bangladesh. However, while the latter saw her kids learning her trade as much more promising for their future than going to school, the borrower in Cambodia needed her children's help to get her shop off the ground.
6 Interestingly, Yunus was prompted to start the Grameen Bank by a similar situation (Yunus, 1999). He lent the woman a small amount of his own money so that she did not have to buy her materials from the middleman any more.
7 There are also roving Fellows who cover a number of organizations and countries within one Fellowship period.
8 Politics were otherwise remarkably absent from the Fellows Blog, with the exception of the 2007 post-election violence in Kenya and some posts about the Rwandan genocide.
9 *Yovo* is the term Béninois use for foreigners.

Bibliography

Adams, V. (2012). The other road to serfdom: Recovery by the market and the affect economy in New Orleans. *Public Culture, 24*(1), 185–216.
Bartky, S. (1996). Sympathy and solidarity: On a tightrope with Scheler. In D. Meyers (Ed.), *Feminists rethink the self* (pp. 177–196). Boulder, CO: Westview Press.
Boltanski, L. (1999). *Distant suffering: Morality, media and politics*. Cambridge: Cambridge University Press.
Bono. (2007, July). Guest editor's letter. *Vanity Fair*.

Bornstein, E. (2012). *Disquieting gifts: Humanitarianism in New Delhi*. Palo Alto, CA: Stanford University Press.

Brown, S. & Morrison, A. (2003). Expanding volunteer vacation participation: An exploratory study on the mini-mission concept. *Tourism Recreation Research, 28*(3), 73–82.

Callanan, M. & Thomas, S. (2005). Volunteer tourism: Deconstructing volunteer activities within a dynamic environment. In M. Novelli (Ed.), *Niche tourism: Contemporary issues, trends and cases* (pp. 183–200). Amsterdam: Elsevier.

Chouliaraki, L. (2010). Post-humanitarianism: Humanitarian communication beyond a politics of pity. *International Journal of Cultural Studies, 13*(2), 107–126.

Conran, M. (2011). They really love me! Intimacy in volunteer tourism. *Annals of Tourism Research, 38*(4), 1454–1473.

Crossley, E. (2012). Poor but happy: Volunteer tourists' encounters with poverty. *Tourism Geographies: An International Journal of Tourism Space, Place and Environment, 14*(2), 235–253.

Elsrud, T. (2001). Risk creation in traveling: Backpacker adventure narration. *Annals of Tourism Research, 28*(3), 597–617.

Ferguson, J., Soekijad, M., Huysman, M. & Vaast, E. (2013). Blogging for ICT4D: Reflecting and engaging with peers to build development discourse. *Information Systems Journal, 23*(4), 307–328.

Fischer, F. (1998). *Making them like us: Peace Corps volunteers in the 1960s*. Washington, DC: Smithsonian Institution Press.

Flannery, M. (2007). Kiva and the birth of person-to-person microfinance. *Innovations: Technology, Governance, Globalization, 1*(1), 31–56.

Flannery, M. (2009). Kiva at four. *Innovations: Technology, Governance, Globalization, 4*(2), 31–49.

Harris, B. (2013). *The International Bank of Bob: Connecting our world one $25 Kiva loan at a time*. New York: Walker & Company.

Kar, S. (2013). Recovering debts: Microfinance loan officers and the work of "proxy-creditors" in India. *American Ethnologist, 40*(3), 480–493.

Karim, L. (2011). *Microfinance and its discontents: Women in debt in Bangladesh*. Minneapolis: University of Minnesota Press.

Karnani, A. (2007). Employment, not microcredit, is the solution. *Journal of Corporate Citizenship, 32*, 45–62.

Lovink, G. (2008). *Zero comments: Blogging and critical Internet culture*. New York: Routledge.

Mathers, K. (2010). *Travel, humanitarianism, and becoming American in Africa*. New York: Palgrave Macmillan.

McGehee, N. (2002). Alternative tourism and social movements. *Annals of Tourism Research, 29*(1), 124–143.

McIntosh, A. & Zahra, A. (2007). A cultural encounter through volunteer tourism: Towards the ideals of sustainable tourism? *Journal of Sustainable Tourism, 15*(5), 541–556.

Mostafanezhad, M. (2013a). The geography of compassion in volunteer tourism. *Tourism Geographies, 15*(2), 318–337.

Mostafanezhad, M. (2013b). "Getting in touch with your inner Angelina": Celebrity humanitarianism and the cultural politics of gendered generosity in volunteer tourism. *Third World Quarterly, 34*(3), 485–499.

Mühlebach, A. (2011). On affective labor in post-Fordist Italy. *Cultural Anthropology, 26*(1), 59–82.

O'Neill, K. L. (2013). Left behind: Security, salvation, and the subject of prevention. *Cultural Anthropology, 28*(2), 204–226.

Panteli, N., Yan, L. & Chamakiotis, P. (2011). Writing to the unknown: Bloggers and the presence of backpackers. *Information Technology and People, 24*(4), 362–377.

Parreñas, R. (2012). Producing affect: Transnational volunteerism in a Malaysian orangutan rehabilitation center. *American Ethnologist, 39*(4), 673–687.

Pedwell, C. (2012). Affective (self-) transformations: Empathy, neoliberalism and international development. *Feminist Theory, 13*(2), 163–179.

Raymond, E. M. & Hall, M. (2008). The development of cross-cultural (mis)understanding through volunteer tourism. *Journal of Sustainable Tourism, 16*(5), 530–543.

Redfield, P. & Bornstein, E. (2010). An introduction to the anthropology of humanitarianism. In E. Bornstein & P. Redfield (Eds.), *Forces of compassion: Humanitarianism between ethics and politics* (pp. 3–30). Santa Fe, NM: SAR Press.

Richard, A. & Rudnyckyj, D. (2009). Economies of affect. *Journal of the Royal Anthropological Institute* (N.S.), 15, 57–77.

Roy, A. (2010). Poverty capital: Microfinance and the making of development. New York and London: Routledge.

Schwittay, A. (2014). Making poverty into a financial problem: From global poverty lines to Kiva.org. *Journal of International Development, 26*(4), 508–519.

Simpson, K. (2004). "Doing development": The gap year, volunteer-tourists and a popular practice of development. *Journal of International Development, 16*, 681–692.

Sin, H. L. (2009). Volunteer tourism: "Involve me and I will learn"? *Annals of Tourism Research, 36*(3), 480–501.

Sin, H. L. (2010). Who are we responsible to? Locals' tales of volunteer tourism. *Geoforum, 41*, 983–992.

Stewart, K. (2007). *Ordinary affects.* Durham, NC: Duke University Press.

Turner, V. (1986). Dewey, Dilthey, and drama: An essay in the anthropology of experience. In V. Turner & E. Bruner (Eds.), *The anthropology of experience* (pp. 33–44). Urbana: University of Illinois Press.

Wearing, S. (2001). *Volunteer tourism: Experiences that make a difference.* Wallingford: CABI.

Woodward, K. (2004). Calculating compassion. In L. Berlant (Ed.), *Compassion: The culture and politics of an emotion.* New York: Routledge.

Yunus, M. (1999). *Banker to the poor: Micro-lending and the battle against world poverty.* New York: Public Affairs.

Zahra, A. & McIntosh, A. (2007). Volunteer tourism: Evidence of cathartic tourist experiences. *Tourism Recreation Research, 32*(1), 115–119.

CONCLUSION

Throughout this book, I have shown how sentiments of aid can constitute everyday humanitarians and microfinance supporters and can mobilize their affective investments. Kiva's success, which builds on the ways in which microfinance has become a popular cause that makes poverty alleviation simple, understandable and actionable for Northern publics, shows that many individuals in the global North feel compelled to care and share to alleviate the poverty of distant others. Not only is this millennium the age of poverty (Roy, 2012), but "giving may well be an ethos of our time" (Bornstein, 2012, p. 15). Indeed, Bornstein asks whether humanitarianism and philanthropy, which I have articulated in the notion of everyday humanitarianism, is the new development. In this final chapter, I present a summary of the main arguments of this book, before exploring the possibilities of a politics of affirmation and hope.

Book Summary

I began this book by laying the theoretical and historical foundations of Northern publics' affective engagements with international development, and particularly with microfinance. Indeed, this book is the first comprehensive analysis of the affective dimension of international development, which until now has been neglected. At the heart of these engagements is the mobilization of affective investments, which are financial, social and emotional commitments by Northern publics to distant others, with the aim to alleviate their poverty. In Chapter 2, I have shown how the constitution of these publics as everyday humanitarians has its roots in the emergence of humanitarianism as a structure of feeling 300 years ago. From there, different modes of engagement have drawn on notions of needy and worthy distant others. The contours of these notions that have changed over time, even as they remained firmly anchored in hierarchical relationships between those who need care and those who give it. These relationships are firmly entangled in the larger cultural and political economy of international development and its historical antecedents.

In the second part of book, I have examined mediated connections between everyday humanitarians in the global North and distant others in the global South. Chapter 3 focused on Kiva.org, the world's first person-to-person microlending website, and I have shown that the organization's microloans and micronarratives, albeit successful on a quantitative level, have only limited structural effects, paralleling the critique that microfinance cannot bring about sustained, macro-level economic change (Bateman, 2010). The scripted and mediated relationships between lenders and borrowers that are at the heart of Kiva, in spite of its rhetoric of business partnerships, mirror broader hierarchical relations between those who suffer and those who care for them. The former are spoken for and their stories are appropriated for the growth of a Silicon Valley social enterprise and for the enjoyment of Kiva fans. Furthermore, microfinance's obligatory success story remains continually reinscribed in Kiva's narrative and visual representations. Visual representations were also the focus of Chapter 4, which situated a number of winning photographs of the CGAP Microfinance Photo Contest in the context of the mutations of microfinance. These mutations are the result of the move to a more minimalist and commercialized financial inclusion approach, reminding us that any discussion of affect and representation needs to be anchored in attention to power, politics and place.

From these virtual and electronic mediations I shifted to visceral and embodied encounters in the third part of the book. In Chapter 5, I chronicled the personal encounters of microfinance tourists, myself included, with women borrowers and their loan officers in Chennai, India. The tour was organized by Opportunity International, a Christian microfinance funding umbrella, which allowed me to examine the role of religion in development and microfinance. During our journey, attendance at borrower group meetings, question-and-answer periods with borrowers and especially photographic interactions created unexpected, joyful moments that reinvigorated tour participants' affective investments. These encounters did not question microfinance's obligatory success story, however, which was reinforced through the controlled and scripted performance of microfinance tourism. Ultimately, encounters with borrowers reaffirmed personal narratives of responsibility, support and brotherly love and reinforced historical relations between givers and receivers of care. Nevertheless, some participants came away from the tour with new questions, whose answers will hopefully complicate the simple story of microfinance success we performed in Chennai.

In Chapter 6, I asked if volunteering as a form of affective labor leads to the mobilization of affective investments and allows for critical engagements with microfinance. Through an analysis of the posts by several hundred Kiva Fellows on the official Kiva Fellows Blog, I examined Fellows' representations of microfinance, poverty and development and their accounts of encounters with their host MFIs' borrowers and staff. What emerged from these posts was international volunteering as an intensely personal journey that resulted in nuanced understandings of micro-finance and its challenges and new perspectives on the relations of international aid. Fellows' direct confrontation with the hardships of many Kiva borrowers, and their attempts to translate these stories into hopeful messages that would continue to inspire Kiva lenders, raised many questions for these predominantly US volunteers. While the blog posts showed how Fellows grappled with answers, they also revealed the limits of that engagement, which remained tenuously tied to Kiva's and micro-finance's obligatory success story. Ultimately, reading these stories from the field enriched my own academic and affective journey, on which I want to reflect at the close of this book.

Epilogue: A Politics of Affirmation and Hope

A question that has followed me while writing this book is whether Northern publics' affective engagement with global poverty alleviation and microfinance can bring about political change that challenges existing structures of power. Many of the scholars who have asked that question before me have answered it in the negative, beginning with Hannah Arendt, who argued that

> forms of human sociality that hinge on compassion are nonpolitical and non-public because the common good is founded on nothing more than indi-viduals' willingness to feel and act on feeling. Such socialities enjoin people in an immediate, intense space of cosuffering and affective communion, and they encompass these people in a relationship not based on universalistic rights but on particularistic, voluntaristic, face-to-face action.
>
> *(2006 [1963], pp. 86–87)*

For Arendt, and subsequently Luc Boltanski (1999), the impossibility of moving from individual feelings to collective rights precludes affect as a basis for political action. Recent scholarship on the role of affect in development agrees: "if senti-ments of compassion ultimately guide political action, political action itself is in danger of becoming anti-political" (Müller, 2013, p. 480). This denial of political effect through affect is usually anchored in the links between affective engagements and neoliberalism. At the conclusion of this book, I continue to partially agree with these arguments.

And yet, over the course of its writing, I have begun to consider other possibil-ities, and what role academic work can play in creating them. They begin by asking: How can representations, of poor people, of microfinance and of inter-national development, be disrupted? When I interviewed Jeanette Thomas, the organizer of the CGAP Microfinance Photo Contest that is the focus of Chapter 4, I pointed out to her that while most of the winners were now coming from the global South, all of the judges were still from the United States. This got her think-ing and in 2013, Bangladeshi photographer Mohammad Rakibul Hasan, who had been a repeated competition finalist, was the first-ever jury member from the global

South. After I emailed him a copy of my *Anthropology Today* article (Schwittay, 2013, a shorter version of Chapter 4) that uses one of his photos, he wrote back that "I believe, after reading your article must lead me to a new dimension while I will be judging entries this year." While an in-depth analysis of how this process has unfolded must wait for another article, my interactions, as a researcher, around the CGAP photo contest have begun to shift its politics in a small way. This happened because of my own commitment to engaged scholarship. It takes effort to make one's work relevant and this book is part of my efforts. The passionate responses to the recent article by *New York Times* reporter Nicholas Kristof – the same Kristof who visited his Kiva borrower in Afghanistan in 2007 – about the irrelevance of the academy show that many other scholars share these sentiments (Kristof, 2007, 2014).

Ultimately, representations of financial inclusion must ensure that generating popular support for microfinance also becomes a process of critical engagement with its many complexities and limitations. For this to happen, everyday humanitarians must be offered more than micro-stories, media soundbites and celebrity tweets. An alternative can be found in testimonies, a narrative genre with the potential for generating critical discussion. According to Paolo Freire, testimony begins with naming, and thereby problematizing, what *is* as a starting point for change toward an *ought*. "Testimonies are centered on personal experience infused with love for the world and hope for the future" (Freire, 1996, p. 87). They are conveyed "through cognitive and affective registers" and thereby become a starting point for the creative forces of affect to bring about change (Roelvink, 2010, p. 114). Testimony also creates a space for the voice of the other to be heard, so that empathy does not become stereotyping, narcissistic or voyeuristic.

What would testimony in the context of Kiva look like? The website already is a hub where visitors learn about hundreds of thousands of borrowers around the world. What if these borrowers were enabled to give testimonies of their lives, their joys and their sorrows, in all their complexities? No longer answering to questionnaires, borrowers could tell their story on their own terms. The technological means for capturing such stories certainly exist. While such testimony would go beyond the remit and organizational capacities of Kiva and partner MFIs, kindred organizations and websites could do this important work. The eagerness with which Kiva fans consume the current truncated offerings on the Kiva site promises an equally receptive audience for fuller stories. When testimonies generate dialogue through collective discussion, relationships are formed. The beginnings of such a discussion already takes place on the Kiva Fellows Blog with its more detailed posts, although these remain circumscribed by their positive, descriptive and normative character. Furthermore, testimony cannot remain limited to the descriptions of Kiva Fellows' experiences but must create equal possibilities for borrowers to talk of theirs. Such dialogue, in turn, can lead to new possibilities of being, especially if it focuses on alternatives to the current status quo (Roelvink, 2010).

Narrative and visual representations of microfinance, and development more generally, are, then, a good starting point to think of political change. From these beginnings, "an emotion can be labeled as political when it incites an *active* response to suffering" (Suski, 2009, p. 217). Conversely, "without emotion, no appeal to action could be legitimate" (Chouliaraki, 2010, p. 115). Throughout this book, I have documented the range of actions that development supporters have taken in response to learning about the plight of distant others, from lending to consuming to clicking to traveling. Even though there are important differences in what these actions ask of their agents and what effects they will have on distant others, what unites them is that they are all manifestations of *everyday* humanitarianism – carried out by everyday people in their daily lives. This anchoring in the everyday is foundational for "theories of affective agency [that] reconceptualize radical agency and reinscribe it in the quotidian and the micropolitical" (McManus, 2013, p. 150). Thus, structural change that attacks the foundations of poverty rather than serving as a band aid for its symptoms can start with ordinary affects at the same time as "attending to the structural and systemic by way of mapping its conditions of possibility within the quotidian or the micro" (McManus, 2013, p. 157). After all, it is people's daily practices that provide effective recipes for intervention, and it was the availability of quotidian recipes that was one of the preconditions for the emergence of humanitarian sensibilities in the first place (Haskell, 1985). Thus, Kiva's neat fit into the ordinary lives of its fans, and especially their pleasurable electronic consumption, is a strength that could be harnessed rather than critiqued.

The result is a different kind of political action. Traditional Marxist politics "derives its reason from the being of the collective united by an instrumental consciousness and orientation to shared goals, towards which the political collective must strive in as co-ordinated a fashion as possible" (Hynes et al., 2007, p. 112). Affect, on the other hand, gives rise to an affirmative and anticipatory politics, which has been embraced by such undeniably political campaigns as the global justice movement (Roelvink, 2010) and the Zapatista uprising in Chiapas (McManus, 2013). Central to the latter are *encuentros* (encounters) that have brought together thousands of Zapatistas with non-indigenous Mexicans and international supporters in "affective experiments in doing politics differently" (McManus, 2013, p. 153). Such encounters materialize the intersubjective character of affect. "Enhancing agency, then, is precisely dependent upon cultivating the kinds of affective encounters that make new socialities, new and joyful modes of relation and composition, possible" (McManus, 2013, p. 153). Encounters also ensure continued attention to the materiality of life.

Affective encounters do not have to be face to face, as Kiva's electronically mediated connections show. They produce Kiva love, which in its ability to transcend and transform has the potential to contribute toward a political use of the term (Hardt, 2011). The work of many Kiva Fellows who are at the center of Chapter 6 is also animated by love. Although their personal encounters with microfinance borrowers and staff of their host MFIs, as chronicled in their blog posts, ultimately reaffirm a belief in the positive benefits of microfinance, it is a cautious and nuanced embrace, sobered by the realities of the minute or missing improvements in borrowers' lives. In addition, the power of a Kiva Fellowship for political change might not lie in experiencing microfinance first-hand, but in the very human relations Fellows must establish during their time in the field. Being cared for and helped by those whom they came to assist was an experience that shook many Fellows to the core, not only because it went against cherished assumptions of autonomy and independence, but also because it made Fellows think about the power differentials in the caring relationship. These meetings also complicated their expectations of people in the global South as needing help and care. As one of the Fellows put it, when he met borrowers in Ghana, he "saw firsthand hope in its most human form amidst struggle." What, then, about hope, as a belief in a better future?

Hope is a central part of an affirmative politics. "Being political affectively must involve building a protest against the affectivities of suffering into a set of techniques that also aim to cultivate 'good encounters' and anticipate 'something better'" (Anderson, 2006, p. 749). The emphasis of this ethos of engagement is on becoming and potentials, as it acknowledges the messy complexity of the contemporary world, but also the possibility of improving it. However, even in hope there is no guarantee, as it can become a tactic of delay and/or a justification for unwanted interventions that create new networks of obligations (Anderson, 2006). Still, "as a politics, affect can create feelings of possibility in the context of hegemonic ideology and hopelessness" (Roelvink, 2010, p. 112). Be it neoliberal dominance in global development interventions or the persistent scorch of poverty, affective encounters with distant others who are subject to them open up spaces of becoming. In this book, I have charted the becoming of everyday humanitarians as one of these spaces. They are the reason why Kiva has been so successful, in spite of all its limitations and shortcomings. It generates new structures of feeling that affect the present in an anticipatory and affirmative way, looking forward to a future where poverty will not be confined to museums or eradicated but room for change has opened up. This also demands a rethinking of what constitutes success, and reform or revolution are no longer the only two options.

This politics of affirmation might not come easily to critical academics. We have been trained to take apart, without an obligation to begin to reconstruct. There are signs of change, though, resulting in part from the multiple subject positions researchers occupy and from different methodologies that accompany these positionalities. Throughout this project, I have – in no particular order – lent money to people, talked to them, read their blogs, observed their work and traveled with them, as a Kiva lender, a microfinance tourist, a critical researcher and an engaged anthropologist. In the last of these roles, I am contributing to what Joel Robbins has described as an emerging "anthropology of the good," which finds expression in three ensembles of recent anthropological works (2013, p. 457). One of these are studies of value, morality, imagination and well-being. Especially relevant for this book are works on empathy, care and the gift, which have mainly focused on the creation of moral selves. However, "it is equally necessary to explore the ways they foster the good in social relations" (Robbins, 2013, p. 458). Third are writings on hope, time and change.

As with the construction of the good, there is a strong temptation to dismiss people's investments in realizing the good in time as more utopianism, to smother their hopes analytically with what Clifford has recently called our own "wet-blanket realism."

(Robbins, 2013, p. 458, quoting Clifford, 2009, p. 32)

While anthropological attention is usually on the subjects of hope in the global South, I have shown that the good that everyday humanitarians are trying to create is equally worth our critical attention. Beyond that, "we are being called to read the potentially positive futures barely visible in the present order of things, and to imagine how to strengthen and move them along" (Gibson-Graham & Roelvink, 2009, p. 342). Affective engagements with international development through microfinance open up spaces of hope that can be filled with critical-constructive knowledge leading to informed practice and meaningful transformations.

Bibliography

Anderson, B. (2006). Becoming and being hopeful: Towards a theory of affect. *Environment and Planning D: Society and Space, 24*(5), 733–752.

Arendt, H. (2006 [1963]). *On revolution.* London: Penguin Classics.

Bateman, M. (2010). *Why doesn't microfinance work? The destructive rise of global neoliberalism.* London: Zed Books.

Boltanski, L. (1999). *Distant suffering: Morality, media and politics.* Cambridge: Cambridge University Press.

Bornstein, E. (2012). *Disquieting gifts: Humanitarianism in New Delhi.* Palo Alto, CA: Stanford University Press.

Chouliaraki, L. (2010). Post-humanitarianism: Humanitarian communication beyond a politics of pity. *International Journal of Cultural Studies, 13*(2), 107–126.

Clifford, J. (2009). Hau'ofa's hope. *Oceania, 72*, 238–249.

Freire, P. (1996). *Pedagogy of the oppressed.* London: Penguin Books.

Gibson-Graham, J. K. & Roelvink, G. (2009). An economic ethics for the anthropocene. *Antipode, 41*(S1), 320–346.

Hardt, M. (2011). For love or money. *Cultural Anthropology, 26*(4), 676–682.

Haskell, T. (1985). Capitalism and the origins of humanitarian sensibilities. *American Historical Review, 90*(2), 339–361.

Hynes, M., Sharpe, S. & Fagan, B. (2007). Laughing with the yes men: The politics of affirmation. *Continuum, 21*(1), 107–121.

Kristof, N. (2007, March 27). You, too, can be a banker to the poor. *New York Times.*

Kristof, N. (2014, February 15). Professors, we need you! *New York Times.*

McManus, S. (2013). Radical political agency: Affective politics in the case of the Zapatistas in Chiapas. In B. Maiguashca & R. Marchetti (Eds.), *Contemporary political agency: Theory and practice* (pp. 137–163). London: Routledge.

Müller, T. (2013). The long shadow of Band Aid humanitarianism: Revisiting the dynamics between famine and celebrity. *Third World Quarterly, 34*(3), 470–484.

Robbins, J. (2013). Beyond the suffering subject: Toward an anthropology of the good. *Journal of the Royal Anthropological Institute* (N.S.), 19, 447–462.

Roelvink, G. (2010). Collective action and the politics of affect. *Emotions, Space and Society, 3*, 111–118.

Roy, A. (2012). Ethical subjects: Market rule in an age of poverty. *Public Culture, 24*(1), 105–108.

Schwittay, A. (2013). Representing financial inclusion: The CGAP Microfinance Photo Contest. *Anthropology Today, 29*(5), 9–12.

Suski, L. (2009). Children, suffering, and the humanitarian appeal. In R. A. Wilson & R. D. Brown (Eds.), *Humanitarianism and suffering: The mobilization of empathy* (pp. 202–222). Cambridge: Cambridge University Press.

INDEX

Page numbers in **bold** denote figures.

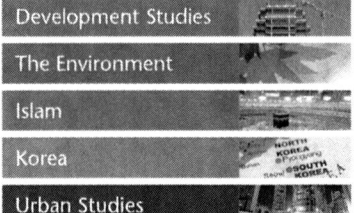